McFarland
Classics

This book is dedicated to
the readers of and contributors to *Views & Reviews*
from that odd period in small magazine publishing
when none of us suspected we were doing anything unusual

The Vanishing Legion

A History of Mascot Pictures
1927–1935

by Jon Tuska

McFarland Classics

McFarland & Company, Inc., Publishers
Jefferson, North Carolina, and London

1007222215

Library of Congress Cataloguing-in-Publication Data

Tuska, Jon.
  The vanishing legion.

  Includes index.
  ISBN 978-0-7864-0749-1 (softcover : 50# alkaline paper)
  1. Mascot Pictures (Firm) I. Title.
PN1999.M3T8 1999   384.8'0979493   81-6014 AACR2

British Library Cataloguing-in-Publication data are available

Front cover: From the 1933 serial *The Three Musketeers* (PHOTOFEST)

Manufactured in the United States of America

McFarland & Company, Inc., Publishers
  Box 611, Jefferson, North Carolina 28640
  www.mcfarlandpub.com

Table of Contents

Acknowledgments

For all their help, in the past as well as in the present, the author wishes to extend his particular gratitude to the executive personnel of Columbia Pictures Television, to Sid Weiner, now retired, formerly Director of Administration, Joe Abruscato, Bob Nilson, Marvin Usevich, and those many persons not named, since without them this book would not have been possible at all. Karl Thiede provided invaluable research and the appendices were especially prepared for this edition by Vicki Piekarski.

All translations from foreign languages, indicated when the title of the publication is rendered in its language of origin, are by the author.

A preliminary version of this book, as noted in the Preface, appeared serially in *Views & Reviews* in 1971-1973.

Preface

An earlier version of the present book appeared originally in the magazine *Views & Reviews*, which I edited and published in the years from 1969 to 1975, a quarterly devoted to the popular arts and motion pictures in particular. The seven installments of the magazine version met with an enthusiastic response from readers and this, in part, encouraged me to contemplate the notion of expanding it into a book-length history.

Prior to publishing the magazine version of *The Vanishing Legion*, I got in touch with Nat Levine, the founder of Mascot Pictures. He was then managing a small theatre in Torrance, California, and he gave generously of his time and assistance to provide me with much of the factual material I needed. When I made the decision to expand my historical account of Mascot Pictures into a book, again I contacted Levine. He was by now retired, living on Social Security. Gone were the millions he had made in the motion picture industry. I asked him what had happened. "When I gambled making movies," he replied, "I made money. When I began playing the horses, I lost ... I lost everything." Somehow it doesn't seem possible to tell the history of the motion picture company he founded without keeping in mind that Nat Levine was first, last, and always a gambler.

Because of the added scope a book affords, I have been able to encompass in *The Vanishing Legion* a critical treatment of every Mascot serial and feature, and not just the eight chapter plays emphasized in the serialized magazine version. Thanks also to cinema historian Richard W. Bann, I was permitted to retrieve a print of *Crimson Romance* (Mascot, 1934) which, without this fortunate discovery, would have otherwise been lost to future generations.

Working on this book brought me into contact with a wide assortment of people who told me engaging and amusing stories of what it had been like to be associated with Mascot Pictures and who evoked for me the vital spirit inspiring everyone employed by that little company, those who, for relatively low pay and forced to function under anything but ideal conditions, managed nonetheless to produce intensely impassioned and, in their inimitable way, quite memorable films. It still shows on the screen whenever and wherever a Mascot picture is projected. Yet this is not to say that I am unaware that as cinema history *The Vanishing Legion* focuses on films that are generally held to be inferior by many critics. Compared to many films today, they were; even compared to many films made contemporaneously with them, they were. But I am not at all certain how relevant a consideration this is. Even "B" pictures deserve recognition. I recall a review of one of my books in the French cinema magazine, *Positif* (September, 1978), in which the reviewer, Lorenzo Codelli, posed the question, "Qui les analysera sérieusement, de façon étendue, en retrouvant, en revoyant tous les films disponibles?" M. Codelli then proceeded to take me to task for insufficiently engaging in "une célébration inconditionelle de ce qui a existé, sans aucune perspective dans l'actualité ni dans l'avenir du cinéma américain." I admit he was justified in this accusation. I had not written in that fashion about the American cinema. But in the present book, for this one time, I intend it to be different; here, I believe, I have tried to achieve what M. Codelli was calling for, an unconditional celebration of a cinematic form as it once existed, written from a perspective that permits little notice of any other actuality lest it be of the personalities encountered along the way, a book not overly weighed down by cognizance of other trends in the development of the American cinema.

In the years while this book was being prepared, I interviewed, for the purposes of oral history, Ken Maynard, Lucile Browne Flavin, Lee Duncan, D. Ross Lederman, Julian Rivero, Joseph Kane, George "Gabby" Hayes, Yakima Canutt, Olive Golden Carey, Ruth Hall Garmes, Maurice Geraghty, Gene Autry, John Wayne, and a number of others who had things to tell me, or whose lives had things to say which I have felt worth relating. I have, therefore, sought to characterize a number of these principals, many of whom are since deceased, with the object in mind of making the whole process of recall as graphic for the reader as it was for me in the doing and hence to provide a sense of *temps en passant* to the entire enterprise. In a way while writing this book I became possessed with looking at the world the way Americans did in the late twenties and early thirties, with that quaint and naive and, in the end, unfounded optimism that so preoccupied American films in that era. Seeing a contemporary film in the midst of this, in fact, would bring about quite a sensation — if not of culture shock then of its temporal equivalent, time shock.

I am not able to leave off without thanking — at least collectively, and hence the dedication of this book — the many readers who faithfully wrote to me following every installment of the far more condensed magazine version with corrections or additional information. Those letters and comments have been at last put to the very best use. Their contents have been interwoven into the new fabric of this text. No book should purport to be more than it is. *The Vanishing Legion* is a recreation of an era in filmmaking that will never come again, certainly not in the same way nor with quite the same improvident, even childlike and exultant, sincerity. It is a freeze-frame of the past held up anew for the present.

One

The Lurking Peril

There was once a chapter play in fifteen episodes titled *The Lurking Peril* (Arrow, 1919). It starred George Larkin who, according to the script, was possessed of "an unusual sort of brain." In a weak and foolish moment, induced by financial hardship, Larkin sold off the right to dissect his brain after his death to a diabolical old professor. Typically, the old professor was overly anxious and unable to wait. He decided to hasten Larkin's demise. For fourteen chapters Larkin led the old professor on a merry chase, always narrowly escaping an impending doom. Despite the hectic pacing, there was still time for a romance between Larkin and heroine Anne Luther — although, to tell the truth, Luther seemed more terrified over the prospect of her lover losing his brain than enchanted by the rhapsodies of courtship.

The storylines of chapter plays may not invariably have been this ridiculous, but they did usually border on the fantastic and, in retrospect, this must have been part of their charm. The first theatrical serial generally cited by cinema historians is *What Happened to Mary?* (Edison, 1912), but it was more an episodic story released to theatres in short weekly installments featuring the same heroine than it was a bonafide chapter play. The notion of the cliffhanger as an incentive to see the next episode wasn't introduced until *The Adventures of Kathlyn* (Selig, 1913) which starred Kathlyn Williams. Over the succeeding decades cliffhangers became as standardized as were many of the plots and a staple ingredient of chapter plays. Producers of serials, almost from the start, took advantage of the

1

weekly interval between installments to conceal a wealth of sins, the most common of which was surely the lack of continuity.

The one serial everyone seems to have heard of is *The Perils of Pauline* (Pathé, 1914). It first introduced audiences to Pearl White as a serial heroine. Not all twenty chapters of *Perils* ended with a cliffhanger, but some of them did. What was truly remarkable about this serial was that, in an age when women were otherwise being stereotyped in films so often as the innocent virginal girl next door or the sexually experienced vamp, Pearl White was attractive, capable, daring, and willing personally — as well as fictitiously in the plot — to meet and surmount the most dangerous predicaments, emerging triumphant, and, for the camera anyway, unscathed.

She was born Pearl Fay White at Green Ridge, Missouri, on March 4, 1889, the third daughter and youngest of five children. Her father was a farmer who eventually moved his family to Springfield, Missouri, where he pursued a business career in real estate and insurance and, for a time, was a deputy assessor for Greene County. Pearl dropped out of high school in her sophomore year and, enamored of the stage, began playing small parts in the local Diemer Theatre stock company. When she turned eighteen in 1907, Pearl left home to join a traveling stock company. By 1910, experiencing difficulties with her voice, Pearl decided to try motion pictures, joining the recently formed Powers Film Company located in the Bronx, New York. Very soon she found herself playing in starring roles and winning critical accolades for both her beauty and her talent.

After a short stint with Lubin in 1911, a film company based in Philadelphia, Pearl signed with the American branch of the French firm, Pathé Frères, at its New Jersey studio. Near the end of 1912 she was starring in short comedies for the Crystal Film Company which distributed its pictures through the Universal exchanges. Her work schedule was particularly heavy and, exhausted, she took a seven month vacation in Europe. What persuaded her to return to the United States and to the screen was the promise of a salary of $250 a week and the prospects of an elaborate publicity campaign offered to her by Louis J. Gasnier, who was then associated with Pathé. *The Perils of Pauline* did for Pearl White all Gasnier had said it would, and more. Chronologically, *Perils* was the fifth chapter play to be produced and released by any film company. It was sponsored by the Hearst newspapers and, overnight, it made Pearl one of the best known film personalities. Throughout the teens, Pearl continued as the reigning queen of the serials. In 1919 she left Pathé to star in features for Fox, but the films did not prove a success. A tour of Europe in a kind of vaudeville act followed before Pearl attempted a comeback in another serial, *Plunder* (Pathé, 1923). The production was plagued with problems, not the least of which were caused by Pearl's failing eyesight, her bad sense of timing, and the pain attendant to an old back injury. Once this serial was completed, Pearl went to live in France in retirement until her death in 1938.

As more and more chapter plays were produced, their identifiable characteristics became increasingly pronounced. The heroine—or hero— was opposed by an obvious villain who was in quest of an object around which all the action was centered. This object might be a missing or buried fortune, a fabulous invention, a secret gold, silver, or oil deposit, a map to a treasure. Pearl White called the object a "weenie," a term which was appropriate enough. All the essential plot ingredients, ideally, had to be introduced in the first chapter, which is to say the principal characters had to be identified, their various factions if there were any, and the "weenie." After that, the heroine or hero had to be plunged at once into mortal danger. Since it was difficult to reasonably draw out a conflict so that every fifteen or twenty minutes the action could be arrested by a cliffhanger, implausibility by necessity had to be disguised through fast and furious action. Perhaps the most significant creative challenge imposed by serials on screenwriters was this requirement to come up with a sufficient number of subplots that would *both* result in a cliffhanger and still advance the main plotline.

Toward the end of the teens, mystery elements were more commonly included. There might be a masked hero, as was the case in *The Lion Man* (Universal, 1919), who kept the audience in suspense as to his identity until the final episode, or there might be a masked master villain such as the veiled woman in *The Veiled Mystery* (Vitagraph, 1920) who turned out to be a man, heroine Pauline Curley's guardian, played by Henry Barrows. In *Fighting Fate* (Vitagraph, 1921), the villain was disguised in a medieval suit of armor and was known as The Iron Mask. In *The Iron Claw* (Pathé, 1916), a Pearl White serial, Harry Fraser portrayed The Laughing Mask, a nemesis to evil-doers who wasn't unmasked until the final chapter.

Louis J. Grasnier who had inaugurated at Pathé what was to become the tradition of the "sportatelic" American girl with Pearl White was also the first to stress colorful and memorable villains. Warner Oland, a Swedish actor with a penchant for portraying Orientals and who would eventually become world famous for his role as Charlie Chan in the thirties, was paid $1,000 a week by Pathé to personate a wide variety of villains. When a serial featured players whose reputations were less than familiar to audiences, the title became all important. It was best, of course, if a serial could have a strong title like *The Lightning Raider* (Pathé, 1919) and, as this serial did, also have Pearl White menaced by Warner Oland. *Raider* was directed by George B. Seitz, the undisputed serial director *par excellence* of the silent era. After Seitz came Spencer Gordon Bennet, W.S. Van Dyke, Robert F. Hill, and B. Reeves Eason who together established most of the high water marks for thrilling chapter plays in the twenties.

Universal entered the chapter play field very early with vehicles co-starring Francis Ford, director John Ford's elder brother, and Grace Cunard. It was Universal that initiated the 100- to 300-foot overlap practice, which served to refresh the minds of viewers with what had occurred at the conclusion of the previous episode and Pathé quickly followed suit, beginning with *Double Adventure* (Pathé, 1921).

Although many of the earliest pioneer producing companies made and released chapter plays along with a number of independent firms that came and went after one or two releases, the twenties were dominated in most markets by only two companies, Pathé first, followed closely by Universal. Of the two, Pathé had the loosest management structure. As a general rule, Pathé preferred to purchase and distribute a serial product that had already been produced. This rather cautious procedure slowly gave way to the point where Pathé participated in part and then in all the production costs for a serial with an independent producer overseeing the production. By 1920 this practice was further modified so that while Pathé would still contract with an independent producer, the producer would then have to depend wholly on Pathé contract personnel like George B. Seitz for direction, Frank Leon Smith for the scenario, and Pathé contract players to bring in the production. The independent producer's function in all this would consist all too often in nothing more than simply handling the money, admittedly a questionable and frequently a disastrous policy. By the time Pathé came to produce *Play Ball* (Pathé, 1925), starring the popular serial team of Allene Ray and Walter Miller, Spencer Gordon Bennet, the director and Seitz' successor at Pathé, and Frank Leon Smith, the scenarist, functioned as the unofficial producers, an experiment that finally resulted in the production by Pathé, during its final years, of its own chapter plays without any outside assistance.

In the early twenties, Pathé serials generally ran to fifteen chapters with a three-reel first chapter, while Universal opted for the first chapter to be of commensurate length with the remaining episodes. By the mid twenties, most serials had become standardized at the ten to twelve chapter length. Usually the first three chapters were the most engaging and interesting, since these were the "sales" episodes shown at previews to exhibitors who would be asked to judge the entire serial on the basis of them. It was also in the mid twenties that Pathé began making feature versions of its serials. In time, two cameras were used to film every scene, one for the feature version and one for the serial version. Most of these feature versions were inferior but a happy exception was *Hawk of the Hills* (Pathé, 1927), which was the equal in its feature form to what it was as a chapter play, and there were others.

Because of the episodic nature of a serial, screen adaptations from novels, which always seem to suffer anyway, were hopeless. But here, too, there were some notable exceptions like *The Green Archer* (Pathé, 1925) based on mystery writer Edgar Wallace's novel of the same title. In fact, Wallace's melodramas were sufficiently episodic as fiction that it is something of a wonder that more of them were not filmed as chapter plays. *Archer* starred Allene Ray and it was on the set of this serial that she was crowned queen of serials, thus replacing Pearl White. Allene Ray was a comely woman of diminutive stature, delicate hands, and rather large eyes whose basic emotion before the camera was registering fear. She was, however, offscreen a woman of exceedingly placid disposition, normally incapable of showing anything approaching fear. Spencer Gordon Bennet, her director, would go to such lengths as to arrange for a prop man to fire a revolver behind the scenery at the requisite moment and, both fortunately and invariably for all concerned, this ruse seemed never to fail. Allene Ray would register fear. The level of acting in the majority of the silent serials seldom exceeded this rather rudimentary performance in one key, nor can it be said to have markedly changed in serials made during the subsequent sound era.

So many chapter plays were made because they made money. A serial like *Blake of Scotland Yard* (Universal, 1927) was budgeted at $125,000, but its director, Robert F. Hill, managed to bring it in for $97,000. Before it was released, Universal had over $900,000 in committed bookings and, eventually, in worldwide release it grossed $3,500,000. Nor was this an isolated phenomenon.

The master villain frequently in silent serials was a surrogate father figure, an uncle perhaps, or a legal guardian, who in order to acquire possession of his ward's wealth plotted her demise. From every death trap he devised, the heroine might be saved by the timely arrival of the hero; but, just as often and much more to the point, the heroine was able to extricate herself and many times found herself rescuing the ostensible hero. On one level, doubtless, such chapter plays appealed to the growing spirit of independence in women, at least in fantasy.

Almost as common, when it came to the villain, he might be a racial outcast. One is reminded of the German historian Oswald Spengler who in *Reden und Aufsätze* (C.H. Beck'sche, 1937) responded in this fashion to the question, is world peace possible? "So long as there is human development, there will be war. If, however, the white peoples should become so weary of war that they are no longer able to bring it to bear to enforce their governments, then the world will become a sacrificial victim to the colored races, just as the Roman Empire fell to the Germans."

During the Great War, military preparedness serials were the order of the day and William Randolph Hearst was in the vanguard, financing *Patria* (Pathé, 1917) which showed the United States being plotted against by the Japanese and the Mexicans. There were a great number of serials, during the war and after, that depicted supposed racial danger, from obvious examples like *The Yellow Menace* (Serial Film Company, 1916), featuring a power-hungry Oriental lusting for world dominion, to a similar use of Native Americans in chapter plays like *In the Days of Buffalo Bill* (Universal, 1922) and *In the Days of Daniel Boone* (Universal, 1923). By stereotyping Native Americans as savages, little better than vicious animals, these chapter plays reinforced the need white Americans had to self-righteously justify before all the world what had happened to the Indians at their hands. The same was true when colonialists were pictured battling against Africans in serials like *The Jungle Goddess* (Export-Import Film Company, 1922). G.A. Atkinson, a cinema correspondent for the *London Daily Express*, launched his criticism of American chapter plays from a perspective not too far removed from Spengler's. "Still more important in this connection," Atkinson wrote, "is the fact that in many serial films the villains are black, yellow, or brown men whose villainy at the expense of the whites is glorified throughout the film, although they are brought to book at the finish; but it may be doubted whether the moral of the eleventh hour vindication of virtue is fully seized by the exultant natives, who have witnessed the triumphs of their colored kind through so many long drawn out previous episodes."

André Bazin, the noted French film critic, wrote in his preface to Jean-Louis Rieupeyrout's *Le Western; ou, Le Cinéma Américain par Excellence* (Éditions du Cerf, 1953): "Le Western est né de la rencontre d'une mythologie avec un moyen d'expression." Nearly a third of all silent serials were Westerns and this percentage, if anything, remained the same or increased slightly in the sound era. But what Bazin said of the Western might be extended to apply more generally to the entire world of chapter plays: they were a meeting of a mythology with a means of expression.

One view of modern psychology is that a myth and a dream are quite similar in intention, although the origin of the one is collective, the other personal. Freud felt that myths, like dreams, have a manifest content, or a surface meaning, and a latent content, or a hidden meaning. Thinking this way, Freud was able to *reduce* the myth of Prometheus' stealing fire from the gods in a hollow tube to something quite different. Equating Prometheus with man in his essay "The Acquisition of Power over Fire" (1932), Freud surmised that "it is not fire which man harbors in his penis-tube; on the contrary, it is the means of extinguishing fire, the water of his stream of urine." Speculating on the function of art in *The Future of an Illusion* (Liveright, 1928), Freud concluded that "as we have long known, art offers substitutive gratifications for the oldest cultural renunciations, still always most deeply felt, and for that reason serves like nothing else to reconcile men to the sacrifices they have made on culture's behalf. On the other hand, works of art promote the feelings of identification, of which every cultural group has so much need, in the occasion they provide for the sharing of highly valued emotional experiences. And when they represent the achievements of a particular culture, thus in an impressive way recalling it to its ideals, they also serve a narcissistic gratification."

However true this might seem, it also relies on too narrow a view of art. I would augment Freud with the position adopted by C.G. Jung. "It would be unjust to assert that ... reduction is wrong in a given case," Jung wrote in his *Two Essays on Analytical Psychology* (Meridian Books, 1956); "but, exalted to the status of a general explanation of the healthy psyche as well as the sick, a reductive theory by itself is impossible. For the human psyche, be it sick or healthy, cannot be explained *solely* by reduction." It was due to his more expansive orientation that Jung, when he came to speculate on the function of art in his essay "On the Relation of Analytical Psychology to Poetry" (1922), felt that the social significance of art consisted in the fact that "it is constantly at work educating the spirit of the age, conjuring up forms in which the age is most lacking. The unsatisfied yearning of the artist reaches back to the primordial image in the unconscious which is best fitted to compensate the inadequacy and one-sidedness of the present."

Were motion picture chapter plays art? They were to those "masses who are engaged in exhausting labor and who have not enjoyed the benefits of individual education" to whom Freud referred in *The Future of an Illusion* and for whom Freud believed most art remained inaccessible. On its most basic level, the chapter play performed the same function Samuel Johnson once attributed to literature: "The only end of writing is to enable readers better to enjoy life, or better to endure it."

Two

The Gambler

The most successful motion picture producers have usually been gamblers. Nearly all the early movie moguls were men who lived by hunches, intuitions and showmanship — exploiters, opportunists, given the right circumstances (or what they thought the right circumstances) men always willing to take a chance. They would be strangers in today's climate of bankers and cautious investors. Nat Levine must have had his share of that reckless early spirit or his Mascot Pictures would never have gotten off the ground.

Born Nathaniel Levine at New York City on July 26, 1899, he graduated from junior high school when he was thirteen years old. His brother knew the secretary to theatre owner Marcus Loew and Nat applied with Loew for a summer job in 1913, just before he was to enter senior high school. He liked the job of office boy and the film industry itself. He liked them so well that he forgot completely about high school and opted to remain with the Marcus Loew theatre chain. He did, however, attend night school, studying business administration and stenography. His starting salary was $5 a week. Levine stayed six years with Marcus Loew, finally working himself up to the position of Loew's personal secretary, his salary increasing to $25 a week.

Levine left Loew in 1919 and went to work as sales manager for Margaret Winkler in Kansas City. The Winkler organization distributed the Felix the Cat cartoons. It was while in Kansas City that Levine met Walt Disney who had his first studio there and who presently began animating the Alice cartoon series which was in turn distributed to independent exchanges by the Winkler organization. Levine's job caused him to form many useful contacts in distribution throughout the country. He came to know the peculiar needs of the independent exchanges — that is, film exchanges that were not affiliated with any of the major producing studios. This experience also naturally oriented him toward the sale and distribution of short films as opposed to features. Levine's ultimate success would come in the short film market.

His employment with both Loew and Winkler taught Levine that maximum profitability, albeit with somewhat greater risk, derived from the production of motion pictures, especially in terms of the grind house circuits with their insatiable need for new product, provided of course that the risk was kept at a minimum through tight budgets. Even though he was destined to work for many years in distribution, including that for his own films, Levine's primary ambition remained to be a producer. He never ventured beyond this point. He was not an empire builder like Marcus Loew or even his subsequent partner, Herbert J. Yates.

The year 1921 found Levine in Hollywood, his nearly ten-year apprenticeship over, hoping to find a picture he could purchase inexpensively and with which to test his aptitude and flair for independent marketing of a wholly-owned Levine property. He was offered a picture, a short programmer of 2,300 feet, starring Dorothy Davenport, an actress married to screen actor Wallace Reid. After raising the $10,000 he needed to buy all rights to it, Levine took the picture back to New York where he had 2,600 feet of subtitles added and then put it into release as *Every Woman's Problem* (Plymouth Pictures, 1921). Directed by Willis Robards from a screenplay by Jack Natteford, *Every Woman's Problem* had Davenport cast as a female attorney who, despite opposition from a yellow newspaper, is elected a judge. A gang of bootleggers, also opposed by the newspaper, decides on a scheme to put the paper out of business. In the meantime, Davenport's screen husband, outraged by the newspaper's conduct toward Davenport, threatens the life of the editor. When the editor is killed in a bomb explosion perpetrated by the bootleggers, Davenport's screen husband is arrested and booked on suspicion. Davenport is elected governor of the state while her husband, joined by the bootleggers, is made to stand trial and is convicted. Davenport is torn between her desire to save her husband's life, through use of her power to pardon, and her sworn duty to see justice done. Her dilemma is solved, conveniently enough, when one of the bootleggers confesses her husband's innocence. It is not explained, however, just how all of this was supposed to be *every* woman's problem.

Despite the melodramatic storyline, the film grossed nearly four times what Levine had paid for it. Levine opined then that he had the first prerequisite of a film producer: he could read the public's wants.

For the next several years, Levine continued buying up pictures that had already been made but which were entangled by liens, usually to processing laboratories, and marketing them on a state's rights basis. This form of independent distribution entailed selling exhibition rights to a film for a specified period of time, generally five years, sometimes less, to the independent exchange servicing a given area. The exchange paid a flat fee to the producer, in this case Levine, and could book the picture as many times in as many theatres as it could within the specified time period. Levine had particular luck with a group of comedies starring Fatty Arbuckle's wife, Minta Durfee Arbuckle, two-reelers which possessed a certain box office attractiveness because of the drawn-out scandal resulting from Arbuckle's arrest in San Francisco in 1921 attendant to the death of Virginia Rappe. In the late twenties Minta Durfee Arbuckle went on to set up a thriving business as a beauty consultant but she lost over a million dollars in the

Wall Street crash of 1929 and, except for occasional character roles during the sound era, the woman who had been Charlie Chaplin's first leading lady died in obscurity in 1975. What impressed Levine about his success with her short comedies in 1925 was that, while the major studios would have nothing to do with Minta because of her association with Arbuckle and the Arbuckle name, there was still some box office advantage in a former star, no matter how faded.

In mid 1926 Levine personally took the plunge, joining with independent producer Samuel Bischoff and other investors in the production of a chapter play. Throughout the early twenties, Bischoff had been producing a series of two-reel comedies for distribution by E.W. Hammons' Educational Pictures for which company Fatty Arbuckle then worked as a director, using a pseudonym so as to hide his identity. Following his association with Levine on this serial, Bischoff produced a group of features starring Silver Streak, the dog introduced to the public for the first time in the chapter play, and then went on to become a production manager at Columbia Pictures, then at Tiffany Productions, founding KBS (Kelly-Bischoff-Saal) Productions in 1932-1933, before joining Warner Bros. as an executive producer. It proved a most advantageous association for Levine. Bischoff taught him the practical fundamentals of production supervision, budgeting, and casting.

The serial had the working title *The Sky Skidder* and was directed by William Craft. Budgeted at $70,000, it was hoped that the canine star, Silver Streak, a German shepherd, would appeal to the same audience that had made Rin Tin Tin so popular. Also cast was Louise Lorraine, a familiar serial heroine, petite, comely, athletic, almost coquettish, but without the following of serial headliners like Pearl White or Allene Ray. The previous year Lorraine had costarred with screen strongman Joe Bonomo in the fifteen episodes of *The Great Circus Mystery* (Universal, 1925). Whatever box office draw Lorraine might have was expected to carry the production, which otherwise had a cast of little known bit players.

The plot told of Anders Rudolph, the inventor of a plan for a silent motor which would revolutionize airplane construction. Malcolm MacGregor, playing Lloyd Darrell, a secret service agent, comes to the small town in the Northwest where Rudolph is working in seclusion with Louise Lorraine, playing Rudolph's daughter. MacGregor, calling himself Bill Smith, falls in love with Lorraine. With the help of the wolf dog, Silver Streak, MacGregor proceeds repeatedly to thwart the schemes of the villains to steal the plan. Hughie Mack, a silent comedian bearing a strong resemblance to Fatty Arbuckle, was added to the plot for comic relief.

Once production was completed, the investors began clamoring to Levine for money. Rather than distribute the chapter play on the state's rights network, Levine offered to sell it to Universal. His asking price was $75,000, or $5,000 above what had been spent on it. Universal retitled it *The Silent Flyer* (Universal, 1926) upon release. The serial was ten chapters in length, which had lately become the standardized length for both Universal and Pathé. This sign of episode cutback was dictated principally by an effort to evoke stronger economy measures in chapter play production costs. According to Kalton C. Lahue in *Continued Next Week* (University of Oklahoma Press, 1964), a sometimes unreliable but generally competent history of the silent serial, "by 1922, the production of serials required a larger expenditure of money, for both costs and salaries were spiraling upward. The minimum spent neared $90,000, and many serials went above $200,000 prior to release." Spencer Gordon Bennet — he had become the principal director on the Pathé serials at the same time Levine started in competition — has said that on the average the Pathé serials that he directed in the mid and late twenties were budgeted at $10,000 an episode.

Levine didn't lose money on *The Silent Flyer* but he cannily recognized the fact that were a producer able to bring in a chapter play for half of what had been spent on this initial effort, and then market it on the state's rights network, he might easily double or triple his profit margin. This inspired him to head for New York with his bride — he had recently married — to found and incorporate Mascot Pictures, a production company intended to specialize exclusively in the making of chapter plays. Next, Levine contacted Harry S. Webb, an independent producer/director in Hollywood. Webb had earlier been working at Universal as an actor and, occasionally, in production, and had had a small role in *Reputation* (Universal, 1921) which starred Priscilla Dean, then a top box office attraction for Universal. Webb was adept at making cheap Westerns, something he began doing in 1924, most of them starring Jack Perrin, low budget affairs released for the independent market by Aywon Film Corporation. Webb was to direct, Levine to supervise and then handle sales and marketing.

The Golden Stallion (Mascot, 1927) went into production in October, 1926. One of the conventions of the silent serial had long been the tendency to feature popular athletes in the role of chapter play heroes. Jack Dempsey in *Daredevil Jack* (Pathé, 1920), Gene Tunney in *The Fighting Marine* (Pathé, 1926) preceded by James J. Corbett in *The Midnight Man* (Universal, 1919) had all been given their chance of trying motion pictures and in 1927 Babe Ruth and Lou Gehrig were offered $40,000 to star in two proposed serials, which offer they declined. Levine couldn't afford first-rate talent, but he did manage to get an athlete for *The Golden Stallion,* Maurice "Lefty" Flynn, a former Yale football star. Hoping to duplicate his success as an entrepreneur of animal stars, Levine also acquired a horse, a stallion he named White Fury for the sake of the credits, and to play the principal villain, the second half of the starring duo for *The Great Circus Mystery,* Joe Bonomo. A retired Coney Island weight lifter and, offscreen, an unassuming and even folksy storyteller, Bonomo eventually wrote a book about himself and his life which he published himself, *The Strong Man* (Bonomo Studios, 1968).

Harry Webb was a heavy drinker and not altogether trustworthy, but he knew now to achieve effects and manufacture stunts which would have been rather costly at a major studio by doing nothing less than taking desperate chances with his screen personnel. Carl Krusada and William Lester wrote the screenplay for *The Golden Stallion*, but they weren't quite sure of how to end it. The plot concerned the secret clue to a fabulous gold mine branded onto White Fury's neck. In the final episode, "The Lost Treasure," Bonomo was instructed by Webb, in a frenzied fight with "Lefty" Flynn, to brandish a club in order to scare off White Fury. What Webb did *not* tell Bonomo, and therefore what still mystified Bonomo when he came to write his autobiography, was that White Fury had been trained to charge at anyone waving a club in his vicinity. Staging for this strategic moment was all-important to Webb, so he set up the location at the edge of a steep barranca, told Bonomo in the course of the fight to start waving the club, and made certain the camera was so positioned as not to miss anything if Bonomo were accidentally to back up so far that he fell off the edge of the barranca. It happened just that way, with the edge of the barranca composed of loose gravel and dry turf giving way and Bonomo careening head over heels into the gully. Unfortunately, not having been let in on the play, Bonomo neglected to drop the club so White Fury, seeing it still waving in Bonomo's flailing hand as he spun and cartwheeled, followed him over the side. Assuming a sitting position part way down to maximize friction, all the terrified Bonomo could do was look back at the enraged White Fury also breaking his own descent in this fashion, wild wrath still in his eyes, sitting and sliding downward after Bonomo.

"Good work, Joe!" Webb was shouting from the top of the cliff as the camera was grinding. "Great ... great! This'll make history."

Since it was a silent film, the technical crew as well as the rest of the company could join Webb in applauding Bonomo — which of course was hardly reassuring to Bonomo until he heard someone, above the din, shout for him to drop the club. He dropped it and then somersaulted off to the side, appearing to have been killed by the fall. White Fury, now that the club was gone, reached the bottom and disinterestingly sniffed around the gully floor.

Webb rather adroitly convinced Bonomo that the scene had been done in the best possible way. Once the serial was released, Webb even went so far as to comment to Bonomo, without any intimation of cynicism, "I've got to admit you're a good actor, Joe. The audiences think you really *were* scared."

Released in January, 1927, *The Golden Stallion*, perhaps due to its formula of hectic, nonstop action and its thrilling finish, did so well on the state's rights market that Levine was able to commence production on two more chapter plays that fall, *Isle of Sunken Gold* (Mascot, 1927) and *Heroes of the Wild* (Mascot, 1927). Of the two, *Isle* went into production first and was by far the weaker and structurally the more slapdash. To star in it, Levine decided to engage Anita Stewart. Stewart had had the female lead in a serial, *The Goddess* (Vitagraph, 1915), following her earlier break in *A Million Bid* (Vitagraph, 1913), a five-reeler with which Vitagraph initially launched itself into the production of multiple reel films. Her subsequent starring vehicles, *The Juggernaut* (Vitagraph, 1915) and *The Girl Philippa* (Vitagraph, 1917), put her not far behind Mary Pickford, Marguerite Clark, and Clara Kimball Young as one of the most popular leading ladies of the teens.

Louis B. Mayer, who by the time Levine was signing Stewart to a contract was vice president in charge of production for Metro-Goldwyn-Mayer, the producing arm of Loew's, Inc., had himself first decided to enter the film production field in 1917 and his first step was to sign the then extremely popular Anita Stewart to a contract whereby she agreed to work exclusively for a new corporation Mayer set up which he called Anita Stewart Productions, Inc. Vitagraph sought to enjoin Mayer from doing so by filing a lawsuit, but Mayer's contract finally prevailed and Stewart was permitted by court decision to go on to star in some fifteen features for Mayer, in addition to two she had to make for Vitagraph in settlement of the dispute. The Mayer films invariably followed the same formula with Stewart, in Bosley Crowther's words in his book *Hollywood Rajah: The Life and Times of Louis B. Mayer* (Holt, Rinehart & Winston, 1960), playing "the poor but decent girl conducting herself with honest purpose, always against temptations and harsh assaults, with a full reward for her virtue bestowed in the happy end." Many years later, Stewart confided to Crowther, "'I have often wondered since if it would not have been better if I had remained in dear old Brooklyn with Vitagraph.'" Mayer chose, when the time came, not to renew Stewart's contract and she was definitely in decline at the box office when Levine hired her, but, this notwithstanding, she would go on to make a number of low budget features in the late twenties for producers like Trem Carr and even one for Harry Cohn's then struggling Columbia Pictures.

Bruce Gordon was hired to play the male lead in *Isle*. He had first come to notice as a chapter play personality in the early twenties. He gave a fairly competent account of himself in *The Timber Queen* (Pathé, 1922) opposite Ruth Roland and was cast opposite Roland again the next year in the ill-fated *Ruth of the Range* (Pathé, 1923). Gilson Willets, the screenwriter on *Ruth*, had died while the serial was in production and shooting had commenced before the script had been finalized. As a consequence no one knew how the story was supposed to come out. Added to this, Roland had had a falling out with Bruce Gordon and insisted he be removed as her leading man. Frank Leon Smith, the ace among the Pathé screenwriters, had been called in to save the situation, and he refused to part with Gordon. The following year Gordon was cast opposite Allene Ray in *The Fortieth Door* (Pathé, 1924), a serial destined to establish Ray's popularity as a heroine more firmly than ever, but it was not until she was joined by Walter Miller that a viable new serial team emerged. Gordon had found jobs scarce after *The Fortieth Door* and responded with alacrity to Levine's offer.

In the story of *Isle of Sunken Gold*, Gordon, a gallant sea captain, comes upon a half map locating a fabulous treasure. He finds the island indicated on the map and is pleased to discover that it is ruled over by a princess of European parentage played by Stewart. She is in possession of the remaining half of the map and the two of them join forces in the face of hostile mutineers and native outlaws. They are assisted in their perils by a mysterious simian figure known as the "Devil-Ape" who turns out in the end to be a half-crazed white man. Duke Kahanamoku, a Hawaiian athlete known for his ability at surfing who was frequently cast in Polynesian-type roles in the twenties, perhaps most notably in *Lord Jim* (Paramount, 1925) based on the Joseph Conrad novel, added a degree of verisimilitude, along with other South Sea islanders as extras.

One of the reasons, to be sure, that Anita Stewart had agreed to make the serial was her hope that it would have the same effect, at this point in her career, that *The Goddess* had had at the beginning, although her role in *Isle* was far more exotic. It was not so very different for Jack Hoxie whom Levine hired to star in *Heroes of the Wild*. His first major break in films had come with the chapter play *Lightning Bryce* (Arrow, 1919). It was an independent production sold on the state's rights network and had been sufficiently successful that Hoxie was signed again the next year to star in *Thunderbolt Jack* (Arrow, 1920). Hoxie's leading lady in *Thunderbolt Jack* was Marin Sais whom he married a year later. In the early twenties, Hoxie continued to star in a number of Western features, independent low budget films all of them, the last group produced in 1922 by Anthony J. Xydias' Sunset Productions. Hoxie's career took a dramatic turn for the better when he was signed to a four-year contract by Universal in 1923 to star in an unlimited series of Western features to be filmed and marketed under Universal's Blue Streak brand name. The Blue Streak Western series, which also in time featured Art Acord and Pete Morrison, other low budget Western players, was designed by Universal to compete with the low budget independent Westerns being produced by men like Xydias for the grind houses and the rural trade.

A good rider, although incapable of reading and able to print only the most rudimentary words, Hoxie projected an oafish, bumpkin image which Universal was convinced would continue to have a solid appeal with the audience for which they were aiming. Like the high budget Universal specials with Hoot Gibson, the most popular movie cowboy in the Universal stable at the time, the Hoxie films were to avoid the sobriety and excessive sentimentality associated with the Westerns of William S. Hart and were to remain in a lighthearted vein at all times. There was, however, one difference in the scripting of the Hoxie pictures as opposed to those with Hoot Gibson: the scripts often called for the fun to be poked *at* Hoxie, rather than as in Gibson's case where the humor came about as a result of a comic situation. A rousing publicity campaign ensued, but the Hoxie star never did rise to expectations and in 1927, his four-year contract up, Hoxie was out of work. Levine snapped him up. It was his intention to get whatever box office value he could from an ex-Universal headliner. Hoxie, for his part, felt much the same as Anita Stewart and others who agreed to make chapter plays; he reckoned that the continued exposure over ten successive weeks in at least ten thousand theatres would help his career. Sadly, or perhaps inevitably, given Hoxie's rather limited screen accomplishments, it did not.

The Golden Stallion, although filmed in Southern California, had been a Northwestern in terms of setting. *Heroes of the Wild* was to be a sagebrush drama and for Harry Webb, who was directing, as the reader might easily guess after seeing what happened on *The Golden Stallion*, that meant Joe Bonomo again as the principal heavy. To this Levine added his own innovation: joining a male star with a horse and a dog to form a triad hero. This had never been attempted before in a chapter play. It was in the December, 1918 number of *All-Story Magazine* that Max Brand's first Western novel, *The Untamed*, had appeared. It told of Dan Barry who is accompanied on his adventures by his dog Black Bart and his horse Satan. Zane Grey had first used such a triad hero in his own first Western novel, *The Heritage of the Desert* (Harper's, 1910), but Brand thrust this triad relationship more into the forefront of the action. Brand's novel was adapted for the screen the next year, under the same title, *The Untamed* (Fox, 1919), starring Tom Mix. Frederick Faust, who wrote under the pen name Max Brand, added two more novels featuring Dan Barry before he brought this mini-saga to a close. *The Night Horseman*, the second of the Dan Barry novels, published in 1920, was also adapted for the screen with Tom Mix, altered in title to *The Night Horsemen* (Fox, 1921). While there was, therefore, no want of precedent in either the kind of pseudo-Western fiction Max Brand wrote or in these early features of teaming a horse and a dog with a Western hero, without question *Heroes of the Wild* was the first serial to do so and, as such, it proved immensely popular. It was a format Levine would continue to use repeatedly over the years and, indeed, the second to last serial Mascot produced before the merger to form Republic Pictures was *The Adventures of Rex and Rinty* (Mascot, 1935), teaming Rex, the Wonder Horse, and Rin Tin Tin, Jr. The tradition Levine had begun was not carried on, however, by other serial producing companies, including Republic.

For the horse, Levine again cast White Fury, but without any fisticuffs scripted between him and Bonomo. For the dog Levine acquired a German shepherd that was given the screen name Tornado, another reincarnation of a wolf dog which would become so marked a prototype for many of the Mascot chapter plays henceforth. Al Rogell, one of Hoxie's regular directors at Universal, had always eschewed close-ups or anything about Hoxie that would even hint at the expression of emotion, simply because Hoxie was incapable of showing emotion. The Mascot script sought to compensate for this disability on Hoxie's part by keeping him in the saddle or involved in physical conflict of some kind along with fast-paced, continuous action and a reliance on the animal stars to help carry the picture.

There was a scene in which Joe Bonomo was supposed to creep up on a ranch house and kidnap a baby. Bonomo thought nothing of it, since he had become quite good friends with Tornado on the set. The scene called for Tornado to leap from a barn loft and attack Bonomo before he could get away with the baby in his crib. Bonomo was armed with a protective arm pad. The scene began and everything went fine until Tornado sank his teeth into Bonomo's arm; Tornado's teeth passed right through the pad and went deeply into Bonomo. Bonomo let out a yell and he jerked up his arm so abruptly that the dog flew off into the air, hitting Bonomo's upper teeth in the process and opening a two-inch gash across Tornado's nose. Yelping in pain, the dog ran whining all the way across the barnyard. Nor would he return under any circumstances and do the scene a second time. When a replacement was found for the scene, production was further delayed when it was discovered that the substitute stand-in for Tornado took directions only in French and everyone had to wait until a trainer who spoke French could be located. Webb, to assuage Bonomo's fears, had him covered with double arm pads on both arms. The scene was finally filmed as written, but for the remainder of the serial Tornado refused to have anything more to do with Bonomo.

White Fury portrayed a horse called The Ghost of the Gauchos, a wild stallion carrying on his leg the key to a vast fortune, the rightful owner of which was the leading lady, Josephine Hill. Hill's uncle and guardian, played by Bonomo, is in league with a bunch of crooks and they plot to snatch the wealth. Fortunately for all concerned except the bad guys, Jack Hoxie playing Jack Hale, joined by Tornado and White Fury, are on hand to protect Hill's interests. Of course, at the fade, Hoxie wins both the girl and the fortune.

When Mascot released *Isle of Sunken Gold* in September, 1927, and followed it with *Heroes of the Wild* in November of that year, independent exchange managers, exhibitors, and patrons all seemed in a consensus that Mascot was producing serials very nearly the equal of those being made by Universal and superior to any of those produced by other independent companies. Part of this enthusiastic response was certainly due to the plotting of the Mascot serials, which even this early in the history of the firm illustrated the peculiar pattern of ingredients that came to characterize the Mascot product. Never long on logic — as what serial ever was? — the Mascot chapter plays packed as much action as possible into every episode, whereas both Pathé and Universal tended to stress story as much as action. But there was another attribute they had, one for which Harry Webb was initially responsible, but which became even more pronounced once he was terminated and was replaced by Yakima Canutt: the fabulous appeal of breathtaking stunt work.

Since Canutt becomes such a central figure beginning with the 1928 season, this is undoubtedly the best place to introduce him to the reader. Born Enos Edward Canutt at Colfax, Washington, on November 29, 1896, Canutt had been mistakenly called Yakima Canutt by a newspaper reporter covering the Round-Up at Pendleton, Oregon, in 1914 — because Canutt originally came from Washington's Yakima Valley — and the name had stuck. In 1917 at the Round-Up Canutt was awarded the title of World's Champion All-Around Cowboy. Yak was also awarded the *Police Gazette* Cowboy Championship Belt in 1917, 1918, 1919, 1921, and 1923; in 1923 he was presented with the Theodore Roosevelt trophy. During his off months from the rodeo circuit, Yak worked as an extra in pictures and then branched out into stunt work. Ben Wilson, who was a production supervisor at Universal where Yak frequently hired on to do stunt jobs, admired Canutt's athletic prowess and his expert horsemanship. He proposed to feature Yak as a player in a series of independent Westerns he was to make to be released by Arrow Productions, the releasing company for Jack Hoxie's first two chapter plays. Canutt's first role was one of support in *Sell 'em Cowboy* (Arrow, 1924) with Yak as second lead. *Branded a Bandit* (Arrow, 1924) with Yak in the lead closed out the year.

Dick Hatton, a character actor in low-grade Westerns whom Levine would occasionally employ at Mascot in later years, could as easily star in one of Wilson's productions like *The Cactus Cure* (Arrow, 1925) with Yak as a bullying foreman named Bud Osborne (an inside joke, since Bud Osborne was also a real person, a rodeo wrangler who would have a long career as a character actor in Westerns), as he could star Yak as a rugged Western hero in a film like *The Human Tornado* (Arrow, 1925). Neither the cast nor the story line mattered much to Wilson. He was contracted to supply a given number of Western features, and that is what he did, films often without distinction. If Film Booking Office, a major releasing company at the time, was impressed with one of Wilson's Westerns, like *The Ridin' Comet* (FBO, 1925) starring Yak, Wilson would sell it to them directly to distribute through their exchange network. If not, there was always the state's rights network. Wilson could write, direct, and star himself in a Western, as he did in *West of the Law* (Rayart, 1926), and then turn around and take a bit part in a major studio production like *Rainbow Riley* (First National, 1926). Following his example, Yak began free lancing, taking any kind of work as long as it guaranteed him his minimum asking price, $125 a week.

The independent producer Hal Roach, today best remembered for the short comedies he produced, especially those with Laurel and Hardy, featured Yak in *The Devil Horse* (Pathé, 1926). Rex who was being billed as the "King of the Wild Horses" had first attained popularity because of the series of features Roach had produced with him. Rex was cast as the devil horse. The picture proved to be one of the most memorable equestrian films of the twenties — rivaling *Just Tony* (Fox, 1922), which featured Tom Mix's horse, and *Wild Horse Mesa* (Paramount, 1925), based on a Zane Grey novel; and what was most significant about it was the harrowing battle Yak staged between Rex and a painted stallion. The footage was so spectacular that Yak found ways of using it in the later chapter play *The Vanishing Legion* (Mascot, 1931), which also featured Rex, and in *The Devil Horse* (Mascot, 1932) when this original story idea was expanded and reworked to comprise a serial of the same title. Ken Maynard borrowed the footage for use in his film *The Strawberry Roan* (Universal, 1933) and Yak, when under contract to Republic in the late thirties, used it repeatedly in pictures like the Three Mesquiteer Western *Hit the Saddle* (Republic, 1937) and even in a Gene Autry opus that same year from Republic. Audiences for serials and Westerns were not discerning or sophisticated enough to recognize that the same footage was being used again and again — or, if they were aware of it, never seemed to object.

For the 1925-1926 season, Canutt starred in four independent Westerns for Goodwill release on the state's rights market. All told, throughout the twenties, Canutt would be credited for performing stunts, either for himself or for another player, in some forty-eight films. Harry Webb's drinking problem and his indifference to rather basic safety precautions irritated Levine to the point where he fired him and as a replacement shrewdly contracted Yak at $50 an episode to take charge of all stunts and all second unit work in the Mascot chapter plays. Further, as part of his contract, Yak was to have acting roles in all the chapter plays on which he worked. He was even billed fourth in his initial effort for Levine, *The Vanishing West* (Mascot, 1928), the second of the two serials produced by Mascot that year.

At the time Levine rented office space at the Metropolitan studios — today known as General Service studios — on Las Palmas Avenue. Harry Webb also had an office there. After parting with Levine, Webb signed a contract with John R. Freuler's Biltmore Productions, a small independent company associated with a Poverty Row conglomerate known as Big Four Productions. Webb was soon again producing and directing low budget Western features with Jack Perrin. However, he was quite friendly with Yak even while Yak was working for Mascot and occasionally he would hire Yak for stunt work and action sequences in this new series, in films such as *Ridin' Law* (Big Four, 1930) in which Yak was also billed second, or Yak might himself star in a Western for another member of the Big Four conglomerate as he did in *Canyon Hawks* (Big Four, 1930) produced by National Players. During the influenza epidemic after the Great War, Yak had contracted bronchial pneumonia. For days his bronchial tubes had bled. His voice had altered. It had gotten weak. He would have to shout to be heard. When his voice had finally come back, it had a rasping quality. Yak realized very early that he did not record well and, since sound was the coming thing, it was a conscious decision on his part to concentrate on stunt work. The consistency of his efforts at Mascot over the next several years not only enhanced his reputation as a creative stunt director, but, as probably will become evident, they accounted to a large extent for the unrelieved and thrilling tempo that came increasingly to characterize the Mascot serials.

In his autobiography, *Stunt Man* (Walker, 1979), Canutt commented about Levine and his years at Mascot: "Nat Levine was not only a sharp operator, he knew how to handle people. He could get more work out of a crew than anyone I have ever known. Sometimes he would come out with the kind of impossible order that would ordinarily send people into tantrums. However, with Nat's crews and actors, it would have the opposite effect. They would laugh it off and Nat would laugh with them. He was a shrewd businessman who had a keen appreciation for what people were going through."

Levine's two serials for 1928 repeated the formulae from 1927: *Vultures of the Sea* (Mascot, 1928) had a sea story background as had *Isle of Sunken Gold* and *The Vanishing West*, like *Heroes of the Wild*, was a Western. Levine hired Wyndham Gittens to work on the screenplay of *Vultures of the Sea* and their association would prove, as Levine's association with Canutt, a lasting one, through most of the years that Mascot was active. Gittens, who had begun in the industry as a film editor with Biograph and who had worked successively for Triangle, Paramount, and then M-G-M, wanted most of all to write. Levine gave him that chance and, presently, Gittens proved so expert at it that Levine made him story editor supervising the scripts on all Mascot productions. Perhaps it was due to Gittens' addition to the staff that *Vultures of the Sea* turned out so well, although part of the credit should certainly go to its director, Richard Thorpe.

Having begun his career in vaudeville in 1915, then going on the legitimate stage in 1921, Thorpe, who was born at Hutchinson, Kansas on February 24, 1896, began directing films in 1923 and among his earliest credits as a film actor was the feature *Burn 'em Up Barnes* (Affiliated, 1921) which Mascot would eventually produce in a chapter play version. Thorpe's initial work as a director was in short comedies and, throughout the mid twenties, he directed some seventy-two Western features for Pathé directly or for Action Pictures which were distributed by Pathé. Following his association with Mascot, Thorpe would go on to direct several high quality Westerns in the Thirties and then become a director of numerous top of the bill features, especially for M-G-M.

For a chapter play, *Vultures of the Sea* had exceptional production values. Johnnie Walker, who had given a fine account of himself in the serial *Galloping Hoofs* (Pathé, 1924) opposite Allene Ray, was the male lead. He was perhaps rather more familiar to audiences for his work in features and, interestingly, the previous year he had even appeared in a Samuel Bischoff production with Silver Streak titled *Where Trails Begin* (Bischoff, 1927). Shirley Mason, a popular ingénue in programmer pictures who had played Jewel in *Lord Jim* (Paramount, 1925), was given the feminine lead. The story involved Walker's father who is falsely accused of murder and sentenced to death. The crime was supposedly committed for the sake of a fortune hidden aboard the ship on which Walker's father had been a crew member. Walker ships out on the vessel to learn the identity of the real culprit, a formidable task with Tom Santschi, remembered for his vicious screen fight with William Farnum in *The Spoilers* (Selig, 1914), Frank Hagney, who was a particularly surly heavy, and—marking his first Mascot appearance—Boris Karloff all among the suspects. Shirley Mason is the owner of the ship but she is held a virtual prisoner. It isn't until the final episode that both Walker and Mason evade death successfully for the last time and find both the hidden gold and the guilty party.

It was an odd talent of Levine's that he could not only take advantage of actors and players on their way down, but also that he could see unusual potentials in the as yet untried, many times before anyone else did and sometimes potentials which might not have occurred to another. The presence of newcomers from Boris Karloff in *Vultures of the Sea* to Gene Autry in *The Phantom Empire* (Mascot, 1935), seven years in the future, or giving men like Canutt and Gittens creative freedom, would surely attest to this penchant for gambling on aspiring talent while *The Vanishing West* with its roster of Western stars from independent productions in the twenties demonstrated Levine's unbiased use of actors whose careers were in a slump. Leo Maloney, Jack Daugherty, Jack Perrin, Yakima Canutt, and William Fairbanks, all of whom had starred in silent Westerns of varying quality, mostly from weak to downright bad, were teamed together. Perrin who was simultaneously working in the Harry Webb vehicles played Mickey Bennett's father, a man who, unjustly accused of a crime, is a fugitive from justice. The repetition of this theme — it was to become even more prominent during the sound era — was an essential psychological ingredient behind the popularity of the Mascot chapter plays. Mickey Bennett was also, significantly, Levine's first attempt to assign child actors major roles in his serials, a practice which he maintained in subsequent productions. A villainous uncle, in hopes of gaining possession of a mysterious fortune, seeks in turn to become Bennett's legal guardian. This, too, was to become a common ingredient. Although Leo Maloney's Western features had been of the lowest grade, many of them produced and distributed independently by the Weiss brothers, Maloney had taken a leaf from Tom Mix in *The Untamed* and customarily appeared with his horse, billed as Flash, and his dog, billed as Bullet. So here again was the triad hero, a man, his horse, and his dog, as had been the case in *Heroes of the Wild*. It is equally worth noting that because of their story lines the Mascot Western chapter plays were making a dramatic departure from the formulary plots of Western features that were still largely mired in the tradition of the ranch romance inspired by Owen Wister's influential novel, *The Virginian* (Macmillan, 1902), and preceded before that by four decades of dime novel Western romances.

The Fatal Warning (Mascot, 1929) was Mascot's last silent serial and the first of Levine's two entries for the 1929 season. Richard Thorpe was again contracted to direct both it and *The King of the Kongo* (Mascot, 1929), the latter slated to become Mascot's first sound chapter play. Levine had been budgeting his serials at $30,000 and seldom exceeded this budget by more than $5,000. To make $70,000 stretch for two serials, one of which would require expensive sound recording equipment, Levine had to avoid using a name cast for *The Fatal Warning* — leaving that for *The King of the Kongo* — but he made up for this deficiency by signing quite capable, if lesser known, players and by providing them with an uncommonly intriguing story.

The Fatal Warning also brought with it the introduction of a serial convention with which Mascot would do more in the next five years than any of its competitors: the master villain who is also a mystery man finally unmasked in the last chapter. This was not a new idea, to be sure, but Mascot's writers seemed to surpass everyone else in thinking up weird and unusual villains to be unmasked. Those from the sound era — The Voice, The Rattler, the Wolf Man, The Wrecker, The Eagle, El Shaitan (a word play on Satan) — are remembered by some viewers far better after more than forty years than are either the casts or the story lines. *The Fatal Warning* opened with George Periolat, playing an executive officer of a bank. He is reading a novel with the same title as the serial when he is confronted by a mysterious intruder; Periolat then disappears. He is suspected of having stolen $100,000. Helen Costello, portraying his daughter, denies this charge and calls on a friend, Ralph Graves, playing a criminologist, to clear her father's name. The lamp of suspicion moves from one character to another until Costello and Graves are incapable of distinguishing between friend and foe.

Foremost among the suspects is Boris Karloff, having returned for his second Mascot serial. Karloff's first serial appearance had been in *The Hope Diamond Mystery* (Kosmik Films, 1921) in which he played the high priest of a strange cult. This chapter play had made use of tinted scenes so that Karloff, when he would rub his hands over the surface of the diamond of the title, seemed to be drawing from it rings of multicolored light. He proves something of a red herring in *The Fatal Warning* and even more so in *The King of the Kongo*. In *Kongo*, every time a fatal catastrophe is about to befall the hero, played by Walter Miller, or the heroine, Jacqueline Logan, there are invariably shots of Karloff's sinister features aureoled by shadows. The last chapter holds, therefore, a double surprise; not only is the real culprit unmasked, but Karloff is revealed to be none other than Logan's father.

The really costly aspect of *Kongo* was that it had to be issued in three versions. The first was silent. The second was a sound-on-disc arrangement to accompany the silent film. The third was the full-fledged sound-on-film version. Levine had the daring to attempt a sound serial well in advance of Universal. Henry MacRae, who was in charge of the Universal chapter plays, had been having an ongoing fight with Carl Laemmle, head of the studio, about making an all-talking serial, Laemmle turning a deaf ear to him because Universal's sound engineers were adamant that it was impracticable, if not altogether impossible, to film a chapter play in the new sound medium. This same rule applied to all the outdoor pictures Universal was producing at the time and, hence, while both Ken Maynard and Hoot Gibson were making Western features for Universal, only some of the sequences — generally confined to interior scenes — were released in a sound format. Following the release of *Kongo*, MacRae succeeded in persuading

Laemmle to renege and proceeded at once to produce his own all-talking serial, *The Indians Are Coming* (Universal, 1930), starring Tim McCoy, which earned over a million dollars for the studio, principally because of the novelty of its being all-talking and definitely not because of any inherent merit it might have had as either a serial or as a Western.

Pathé, on the other hand, was all but defunct by 1929 primarily because of the stock manipulations of Joseph P. Kennedy. A banker and financier from Wall Street who had made a fortune in bootlegging, Kennedy was in Hollywood a total of thirty-two months, during which time he accumulated $5,000,000 as a result of taking over Film Booking Office and then merging its facilities with Pathé, combining this group with the Keith-Orpheum theatre circuit, and selling this miniconglomerate to General Sarnoff's Radio Photophone Company to become RKO Radio Pictures. Kennedy's work promoting Fred Thomson and Tom Tyler as matinee idols taught him a whole new set of techniques he would put to even more effective use years later when he decided to seek political careers for his sons.

As a consequence of Kennedy's mergers, Pathé's reigning serial team of Walter Miller and Allene Ray were released from their contracts. Levine responded swiftly, hiring Miller to star in *The King of the Kongo*, while Universal reciprocated by contracting Allene Ray to costar in *The Indians Are Coming*. But the coming of sound did not prove auspicious for either; Miller was quickly relegated to character and heavy roles, while Allene Ray, because of voice and acting problems, slipped even more readily into secondary roles and then, unable to secure screen work of any kind, into retirement.

For *Kongo* Levine hired Lee Zahler, a commercial film score composer, to compose and synchronize an accompanying musical score for the serial and a theme song, "Love Thoughts of You," which Zahler dedicated to heroine Jacqueline Logan. Henceforth, Zahler would compose the music for the opening credits on all the Mascot serials and, where needed, devise musical interludes during the course of the action. His music, exciting and often spellbinding, aptly added to the memorable visual impact of the chapter plays.

Kongo went into general release in August, 1929. The previous month what was left of the Pathé organization had put into release the last chapter play the company had made, starring Walter Miller and Allene Ray, the silent *The Black Book* (Pathé, 1929), and Mascot was right in position to take advantage of Pathé's publicity campaign with their serial, which had the virtue of sound in addition to Walter Miller. In *Kongo* Miller plays a secret service agent who journeys to a jungle temple to solve the disappearance of his brother who is also in the secret service. Jacqueline Logan is in the same jungle, in her case searching for her missing father. Miller's only clue is a trinket of gold, indicating the possible location of a buried treasure near the temple. Miller is drawn to Logan immediately when he discovers that she possesses a trinket similar to the one he has. A gang of ivory thieves are in control of the temple, ruthlessly in pursuit of the treasure, while in the temple's depths a man who knows the secret of the treasure but will not reveal it is being held prisoner by the gang. The menacing king of the kongo, referred to in the title, is a giant gorilla who plagues Miller and Logan at every turn.

Levine usually left his wife Frances in charge of the office in New York while he was out on location during the production of a serial. *Kongo* proved to be a solid success, financially if not altogether artistically, and put Mascot in a solvent condition to withstand the initial tremors of the stock market crash in October, 1929. Leo Maloney, who had starred in *The Vanishing West* for Levine, was in New York about the same time *Kongo* was being filmed, trying to market an independent feature he had produced, directed, and in which he had starred with Jack Perrin, Wally Wales, who was another star of low-grade independent Westerns in the mid twenties, and Allene Ray, titled *Overland Bound* (Rayton/Presidio, 1929). The significiant thing about *Overland Bound* was that it was an all-talking Western, coming quickly in the wake of *In Old Arizona* (Fox, 1929), made earlier that year, directed by Raoul Walsh and Irving Cummings, and starring Warner Baxter, who was to win an Academy Award for his portrayal in it of the Cisco Kid. With the collapse of Pathé, which had hitherto been distributing Maloney's Western features, Maloney had decided that he could very well produce and distribute his own Westerns. There was, however, a major problem with *Overland Bound*, and it was not the story, written by Ford Beebe and Joseph Kane; rather it was the primitve sound—so inferior as to be uncomfortably distracting. Despite this, Maloney was still able to sell the picture on the state's rights market under the Presidio banner. Triumphant with his success, Maloney, who had long been a heavy drinker, took to celebrating his victory in ebullient fashion. It proved too much for his heart, apparently, since on November 2, 1929, it was reported in the trades that he was dead from a heart attack while staying at the Astor Hotel. Leo, Starlight, and Bullet had taken their last ride together.

Levine had little time for sentimentality. Too many things were happening to him, too many good things. Marcus Loew, with whom Levine had begun in the business, had died in 1927 and Nicholas Schenck had succeeded him as president of Loew's, Inc. "He would have been successful in a legitimate business," Will Rogers had quipped about Loew. But he had reasons to quip. Loew had not changed his will since 1912 and it began as follows: "In the event that the net value of my estate exceeds $200,000...," an irony in view of conservative estimates valuing Loew's estate at $30,000,000. Levine kept this image of wealth and grandeur before him as the twenties ended and the Great Depression began and with it that strange, unprecedented period in American films.

Three

The Voice Speaks

Now that the Mascot serials had found a voice, Levine worked harder than ever, and he worked all the time, especially when in production. In this he served as an example to his cast and crew members who were regularly asked to work overtime and Saturdays in order to complete a serial on schedule.

Rin Tin Tin had certainly been one of the most successful actors of the silent era, although his drawing power and popularity might be almost unthinkable today. The dog—that is, the real Rin Tin Tin coupled with his many doubles—had an intuitive responsiveness before the camera, a striking perceptiveness, and a nearly human range of emotions, able to depict by physical posture and facial expressions, even the way he held his ears or tilted his head, very subtle feelings and sudden shifts in mood. And then there were his eyes, deeply sensitive, variously bright, fierce, sad, a mirror to feelings ostensibly beyond the ken of his canine comprehension. That he was also an action star may be less consequential in forming a judgment of him than acknowledgment of the fact that his success stemmed most precisely from the touching, tragic, and tender moments he portrayed on the screen.

In Volume V of his *Collected Works*, titled *Symbols of Transformation* (Princeton University Press, 1956), C.G. Jung found reason to observe that the "lack of discrimination in the child makes it possible for the animals which represent the instincts to appear at the same time as *attributes* of the parents, and for the parents to appear in animal form..." (the italics are Jung's). After sound, dog pictures never inspired the following they did in the twenties, with the possible exception of the Lassie property. There were a wealth of literary precedents prior to the twenties, for one thing. Jack London's *Call of the Wild* (Macmillan, 1903) had become a classic; a dog story on the surface, beneath that surface it is an allegory of modern man's struggle to dominate nature and in it nature and the wilderness finally triumph when Buck, a wolf-dog, accompanies the wolf pack into the wastelands and becomes their leader. London followed this novel with *White Fang* (Macmillan, 1906) where he told of a dog that comes to choose domestication over running free, reversing the ending of *Call of the*

Wild. London's last dog stories, *Jerry of the Islands* (Macmillan, 1917) and *Michael, Brother of Jerry* (Macmillan, 1917), were but pale imitations of his earlier works. But there were others to carry on his tradition, although perhaps none to ever quite equal him at his finest. James Oliver Curwood, a popular author of stories set in the Canadian Northwest, created Kazan, his dog of the North. Max Brand produced many dog stories for pulp publication, although his best was *The White Wolf* (Putnam's, 1926). Western writer Hal G. Evarts, Sr., wrote *The Cross Pull* (Knopf, 1920), which was filmed the next year under the title *The Silent Call* (First National, 1921) with a German shepherd named Strongheart in the role of Flash.

Strongheart proved an immense success — soon there was a dog food named after him, which is still being sold today. Other studios sought to compete. Rin Tin Tin made his debut in a film story attributed to James Oliver Curwood when he appeared in *The Man from Hell's River* (Western Pictures, 1922). Once Rinty was featured in *Where the North Begins* (Warner's, 1923), Warner Bros. decided to promote him into a major property. Even though he had been first, Strongheart was soon outshown, as were all of Rinty's competitors, Klondike, Peter the Great, Kazan who had also preceded Rin Tin Tin with his appearance in *Kazan* (Export/Import, 1921), the Bischoff/Levine creation Silver Streak, Levine's own Tornado, Leo Maloney's Bullet, or even Bart the Great Dane whom Tom Mix occasionally used, outshown because while they might all have an interesting bag of tricks, none could breathe human meaning into his performances for the screen as could Rin Tin Tin.

In *The Lighthouse by the Sea* (Warner's, 1924), the keeper of the light, played by Charles Hill Mailes, has gone blind. This fact is hidden from his superiors by his daughter, played by Louise Fazenda. A storm rages and Rinty in company with his master, William Collier, are ship-wrecked only to be rescued by the light keeper's daughter. Collier and Fazenda fall in love. But it is Rinty who comes to the old man's aid when rumrunners overpower him and it is Rinty who once more kindles the light. Darryl F. Zanuck, later the head of production at Twentieth Century-Fox, did the screen adaptation. "Rin Tin Tin could do anything," Mel Gussow quoted Zanuck as saying in *Don't Say Yes Until I Finish Talking* (Doubleday, 1971), "... or rather Rin Tin Tins could do anything. Actually there were about five or six Rin Tin Tins at one time ... one for long shots, one for closeups, one to play gentle parts, one to fight. Another could jump and do terrific stunts. Another had marvelous eyes."

It was this combination of Rin Tin Tin incarnations that in the public's mind came to represent a single animal. During the last months of the Great War, Leland Duncan, a sergeant with the American Ex-peditionary Force in France, discovered a German shepherd and her litter of five puppies in the wreckage of an airfield. Duncan saved the dogs' lives and, reputedly, only brought one of them back with him to Southern California, the original Rin Tin Tin. He supposedly bred his Rin Tin Tin retinue and trained all the dogs in various skills. Whatever the case, in *The Night Cry* (Warner's, 1926) Rinty is accused of turning criminal when a herd of sheep is preyed upon by a giant condor. He is sentenced to die. John Harron is Rinty's owner in the film, June Marlowe is Harron's screen wife. Harron hides the dog. When the condor steals their child, Rin Tin Tin races after him, rescues the child, and after a terrible fight kills the bird. No man has ever stood accused before the bar of justice, and been innocent, yet borne up so well under his torment as did Rinty in this picture.

Rin Tin Tin, in addition to earning Lee Duncan some five million dollars, has been cited as having been responsible for supporting Warner Bros. long enough, despite the studio's penchant for expensive, money-losing silent pictures with Broadway actors like John Barrymore, for Warner's to take full advantage of the Vitaphone process and be in the vanguard of talking films. One of the reasons behind Rinty's box office may have been his ability to win enduring favor, most of all with juvenile audiences, because he was able, at least in part, to project a nobility and degree of loyalty that would be somewhat incredible in a human being. To echo Jung's words in a slightly different context, a dog doesn't have such a highly developed ego which must go before all else in his life, and so his behavior may actually *be* altruistic at times.

Competition may not have hurt Rinty, but the coming of sound did. He made *Frozen River* (Warner's, 1929), a part-barking, part-talking film, and *The Million Dollar Collar* (Warner's, 1929) was part-barking. It was based on an idea supplied by its director, D. Ross Lederman, and, as he told me late in life, of all the actors he ever worked with in his long career, Rin Tin Tin was the most capable. "You probably think his trainer, Lee Duncan, always told him what to do," Lederman said. "He may have in the beginning. I don't know. But when I worked with him we needed very few retakes and almost no extensive rehearsing. That dog knew just what was expected of him. He would watch Duncan for a signal, if movement was required. He couldn't tell time. But as for emoting, or playing a scene right, he didn't need any coaching. That's the unusual thing about that dog. He actually seemed to understand the story line well enough to bring off his role better than most of the other actors in the picture. I had more trouble with Tim McCoy and Buck Jones later at Columbia than I ever had with Rinty at Warner's. He was one of the few truly professional actors we had in Hollywood at that time. He just went about his business."

Prospects for work did not look particularly appealing for Rinty when his Warner's contract expired until Nat Levine summoned him to Mascot to make the first all-talking, all-barking serial in canine or human history. Levine offered Duncan a flat $5,000 on a term-of-the-picture contract. Since Rinty had earned much more while at Warner's, Duncan supressed mention of this sum when he came to write his autobiography some years later. Yet, with this "star" cost and full sound recording equipment, which Levine leased from Walt Disney now that Disney had come to Hollywood—consisting of a mobile truck unit for location work and a dubbing service that Disney also rented out when not preparing one of his cartoons for Columbia release — production estimates to bring in the serial, to be titled *The Lone Defender* (Mascot, 1930), exceeded $40,000. Richard Thorpe again directed.

Perhaps, at this point, a distinction should be made between *The King of the Kongo* and *The Lone Defender*. Even though *Kongo* was advertised and sold as being all-talking, it would, by contemporary standards, be termed a "soundie," some talking but music and effects all the way through. *The Indians Are Coming* from Universal had a similar format. In *The Lone Defender* there were no moments where music was used as a bridge or effects alone were employed. Although many scenes were obviously still filmed silent, talking was dubbed into them. It is quite evident to a modern viewer every time this occurs, but probably for audiences in 1930 the novelty itself was such that little attention was paid to the mechanics of just how the talking effect was achieved.

Walter Miller was signed for the male lead along with Buzz Barton, a former silent child star at Pathé. Buzz was by this time in his early teens and Levine, wanting to have both a teenage boy *and* a girl, somewhat dubiously cast June Marlowe, who had played John Harron's wife in *The Night Cry* four years previously, as a teenager. The plot involves the murder of Rinty's owner, a desert prospector with a secret gold mine. The culprits are Lee Shumway, who is actually a notorious bandit known as The Cactus Kid, and Bob Kortman — Kortman would henceforth become a regular in the Mascot stable of screen heavies. Rinty recognizes Kortman as the murderer of his master but, when he attacks him, he is pulled off. Harking back to Rinty's performance in *The Night Cry*, at one point he is suspected of having killed a young colt when, in fact, he sought to protect him from being menaced by a wolf. The dog is sentenced to death but Walter Miller, who turns out to be a special deputy in the Department of Justice, steps in to save him at the last minute. The villains then seek to kidnap Rinty and force him to lead them to the secret mine, but they are hindered in this also and, by the fade, the mine is restored by Miller to its rightful owner, June Marlowe.

Release of *Phantom of the West* (Mascot, 1931) was postponed until New Year's Day. Unlike *The Lone Defender*, which was in twelve episodes, *Phantom* had only ten, an economy move undertaken to offset rising production costs. D. Ross Lederman, who was at the time very much in need of a break, was hired to direct *Phantom* and it was on the basis of this credit that he angled himself a job as a contract director at Columbia Pictures, directing their series Westerns with Tim McCoy.

To star in *Phantom*, Levine cast Tom Tyler who, before the merger of FBO into RKO Radio Pictures, had been a Western headliner for Joseph P. Kennedy at Film Booking Office. Born August 9, 1903, at Port Henry, New York — his given name was Vincent Markowski — Tyler's first silent Western feature was *Let's Go Gallagher* (FBO, 1925) in which a young Frankie Darro, who would also soon be working at Mascot, had a substantial role. Released from FBO in early 1929, Tyler contracted with a low-budget Poverty Row producing company called Syndicate Pictures to make a total of six Western features, of which the last films had synchronized music and effects tracks, before Syndicate thought they would try their hand at producing all-talking Westerns. After three such entries, the series was dropped. Following his appearance in *Phantom of the West*, Tyler was hired by Universal, as was Yakima Canutt to handle the second unit direction, for *Battling with Buffalo Bill* (Universal, 1931). The exposure he gained from these two chapter plays released in the same year proved he was capable of transition to the sound medium and led to a starring series for Trem Carr at Monogram Pictures. Tyler would eventually be replaced in the Monogram Western series by John Wayne, who would remake many of Tyler's 1931 Monogram entries in 1934. Chapter plays over the next decade, despite several series of very, very low-budget series Westerns, became a staple for Tyler and he would go on to star in *Jungle Mystery* (Universal, 1932), *Clancy of the Mounted* (Universal, 1933), *Phantom of the Air* (Universal, 1933), *The Adventures of Captain Marvel* (Republic, 1941), and *The Phantom* (Columbia, 1943) — indeed, it is surprising with what regularity the word "phantom" keeps turning up in the titles of Tyler's serials. John Ford would cast Tyler in *Stagecoach* (United Artists, 1939) where he is shot by John Wayne and it was John Wayne whom Tyler himself would in due course replace in Republic's Three Mesquiteers series in the early forties after *Stagecoach* had made Wayne too big a star to work any longer in a minor "B" series.

In *Symbols of Transformation*, Jung suggested that in myths and dreams wrapping oneself in a cloak can signify invisibility, or hence to become a spirit. *Phantom of the West* was the first Mascot serial to feature a masked and caped mystery villain, suspected at one time or another to be just about every person in the cast. The Phantom is somehow connected with the Mystery Riders, a group of cloaked men who ride in and out of the action singing; it is not until the final episode that we learn that they are actually vigilantes on the Phantom's trail. Zane Grey was probably the first one to employ this imagery in Western fiction when in his *Riders of the Purple Sage* (Harper's, 1912) we are told that one of the characters "recognized the huge bulk and black-bearded visage of Oldring and the lithe, supple form of the rustler's lieutenant, a masked rider. They passed on; the darkness swallowed them. Then, farther out on the sage, a dark, compact body of horsemen went by, almost without a sound, almost like spectres, and they, too, melted into the night." Even more germane may have been the very successful horror feature made by Lon Chaney, *The Phantom of the Opera* (Universal, 1925), based on Gaston Leroux' *Le Fantôme de l'Opéra* (Paris, 1910). But another reason a phantom was used in this serial was because Carl Krusada worked on the screenplay. He had worked on the scenario for *The Golden Stallion* but, more importantly, the previous year he had scripted *The Phantom of the North* (Biltmore, 1929) for Harry Webb. What would be more natural than doing *Phantom of the*

West the next year? Of course, Harry Webb had cast Joe Bonomo as a heavy in *The Phantom of the North* and Bonomo was on hand for *Phantom of the West* as a heavy.

It might be that Levine opined no one would ever suspect character actor Tom Dugan of being the Phantom. If that was the case, he was probably right. Dugan, who had a long career ahead of him in comedy roles, stuttered and was treated as a buffoon throughout the serial until the last chapter when he was unmasked. Only serial logic could possibly have given him away. What is serial logic? Just this: who is the person least suspected? When the Phantom throws one of his darts into a crowded saloon, containing a warning to everyone, is Tom Dugan in the forefront? He is. Now, ordinary logic would discount Dugan on the basis of his inability to be in two places at once. Not serial logic. Serial logic holds that he not only is capable of being in two places at once but since, at some point during the serial, everyone except Dugan has become a suspect, it must of a certainty be Dugan. Nor am I ridiculing a chapter play convention. Serial logic became a highly developed art among chapter play patrons and if school children were learning Euclid's geometry in school they were learning serial logic in the theatres.

In *Phantom*, a man is wrongly accused of having murdered Tom Tyler's father. He escapes from prison and, while a fugitive, leaves a note for Tyler proclaiming his innocence and insisting that there are seven men in town who know the identity of the real murderer. For the remaining episodes, variously plagued by the Phantom or his minions, assisted and intimidated by the Mystery Riders, Tyler is engaged on a quest in search of his father's slayer. However, this is a motion picture chapter play and not Greek tragedy; in a serial, any serial, when a father is killed, or a father figure, it cannot be by the hero, just as when a father or a father figure is wrongly accused of a crime, he can never be found guilty. At the end, Dugan is carried off by the Mystery Riders, thus giving the whole sequence of events a dream-like unreality.

Perhaps much of the action and the staging would have been far more effective than it was had it not been for D. Ross Lederman's direction. As a director, Lederman was something of an oddity. His principal concerns, throughout his career, even throughout his many years at Columbia, remained budget cutting for its own sake (something which, however, endeared him to producers and production supervisors), getting actors to do their jobs themselves with only minimal interference, and, most of all, a concern for his own personal income. Unfortunately, he himself took no particular pride in the many films he directed. All which may well explain why Richard Thorpe was once more engaged to direct Levine's next serial, *King of the Wild* (Mascot, 1931).

To begin the new season — *Phantom of the West*, despite its release date, was a 1930 production — Levine wanted a blockbuster and he wanted to cast in it Harry Carey and Edwina Booth, both of whom had just returned from several months in Africa shooting *Trader Horn* (M-G-M,

1931). He had a jungle story fashioned for the two in hopes of cashing in on Metro's massive publicity for their jungle picture and, with this in mind, both Carey and Booth were signed for one serial each and an option, to be exercized by Mascot at its discretion, for them possibly to make two more. Production problems at M-G-M, however, prohibited either of them from coming to Mascot as scheduled — much of the animal footage from Africa had proved useless and the cast and crew of *Trader Horn* were dispatched to Mexico to shoot new sequences. Levine hastily substituted Walter Miller in the role originally intended for Carey and Nora Lane, a leading lady in Westerns in the late twenties, was signed for Booth's part. *King of the Wild* also marked Boris Karloff's last chapter play at Mascot. He was cast as a suspicious-looking sheik named Mustapha. Presently he would be signed by Universal to play the monster in *Frankenstein* (Universal, 1931) and become too high-priced for chapter play productions. This serial was laid in India, in the Arabian desert, and in the heart of darkest Africa — although, in truth, most of it took place on rented sound stages and at Yuma, Arizona, making *King* the first serial Levine would choose to shoot anywhere save in Southern California.

The plot had some intriguing aspects to it. Walter Miller, while in India, is falsely accused of murder and sentenced to life imprisonment. Naturally he escapes and by the end of the first chapter finds himself on board a ship bound for Africa. Also on board ship are cages filled with wild lions, tigers, and leopards, all of which are let loose when the ship begins to sink, tossed about by a tropical storm, attacking the passengers and crew. Karloff, as Mustapha, is at his camp on shore when his bearers bring Nora Lane's young screen brother to him. The brother, played by Carroll Nye, is delirious and raves about having discovered a fabulous diamond field. Karloff is willing to let the young man recover from his fever before forcing him to talk and divulge the secret of the diamond field's location. At this point, one of Karloff's men arrives to inform him that a strange beast unheard of in Africa — it's a tiger; Wyndham Gittens, it would seem, liked the idea of displacing wild beasts from their native habitats — has been captured in a pit. Karloff, upon seeing the beast, concludes that it must have made its way to shore from the sinking ship. Amid the superstitious jabberings of his people — Hollywood almost always presented African populations as jabbering! — Karloff decides that he will fling Carroll Nye into the pit with the tiger if he will not talk. Returning to his tent, Karloff puts it to the young man, talk or else. Of course, it's else, and he is flung into the pit. Serial logic dictated that, no matter how valuable a person, if he was not acquiescent when importuned by a villain, he would be thrown to the lions — or, in this case, a tiger. There was no provision in serial logic to resort to more subtle and less foolishly fatal methods. This concludes the second chapter. By the third, the young man is seen, after summoning superhuman resources, to climb out of the pit.

Karloff, however, is important to the story for another reason. He possesses a letter, written in *invisible* ink, which ascribes the crime for which Walter Miller is accused to a convict named Dakka, played by Mischa Auer. Only Karloff knows how to bring out this invisible writing. Tom Santschi, playing a man named Harris and accompanied by a creature half human, half beast, called Bimi, is in pursuit of this letter for his own ends. Karloff easily puts him off by giving him a forgery, keeping the real letter, which was originally taken from Walter Miller, hidden. When, later on in the course of the action, Karloff is threatened by a leopard, and Miller saves his life, Miller demands the return of the letter. This Karloff does, reluctantly, and with an evil glint in his eyes, since he sees his blood-thirsty tribesmen — jabbering tribesmen were also invariably bloodthirsty — approaching through the jungle. He and Miller engage in fisticuffs, Miller readily knocking him down and escaping, the enraged tribesmen howling after him in pursuit.

By the end of the chapter play, Miller and Carroll Nye are finally rescued by an army of troopers, the jungle equivalent of the U.S. Cavalry racing to the rescue of white settlers surrounded by whooping "redskins." In the mêlée, Santschi snatches the exonerating letter and attempts an escape on horseback. The horse becomes frightened, rearing, and Santschi falls off, plunging to his death over a cliff. The brutish Bimi retrieves his master's body, struggling to comprehend the meaning of death. The script reads at this juncture:

> 127. LONG SHOT TOWARD THE SETTING SUN as beautiful as we can make it. Bimi with Harris' body in his arms, goes from camera up the rocky hillside moaning his sorrows to the open sky on and on and on as the scene slowly fades into darkness.

I have recounted these incidents from the screenplay because, I think, they are indicative not only of the powerful and strange story lines of the Mascot chapter plays, but more, they give us some insight into the minds of the audiences that made for their popularity. Here, at the nadir of the Depression, Americans seemed to be fascinated with the notion of the brutish and bestial seeking sympathy and human understanding. Boris Karloff's monster in *Frankenstein* would make this appeal. Bela Lugosi, leading a group of crazed brutes seeking revenge on Dr. Moreau, the vivisectionist responsible for creating them, played by Charles Laughton, in *Island of Lost Souls* (Paramount, 1933), would chant, "half human, half beast." The giant ape in *King Kong* (RKO, 1933) was another outgrowth of the same fascination. Yet this had long been a staple of the Mascot chapter plays, variously from the "Devil-Ape" in *Isle of Lost Souls* who turns out to be a man, to the giant gorilla in *The King of the Kongo*, to the nearly human characterizations of animals in *Heroes of the Wild*, *The Vanishing West*, and *The Lone Defender*. Conversely, the treatment accorded Native Americans in *Heroes of the Wild* and native peoples in serials like *The King of the Kongo* and *King of the Wild* only further supported the common American paranoia concerning any other culture not conforming to American middleclass values. Mascot may have inherited this racial stereo-typing from the Hollywood milieu, to which it has always been so profoundly typical, and is therefore not to be singled out for blame. But it is, I suspect, more than a curiosity that while supporting such stereotypes effectively in one direction the company in its serials should have been in the vanguard in another direction, elevating animals anthropomorphically to an almost human level of sensitivity and perception. It was perhaps only another aspect of the tendency to create triad heroes. "The Crucified," Jung wrote in *Symbols of Transformation*, "is traditionally flanked by two thieves, one of whom ascends to paradise while the other descends to hell. The Semetic gods had two *paredroi*; for instance, the Baal of Edessa was flanked by Aziz and Monimos (Baal astrologically the sun, and Aziz and Momimos, Mars and Mercury). The Babylonians grouped the gods into triads. Thus the two thieves somehow go together with Christ." Is it really so far from these myths of the ancient world to the patterns in the Mascot serials? In *King of the Wild*, Karloff and his Africans are consigned to the nether regions, Tom Santschi among the villains quite literally, while the brutish Bimi is transformed by a — for him — nearly divine enlightenment whereas the heroes are redeemed by a legion of would-be angels in military garb.

There was such a legion in *Phantom of the West*. There was presently to be another; indeed, from it was derived the title of the second production for that year, *The Vanishing Legion* (Mascot, 1931). This serial also posited another variation on the triad hero, one part of which was the leading man, in this case Harry Carey, another part of which was an animal, here being Rex, still billed as the "King of the Wild Horses," and a third part of which was, as it had been in *King of the Wild*, a young man or boy, in the case of *The Vanishing Legion* the role assigned to twelve-year-old Frankie Darro.

The Mascot production schedule for 1931 had been standardized at twenty-one days for approximately 25,000 feet of finished film. *The Vanishing Legion* was begun in May and required only eighteen days to complete. *The Galloping Ghost* (Mascot, 1931), which would follow it into production, would be shot in seventeen days during the summer, and *The Lightning Warrior* (Mascot, 1931), which would close out a bountiful year, would be filmed in twenty-three days in November. However much Gittens and his staff of writers might work on the story line, when it came to action sequences in the scripts, a blank space was left with a notation, "See Yak." Among Yak's directors when he was starring in silent Westerns had been Richard Thorpe and, accordingly, the two worked easily together at Mascot.

Following *King of the Wild*, Thorpe left for better things and Levine replaced him with B. (for "Breezy") Reeves Eason. During the silent era, Eason had been a director known for his ability to handle action sequences — he had been in charge of the second unit direction, for example, on *Ben Hur* (M-G-M, 1926), whereas Yakima Canutt would be charged with the same responsibilities when it was remade in 1959. Born October 2, 1886, at Pryore Point, Mississippi, Eason in appearance was a man of five feet, eight inches with red hair and intense blue eyes. He had begun as a stage actor in stock companies and graduated to vaudeville before joining the American Film Company in 1913 as a director. By 1918 he was hired by Norwood Productions as a producer-author-actor and that same year directed his first feature film, *Nine-tenths of the Law* (Atlantic, 1918). His first experience directing a chapter play came with *The Moon Riders* (Universal, 1918), an eighteen chapter opus starring Art Acord. Eason shared the directorial credit with Albert Russell. By the late twenties, Eason had become very good friends with Hoot Gibson and customarily directed most of Gibson's specials for Universal release. Universal, convinced that Western features had no box office potential in the sound era, released Gibson after the 1930 season and, with him, Breezy Eason. Levine thought he would give Eason a try. Eason had long been a roustabout, a heavy drinker, and did not always show up on time when in production because of his frightful hangovers, but he could readily make up for lost time, once he did arrive, by breakneck shooting.

For the title *The Vanishing Legion*, Mascot borrowed from Universal's *The Vanishing Rider* (Universal, 1928), as it had once before when making *The Vanishing West*. *The Vanishing Rider* had starred William Desmond, who had been released from his contract with Universal and Levine had hired him for a character role for *Phantom of the West*. Desmond's association with chapter plays had reached its zenith with *The Riddle Rider* (Universal, 1924) and *The Return of the Riddle Rider* (Universal, 1927), and his costuming for his role as sheriff of Milesburg in *The Vanishing Legion* was his Riddle Rider outfit.

Not having had Harry Carey and Edwina Booth for *King of the Wild*, Levine had no choice but to cast them here. Despite the fact that Booth had been paid only $75 a week by M-G-M and had not had a single line of comprehensible dialogue in all of *Trader Horn*, she nonetheless saw herself by now as a great star. She was in the process of suing M-G-M for $10,000,000, insisting she had contracted a jungle disease while in Africa, although gossip on the set at Mascot had it that she had either suffered a miscarriage or had an abortion and was trying to cover it up. At any rate, the whole business added scandal and notoriety to the fame she was getting from the success of *Trader Horn*. Carey had been cast as Horn and Duncan Renaldo, later to play Spanish American types, the best remembered of which is the Cisco Kid, despite the fact that he was of Rumanian descent, had been the young male lead. The scandal only intensified once Renaldo made a low budget programmer with Booth, right after her appearance in *The Vanishing Legion*, titled *Trapped in Tiajuana* (Mayfair, 1932). Renaldo's wife at that time commenced an alienation of affection suit and, feeling somewhat vengeful, exposed him to the U.S. Board of Immigration as an illegal alien. Renaldo was, for a short time, even imprisoned as a result of the immigration problem, although totally pardoned by President Franklin D. Roosevelt. When Renaldo returned to the screen, it would be working for Herbert J. Yates and Nat Levine at Republic Pictures.

In view of the importance of *Trader Horn* to serial production and to

Mascot Pictures in particular, it would perhaps not be going too far afield to say a few words about it here. "One day Mrs. Ethelreda Lewis was sitting on the porch of her house in South Africa," read the front flap on the dust jacket of *Trader Horn* (Simon & Schuster, 1927) by Alfred Aloysius Horn and Ethelreda Lewis. "Out of the quiet a strange old man walked up to her. He was a straight old man bearing a heavy pack of goods and looked as though he were bearing only frying pans and coffee pots for sale. Actually, he bore the strangest story of romantic adventure, of dangerous exploration, that has burst upon a hungry world in a generation. It's a story of a Rip Van Winkle who awoke from a sleep in Africa and bore a tale more marvelous than Marco Polo's." Although first printed at a modest 3,500 copies, within a year it had sold over 150,000 copies. The book consisted of Horn's reminiscences of the Ivory Coast in the 1870s, as related to Mrs. Lewis. Colonialism was then at its height. The savagery of the land, the primitivism of its aboriginal peoples, the timelessness that accompanies a ritual culture where memory is erased and consciousness obscured by group forgetfulness, these were the things Horn described, these and the quest for a white woman who had been made into a tribal fetish.

It is this last part, the fetish, that is bothersome. When Horn first met Mrs. Lewis, a South African novelist, he was not totally untutored. He was familiar with the Tarzan stories and mentioned them to her in conversation. He spoke frequently of the cinema and probably had seen more than a few of the pictures supposedly set in Africa. A cycle of such films had begun with the release of the chapter play *Miracles of the Jungle* (Warner's, 1921). Elmo Lincoln, who had first played Tarzan in *Tarzan of the Apes* (First National, 1918), continued this cycle with *The Adventures of Tarzan* (Numa Pictures, 1921), a fifteen chapter serial produced by the Weiss brothers that was edited to ten episodes and reissued by the Weiss' newly formed Artclass company in 1928 with synchronized sound effects in the wake of *Trader Horn's* popularity. Next followed *With Stanley in Africa* (Universal, 1922) in eighteen chapters. But it was reserved for Colonel William Selig to produce the crowning achievement of the cycle in *The Jungle Goddess* in 1922, the serial that inspired G.A. Atkinson's comments about Hollywood chapter plays in a column for the *London Daily Express* quoted in the first chapter of this book. Selig spent money on *The Jungle Goddess*, including funds for the use of some 470 wild animals. The story told of the young daughter of an English lord who is kidnapped and thrown into the basket of an aerial balloon. Cut loose by accident, the balloon is shot down over darkest Africa and the girl, played by Vonda Phelps, is captured by cannibals and made into a tribal goddess. Many years pass before her childhood friend, portrayed by Truman Van Dyke, mounts the search for her rescue, which he finally accomplishes in fifteen chapters.

The point is, had Horn seen Selig's film? If not, it was nonetheless reissued in 1929, like *The Adventures of Tarzan* the previous year, because of the intense interest in things African incited by *Trader Horn*. It would be amusing to learn that the film gave birth to Horn's tale, just as the publication of his tale brought new life to *The Jungle Goddess*. The abduction of Nina T—and her ultimate rescue by Horn and Peru, the young man who assists him, occupy less than an eighth of the book's twenty-six chapters. "The English set a great store by facts," Horn told Mrs. Lewis, "but if a book's to be sold in American you must keep your eye on the novelties." Elsewhere he remarked, "I think I told you that that girl Nina T---- will be the pivot of the book. It sure was a bit of a shock to find the daughter of a good English family doing her duty as goddess to Isorga." Mrs. Lewis was circumspect enough to follow each chapter written by Horn, retaining his misspellings and outrageous syntax, with quoted conversations between them. Horn appears to have been quite concerned as to the prospects of producing a best seller. "Aye," he is quoted. "Come to Nina's story, I would have crammed the whole narrative into three ... chapters. There was little enough of it." In the end, that is all Nina's story took, but with a lot in between. The motion picture screenplay concentrated on those three chapters.

However spurious this particular story, in defense of Horn it should be said that he did provide a vivid portrait of life in Africa as he had known it, animals preying upon each other for survival, black tribes preying upon the animals, white men preying upon both and the natural resources. It was a world characterized by murder, by the white man's insatiable need to pillage, and by a silence beneath the blazing sun. Other authors, mostly Europeans, had been horrified by the spectacle of the slaughter they saw in colonial Africa. Conrad recorded his recoil in *The Heart of Darkness* (Doubleday, 1910). Horn spoke as fundamentally, if with less poetry: "Best not to throw too high a light on some of my experiences on the Coast. It never does to give good folk a shock. Aye. Talk of dreadful scenes ... a young lad brought up never to think of evil nor read it in a book—and he gets to the Coast at eighteen ... seventeen, it might have been... He feels Revolt ... the shock of it's like to make him sick."

Horn's account, as I have said, had a tremendous impact on the United States. Irving Thalberg at M-G-M was impressed by the story of Nina and perceived its cinematic possibilities, especially if filmed in Africa. Louis B. Mayer agreed. Once the film was in release, M-G-M made a small fortune selling stock footage that had been shot in Africa. Pauline Hemingway's Uncle Gus financed her husband's trip to Africa with her so Ernest Hemingway could write *Green Hills of Africa* (Scribner's, 1935), in which Hemingway called Pauline "P.O.M." (Poor Old Mama); it also provided the background for Hemingway to write one of his best short stories, "The Short Happy Life of Francis Macomber," and in another short story, "The Snows of Kilimanjaro," parody his resentment of Pauline's family's wealth. Isak Dinesen, the Baroness Blixen, whose husband Hemingway met in Africa, would write after her divorce from Blixen *Out of Africa* (Random House, 1937), which has since become a literary classic. "Aye," Horn said once in regard to Africa's greatest lesson for him, "the first thing education teaches you is to walk alone ... you can sure stand on your own spear when you've learnt the word goodbye, and say it clear."

Thalberg and Mayer wanted Wallace Beery for the role of Horn, no doubt because of Beery's portrayal of Professor Challenger in *The Lost World* (First National, 1925). Beery would have nothing to do with it. He didn't want to go to Africa. So Harry Carey, who was playing vaudeville in East Hampton to recoup losses he suffered to his $750,000 ranch during the St. Francis Dam break in California, was approached. Carey was born January 16, 1878, in New York City and had begun his career in 1906 writing and acting in stage melodramas. He entered the film industry in 1908 as an actor working for D.W. Griffith at Biograph. In 1911 Carey started going to the West Coast with Griffith's outdoor troupe to make Westerns and outdoor pictures and in 1915 he was signed by Universal to star in a series of Western two-reelers and features. Several of these two-reelers had been directed by John Ford and Ford's first Western feature, in fact the first feature he was to direct, was *Straight Shooting* (Universal, 1917) with Harry Carey. A taciturn, strong personality, much in the vein of early movie cowboy William S. Hart, Carey had suffered in the twenties, as did Hart, when contrasted with the glamour exhibited by the ascendant Tom Mix and Mix's imitators. Carey left Universal in 1922 and starred in several low budget Western series, including a series for Pathé before its merger. He had starred for M-G-M in *The Trail of '98* (M-G-M, 1929), a Western with music and sound effects, and so he was fresh in Irving Thalberg's mind. Thalberg told Carey his top price was $600 a week. Olive Fuller Golden, Carey's wife, thought it too little, what with Africa and all. They argued, took their argument to a friend, Will Rogers, and Rogers took it to his wife, a practical soul. Carey was signed.

Horn, somewhat ironically, had commented to Mrs. Lewis that American readers would likely be surprised to learn that his elocution instructor at St. Edward's was Edwin Booth, "the brother to the feller that shot Lincoln." It was while Thalberg was testing several contenders for the female role of the goddess, Bessie Love, Thelma Todd, and Jeanette MacDonald among them, that a young starlet created quite a commotion at the administration building about not being paid for having posed for a series of stills, a job that was done usually for nothing even by name stars. But Edwina Booth, from the beginning, felt she was someone special, and she wanted compensation. Thalberg had her tested. He liked her. Mayer liked the price, $75 a week and found, the "found" being all the trappings of an M-G-M cinema queen. W.S. Van Dyke, engaged to direct the picture, found Booth obnoxious and said so in the book he subsequently wrote about the making of the film, *Horning into Africa* (California Graphic Press, 1931).

Olive Carey was also given a part, and she came out the best of all. When the expedition returned to the States, Mayer fired all of them. Seven months in British East Africa (not the Ivory Coast!), and they were no closer to having a finished picture than when they began. Two M-G-M producers, Bernie Hyman and Paul Bern, after viewing all the footage at M-G-M's Culver City studio, convinced Thalberg that the picture could be saved, and Thalberg convinced Mayer. The principals were all rehired at their same wages — hence Levine's disappointment about having Carey and Booth in *King of the Wild* — all, that is, save Olive Carey. She had had only a small part as a woman missionary and Thalberg thought he could dispense with her entirely. Only he couldn't, and keep the valuable original footage of her death and supposed burial at Murchison Falls, something Horn himself would never have proposed since the "natives," as he described them, would have dug up her white body and turned it into a fetish anyway. Thalberg offered Ollie, as she was familiarly called, $300 to complete the sequence, the same she had been paid for the whole expedition. Ollie balked. Thalberg had originally planned to replace Ollie with Marjorie Rambeau, whom he had been willing to pay a thousand dollars a day. Ollie held out for the same price. Finally Thalberg gave in. She received $5,000 for as many days' work.

Van Dyke, in his book, claimed that the African actor Mutia Omoolu, who had played Renchero, was a natural performer before the camera and that he nearly stole the picture. If he did not do that, he came very close to it, in starkest contrast to the savagery with which the other Africans were invariably depicted. His quiet person, infused with and projecting an inner sense of civilization that was visually denied to his culture by all the imagery in the film, he leaves the viewer of *Trader Horn* even today with the idea of spiritual fortitude, the way Van Dyke felt about him when he asked of "the white and black men of our country ... who laugh, [how many] would step in front of their employer and take the thundering charge of a rhino, ... would stand fast and firm with a huge lion hurtling at them in the air, ... would ever be ready to stop drinking water themselves that the man for whom they carried a gun might not lack...?" The happy ending of Peru, played by Renaldo, and Nina, played by Booth, was written in Hollywood; Van Dyke, using Mutia Omoolu, created another ending, no less romanticized maybe, but completely visual, told by the camera and Mutia Omoolu himself. Not romantic love, but human nobility itself, white and black, surely this was Van Dyke's intention when, at the end, we see Horn, portrayed by Harry Carey, heading once more up the river, Mutia Omoolu's face superimposed on the horizon making the wild denizens less wild, and the heart of man less dark.

"That is, he dreamed a new human relationship. A stark, stripped human relationship of two men, deeper than the deeps of sex. Deeper than poverty, deeper than fatherhood, deeper than marriage, deeper than love. So deep that it is loveless. The stark, loveless, wordless unison of two men who have come to the bottom of themselves. This is the new nucleus of a new society, the clue to a new world-epoch." Are these familiar words? They might be. They are the words of D.H. Lawrence used in his book *Studies in Classic American Literature* (Thomas Seltzer, 1923) to describe another friendship, that between Natty Bumppo, Hawk-eye, and Chingachgook, the great serpent, in James Fenimore Cooper's Leatherstocking Saga, a role, that of Hawk-eye, which very shortly, in 1932, Harry Carey would portray at Mascot; but these words apply equally to the concluding image

Van Dyke wrought for *Trader Horn* as a film, an image Lawrence termed "the myth of America."

And now they were at Mascot, at least Harry Carey, Edwina Booth, and, portraying a character assigned the screen name Miss Lewis (!), Olive Fuller Golden. Joining the by now familiar heavies, Joe Bonomo and Bob Kortman, was Dick Dickinson, whom Canutt introduced to Levine, and Pete Morrison who, like Jack Hoxie, had once made Universal Blue Streak Westerns. Tom Dugan was also back, as was Lafe McKee, the latter having long played venerable elderly gentlemen in films. McKee's role for *The Vanishing Legion* was offbeat for him, to say the least, since he is revealed in the final reel to be the master villain, The Voice, who is behind all the trouble; he is horribly stamped to death by Rex. Bob Kortman appealed to Levine for the same reason Boris Karloff had, namely his jaggedly coarse features; he was The Voice's right hand. Throughout the serial, until McKee is exposed, the audience never sees The Voice, but only hears his spoken orders via a shortwave radio. He speaks in a whisper and almost magical power is attached to his verbal conjurings, Chapter One going so far as to be titled "The Voice from the Void," more than a little suggesting a symbol for the unconscious. The dark and startling plot of The Voice and his gang to sabotage the Milesburg Oil Company is set, however, against a backdrop of the most standard of sets. The serial was shot on location at the Prudential lot outside Newhall, California, where Hal Roach had located *The Devil Horse* with Yak and Rex so that now Yak could optimally match old footage from the Roach picture with the new, while The Voice's men hid out on a set at Universal's Studio City lot which had been used earlier that same year as Grogan's tenement building in *Heroes of the Flame* (Universal, 1931), a Tim McCoy serial. In Chapter Two, "The Queen of the Night Riders," stock footage from Tom Mix's *The Great K & A Train Robbery* (Fox, 1927) was interpolated into the Mascot action footage.

Edward Hearn, who had costarred with Ruth Roland in *The Avenging Arrow* (Pathé, 1921), a fifteen chapter serial on which W.S. Van Dyke had been the codirector, had appeared in Mae West's homosexual stage play *The Drag* in 1927, the same year he had played George Washington in *Winners of the Wilderness* (M-G-M, 1927) with Tim McCoy and Joan Crawford, also directed by W.S. Van Dyke—Tim McCoy once confided that Van Dyke was one of Hearn's champions in the motion picture industry in spite of Hearn's sexual inclinations. Levine also supported Hearn and regularly cast him in Mascot productions. In *The Vanishing Legion*, Hearn played Frankie Darro's screen father, falsely accused of murder. Although, by the end, he is freed of all guilt through the efforts of Darro, Harry Carey, and Rex, the triad hero, the scenes where he fondles and kisses Darro, and there are several of them, are either amusing or in poor taste, depending on your point of view. Edwina Booth, it turns out, is the rightful heir to the Milesburg Oil Company, working undercover as Hearn's private secretary, and the Vanishing Legion, much like the Mystery Riders in *Phantom of the West*, is a vigilante group dedicated to serving her interests and seeing to it that she receives her rightful inheritance; in this capacity, in the final episode, the Legion drives off The Voice's gang, thus rescuing Carey, Darro, Hearn, and Philo McCullough, the leader of the Legion, from death at the hands of The Voice. Booth at last can make the grand gesture, sharing her wealth with Carey, Darro, Rex, and the Legion.

"The Voice has spoken" is the eery susurration by the master villain at the conclusion of every message to his gang. When, at one point, a receiver falls into the hands of the law, The Voice is able to make it explode by remote control. This notion was soon to be elaborated at Mascot, and later at Republic, until the master villain was able, in time, to blow up gang members when they were captured and before they could reveal his secret identity, truly a demonstration of how science can become the handmaiden of magic and the will to power.

Harry Carey died in 1947 of a heart attack. Sometime after his death, his widow, Olive Fuller Golden Carey, moved to her present home, outside Carpenteria, on the Coast highway from Santa Monica to Santa Barbara. In winter, 1971, I drove there to see her. She looked not much different from the way she had when she appeared in John Ford's *The Searchers* (Warner's, 1956) or the same year in Sam Fuller's *Run of the Arrow* (RKO, 1956), although her hair was whiter and she had grown somewhat stout. Leading me through an outer porch on the back wall of which were many stills of her husband from various Western movies he had made, Ollie made herself comfortable in a cozy living room and told me to have a seat. She lit a cigarette.

"Harry always said I smoked like a chimney," she chuckled in delight, "but I'm still here." She was in her eighties.

"How does it come that you know so much about what happened on Harry's pictures and even on his Mascot serials?" I asked.

Because I was there on the set with him almost every day," she said animatedly.

"Wasn't that a little unusual?"

"Not at all! Harry couldn't drive. I had to drive him to work and pick him up at night."

"Didn't he ever learn how?"

"Never!"

"But, Ollie, I saw him driving a car in *The Vanishing Legion*."

"You did not. You saw him steering a car they were tugging with ropes. Oh, he tried to learn once, but he ground the gears and the transmission collapsed. He swore he'd never try to drive again and he was a man of his word."

I paused to light a cigarette. "Ollie, I've asked this question of a lot of people, including Nat Levine. What made for his astonishing success?"

"That's an easy one. And you can tell Nat Levine I said so. As long as he ran his office out of his vest pocket, he was a good businessman. When he started hiring others and moved into an office himself, he wasn't so good. He was the kind of man who worked best when he was right there, while they were shooting, making the picture. Once when Harry was doing *The Vanishing Legion*, Bob Kortman needed a business suit. He'd forgotten to bring one with him. The scene had to be shot. Nat jumped into a rain barrel, took off his own pin stripe, and gave it to Kortman."

"You can't be serious, Ollie."

"You can laugh if you want to," she said, "but it was that kind of spirit that made Nat Levine everything he ever became."

Four

The Lightning Warrior

After his experience on *The Vanishing Legion*, Levine worked out a new budgeting system. The first chapter of a serial which was now standardized at three reels was budgeted at $5,000. The remaining chapters were budgeted at $3,000 each. He couldn't hope to beat Universal on polish or budgets, stars or a far-flung exchange network, but he consistently could and did on price. Carl Laemmle's son, known on the Universal lot as Junior Laemmle, had taken over from his father the job of head of production and he was intent on becoming another Irving Thalberg. Thalberg, in fact, had at one time worked for Carl Laemmle in that very position, before Louis B. Mayer had hired him away to head up production at Metro-Goldwyn-Mayer. It was Junior's ambition to upgrade the Universal product to vie with Metro and Paramount, and his film *All Quiet on the Western Front* (Universal, 1930), directed by Lewis Milestone, was an auspicious start. Henry MacRae, when you get right down to it, was a very limited director and as a production supervisor he had great difficulty maintaining uniformity and quality in his serials at Universal. Uniformity, on the other hand, was Levine's long suit.

Also in Levine's favor it ought to be stressed: Mascot did have a good product. Levine had found his market and strove to hold it. With a definite format, a rigid budget, an almost inflexible production schedule, working his crews from the first rays of morning sunlight until far into the night — lighting scenes with torches, if necessary; after all, who judged a serial on the basis of photography? — with his growing staff of writers under Gittens' supervision, his second unit under Yakima Canutt, the stable of regular character players, the triad hero concept with one name star, customary directors, and effective distribution on the state's rights market, Levine was accomplishing in his narrow sphere what every Hollywood mogul had at that time as an objective: he had an assembly-line product which was controlled as to consistency and guaranteed as to market. If his serials failed as works of cinematic art in the conventional sense, they nonetheless made money, some less, some more, but never was Mascot in the red. Mascot had a following. The serials might be flawed by technical crudities, but never for want of visual and emotional impact.

There was also another factor to be taken into account. Levine had

41

arranged for all his laboratory processing work from negatives and work prints to release prints to be done at Consolidated Film Industries, which was owned by Herbert J. Yates. Yates, born August 24, 1880, at Brooklyn, New York, was fully twenty years Levine's senior. He, too, had the reputation of being an entrepreneur. At the turn of the century, he ventured into the tobacco industry, first at American Tobacco and then at Liggett and Myers. He had been a witness to that trend of consolidation in the marketing and manufacturing of smoking tobaccos which characterized nearly all American industries. In *The Iron Heel* (Macmillan, 1907) novelist Jack London declared that combination is stronger than competition and for this reason the formation of combines, syndicates, and, finally, trusts is inevitable in capitalistic enterprise. Yates saw all the small tobacco manufacturers driven to the wall and crushed by the giant combines. With the advent of mass production, better utilization of manpower, and lower prices due to reduced costs of manufacture, larger firms made competition impossible and took to buying up popular brands from smaller companies on the brink of bankruptcy. These new brands and, where they existed, the manufacturing facilities were merged into the parent company.

In 1916, on the basis of his expertise at business management, Yates deserted tobacco and joined Hedwig Film Laboratories. By 1918 he was ready to strike out on his own, convinced that there was even a greater fortune to be made in the film industry than in tobacco. He bought Republic Laboratories and pursued an aggressive policy of acquisition. In 1919 he formed the Allied Film Laboratories Association. By 1927, after several more mergers, he organized Consolidated Film Industries. Yates knew from tobacco that in the process of intelligent and careful mergers the controlling company in time could remove former managements, the take-over becoming complete. His son, Herbert J. Yates, Jr., went to work in accounting for what was left of the Biograph Company for which pioneer film director D.W. Griffith had once worked. The company, indeed, continued to reissue Griffith's old films throughout the silent era and leased space for new productions at the Biograph studio in the Bronx. Presently, Yates gained a majority interest in the firm and in 1928 his son left Biograph and came to work for his father at Consolidated. Whenever Levine ran short of cash, Yates was pleased to extend him credit, or even lend him money. Yates wanted his own motion picture production company and Mascot was a comer.

The concept of two directors working simultaneously on a chapter play was an innovation begun by Pathé that Levine refashioned to suit his own peculiar needs. In the mid twenties, George B. Seitz at Pathé generally handled the dramatic, indoor episodes, Spencer Gordon Bennet, first his understudy and later his successor, the action. Levine would contract with his actors for the vague period of one month. working them constantly, while his directors, beginning with *The Galloping Ghost*, would take turns, on a day, off a day. Breezy Eason had alternated with Yakima Canutt on *The Vanishing Legion*, breaking up the entire serial into various segments between them. Levine felt Eason unreliable because of his penchant for coming to work late or hung over and this, in his opinion, placed too much of a burden on Canutt. For *The Galloping Ghost,* Levine hired Armand Schaefer to codirect with Eason. Schaefer was born August 5, 1898, at Tavistock, Ontario, and entered the American motion picture industry in 1924 as an assistant prop man at the Mack Sennett studio. He went on to become an electrician, a grip, a set dresser for other studios until he was hired on as an assistant director at Pathé, where he assisted on some fifty Western features and several action serials.

It was Levine's idea to divide the production load between Schaefer, Eason, and Canutt. However, when Eason showed up four hours late on one of his "on" days after having been out celebrating the previous night, Levine let his temper get the best of him and he fired him, promoting first cameraman Benjamin Kline to the position of assistant director to Armand Schaefer. What this promotion really meant was that Kline, for additional pay, was to take over all of Eason's responsibilities but without a director's credit. The new arrangement was for Schaefer to work on all interiors on his days, Kline on all exteriors on his days, and Canutt to work every day organizing stunts, whether indoors or outdoors. While Schaefer was filming his interiors, Kline would be setting up and planning out the next day's exterior shooting. When Kline was shooting, Schaefer would be overseeing set design, available space, props, and viewing both his rushes and Kline's from previous days' shooting so he could properly match his interior shots with Kline's exteriors.

The title for *The Galloping Ghost* was not conceived by the writing department. It was an appellation accorded Harold "Red" Grange by the press from his three years as Number 77 on the University of Illinois football team, where he proved to be one of the swiftest backs in the game. To give but one example: in the Michigan vs. Illinois game of 1924, "Red" took the opening kick-off and returned it 95 yards for a touchdown. In the next twelve minutes of the game, he went on to score three more times. In "Red" Grange, Levine at last had what he had wanted in *The Golden Stallion*, a top name athlete to star in one of his chapter plays. Grange had previously appeared in two feature films, both of them silent, *One Minute to Play* (FBO, 1926) and *A Racing Romeo* (FBO, 1927). In the latter, "Red" had played an amateur race driver who by the fade had won both the sweepstakes and the girl. At Mascot, he was cast, as he had been in *One Minute to Play*, as a super hero of gridiron.

I recall a conversation with film director Edward Dmytryk about how he achieved a certain special effect in the film *Murder, My Sweet* (RKO, 1944) which he directed. In a dream sequence, Dick Powell, playing Philip Marlowe, a private detective, is seen to fall through the air. To get the effect, Dmytryk placed Powell on a platform covered with black felt and filmed him with a revolving lens, zooming the camera away. Dmytryk was aware that a falling body will accelerate as it falls, and that there is air resistance. To achieve this additional perspective, Dmytryk then, before optical printing, matched the original piece of revolving film with another piece filmed with a camera zooming away faster and faster and merged these dual images through double exposure. At the time *Murder, My Sweet* was released, David O. Selznick was producing *Spellbound* (United Artists, 1945) directed by Alfred Hitchcock. *Spellbound* had a similar dream sequence and Selznick inquired of Dmytryk how he got his falling effect. Dmytryk would not tell him; *Spellbound* was not his picture.

The incident is significant because Mascot created a very similar technical feat at the end of Chapter One of *The Galloping Ghost*. "Red" Grange and leading lady Dorothy Gulliver bail out of an airplane. Only Dorothy has a parachute and Grange hangs onto the straps of the parachute once it opens. However, as they are descending together, the straps begin to tear and Grange, being a hero, decides to sky dive the rest of the distance, about a quarter of a mile. As the episode concludes, we see Grange falling helplessly through the air, spinning downward to certain death.

I have quoted Yakima Canutt commenting on how the crew would laugh when presented with an impossible situation like this which, somehow, had to be filmed. By using a variation of Dmytryk's technique, not only was a shot manufactured in which Grange appeared to be falling through the air but, for the next week, in order to save Grange from his doom, an additional shot was managed in which Grange was seen to land presumably on top of another airplane, grabbing onto the top wing of a biplane while both were suspended in mid air. Since Benjamin Kline was responsible for this bit of cinematic sleight-of-hand, Levine gave him screen credit in first position for the photography. This was before the days of the guilds and, although Eason had been fired from the picture, by contract he received sole director credit; Armand Schaefer was listed on the credits as associate director.

Dorothy Gulliver had been the heroine in *Phantom of the West*. As early as *The Lone Defender*, it was characteristic of Levine that he would keep the heroine in skintight riding pants as much as possible in a Western chapter play. Gulliver had been so clad in *Phantom of the West* and while for most of *The Galloping Ghost* she wore a print dress, the aerial sequence did permit Levine to costume her for a time at least in riding pants. Francis X. Bushman, Jr., son of the silent screen matinee idol, had appeared in the chapter play *The Scarlet Arrow* (Universal, 1928). In *Ghost* Levine cast Bushman as "Red" Grange's friend, Buddy. Bushman, in fact, is pivotal to most of the action since the screenplay has him secretly married to Gwen Lee. Should this become generally known, it will mean Bushman's finish as a football player; apparently, being married is against the rules. Walter Miller was back, this time as the head of a gambling ring who is intent on controlling the results of each football game. Miller's headquarters is at the Mogul Taxi garage. Tom Dugan, this time cast as a stuttering cab driver working for a rival taxi company, is Grange's ally. Dugan's company is known as Red Top Cabs. Like the Mystery Riders in *Phantom of the West* or the Vanishing Legion, the Red Top cabbies are on hand to race to

Grange's rescue whenever "Red" is set upon by Miller's henchmen from Mogul Taxi.

Theodore Lorch played a hunchback identified by Lafe McKee, who narrated on the sound track the plot from the previous chapters, as a "mysterious cripple." Being crippled, in short, makes one suspect of being evil and in *The Galloping Ghost* was a role equivalent to that of the "Devil-Ape" in *Isle of Sunken Gold.* Each chapter ends with Lorch, given the character name of Dr. Julian, laughing fiendishly. Rather incredibly, although totally consistent with serial logic, a blow on the head causes Bushman to lose his memory through amnesia. In the final episode, Dr. Julian proves to be a brain surgeon who has been trying for years to avenge his son who killed himself because he threw a football game for Walter Miller and his gang. Julian performs a successful operation on Bushman, restoring his memory.

Besides Tom Dugan's slapstick comedy, Lincoln Perry was also on hand with his Stepin Fetchit characterization, in which the humor, if it can be called that, is derived from racial stereotyping of blacks who sit on the sidelines of the football games, staged at Clay College outside Los Angeles, and marvel at the agility of the white athletes. "Red" Grange is portrayed as possessing such superhuman prowess that, at one point, when character actor Ernie Adams, one of Walter Miller's minions, gets six men to stop Grange, Miller advises him to get more; and even with more men, Grange cannot be stopped.

Perhaps the most interesting aspect of the story is the way the women are depicted. Gwen Lee's only objective in marrying Bushman is to cost him so much money that he is tempted to listen seriously to Miller's promptings that he throw a game. Dorothy Gulliver, on the other hand, cast as Bushman's screen sister, refuses to believe in "Red" Grange's innocence when Grange is framed by Walter Miller and Grange spends the better part of the twelve episodes trying to prove to her that he is a hero worthy of her admiration and love. In psychological terms, what this means is that a hero is constantly in the position of having to perform to impress a heroine. It is hardly a new idea, to be sure, but it is a destructive idea and the hostility one increasingly begins to feel toward Gulliver, who is being courted successfully by Walter Miller while Grange is knocking himself out to impress her, is readily transferred to the Gwen Lee character. Serial logic would seem to dictate, in the early thirties and as opposed to the Pearl White era, that women are either vicious parasites or virtuous fools.

It may be worthwhile noting that Francis X. Bushman, Jr., had been cast earlier that year by Henry MacRae as the star of *Spell of the Circus* (Universal, 1931). At Mascot, he rated only second lead opposite "Red" Grange. After *Phantom of the West,* Universal had immediately cast Tom Tyler in *Battling with Buffalo Bill.* The other two serials from Universal in 1931 were *Danger Island* (Universal, 1931) starring Kenneth Harlan, a character actor from the silent era known principally for his title role in the second make of *The Virginian* (Preferred Pictures, 1923), and *Finger Prints*

(Universal, 1931), again starring Kenneth Harlan. Other than *Battling with Buffalo Bill*, none of these serials could command the audience that the Mascot entries did, and they constituted Mascot's only competition. Mascot's final entry for the year was *The Lightning Warrior* (Mascot, 1931), in many ways the best chapter play the studio had so far produced. But before we come to it, a few words should be said about *Danger Island*, in view of the plot of *The Galloping Ghost* and the critical objections that can be raised concerning it.

The story line has it that, dying in his daughter's arms, Professor Gerald Adams, played by Tom Rickells, tells his daughter, played by Lucile Browne, that he has discovered a rich radium deposit on an African island, the Danger Island of the title. Walter Miller and Beulah Hutton conspire to learn the location of the deposit by befriending Browne. Captain Harry Drake, played by Kenneth Harlan, is in love with Lucile Browne and agrees to lead the expedition to the island. Beulah Hutton makes a strong play for Harlan and discredits him in Browne's eyes. It isn't until later on in the serial, after Miller threatens her life, that Hutton reforms and joins forces with the by then exonerated Harlan and Lucile Browne. It appears that the same serial logic which divided women into two distinct groups in *The Galloping Ghost* was equally at work in *Danger Island*. It was unfortunate, in retrospect, that young people being educated in serial logic should carry with them as a legacy from their time spent in darkened movie houses watching chapter plays like this the conviction that women had either to be protected or were motivated primarily by greed. Chapter plays were scarcely the only kind of screen entertainment demarcating women in this fashion but, as in the depiction of blacks in *The Galloping Ghost* or Africans in *Danger Island*, women clearly joined the ranks of the socially oppressed, a reversal, as I have said, from those trends in serial plot lines which had once permitted serial queens to proudly shatter such stereotypes.

For *The Lightning Warrior*, Levine promoted Benjamin Kline to codirector status with Armand Schaefer. As a consequence of his work on *The Galloping Ghost* and here, Kline was hired by Sam Briskin of Columbia Pictures' "B" department to head up Columbia's outdoor camera unit. Kline stayed under contract to Columbia for many, many years, filming all the exteriors for their Buck Jones and Tim McCoy series Westerns, but again without directorial credit—this was usually reserved for D. Ross Lederman—and went on to contribute substantially to Columbia's own chapter plays when they entered the chapter play field in 1937. One of Columbia's most memorable Western chapter plays, *Overland with Kit Carson* (Columbia, 1939), not only had Kline as head cameraman, but the executive producer on it was Jack Fier, another Mascot alumnus who got his start with Levine when Nat culled him from the ranks of the publicity department at National Screen Service and put him to work as his production assistant.

The screenplay for *The Lightning Warrior* was written by Wyndham Gittens, Ford Beebe, and Colbert Clark. They produced an imaginative and intriguing story for Rin Tin Tin's second serial for Mascot and his last motion picture. When *Clash of the Wolves* (Warner's, 1925) had been released, the *Photoplay* reviewer had commented: "This dog is the most sympathetic and human creature on the screen today. There are times when we think the dog actually sheds tears — and if he doesn't make you...." *Clash* had costarred Charles Farrell and June Marlowe, Levine's leading lady in *The Lone Defender*. At one point in the story, Rinty wants to summon June Marlowe from inside a house and he places his paws against the outside of a window pane and raps lightly with his right paw until he attracts her attention. At another point, when Rinty is being pursued by a posse, he leaps across a yawning chasm. In order to conceal his identity from the towns-people, Rinty is even disguised for a time in a beard and leather booties!

In *The Lightning Warrior*, Rinty was called upon to do very little of the serious acting that had won him legions of admirers, less even than he had to do in *The Lone Defender*, save perhaps for a scene or two in the first episode. For *The Lightning Warrior*, Rinty was strictly an action star which, because of his age, meant an even greater dependence on doubles, including a stuffed wolf dog which Lee Duncan used for unusually harrowing stunts.

George Brent had come to Hollywood from the Broadway stage. He had been tested at several studios and had been found to have an excellent screen voice, but he had not as yet been signed anywhere. He presented himself to Levine and Nat perceived in him the makings of a fine actor. Levine signed him to play the male lead in *The Lightning Warrior*, comprising the male adult part of the triad hero, which of course included Rin Tin Tin at $5,000 for the serial and young Frankie Darro, who had received $1,000 for his role in *The Vanishing Legion*, now raised to $2,000. The exposure from his work in this serial was all that Brent needed, apparently, since he was, after its release, placed under contract at Warner Bros., becoming one of the most popular leading men in the late thirties and early forties.

As the heroine, Levine cast Georgia Hale. She had been Charlie Chaplin's leading lady in *The Gold Rush* (United Artists, 1925) but had had some difficulty finding employment since the advent of sound pictures. Her acting skills, while not spectacular, were far superior to those of Edwina Booth and definitely the equal of Dorothy Gulliver's. Theodore Lorch, the "mysterious cripple," was back, this time in a dual role, that of Lafarge, an escaped convict suspected of being the master villain known as the Wolf Man, and that requiring the neat trick of impersonating the Wolf Man throughout the serial even though in the final chapter it is Frank Brownlee who is unmasked whereas Lorch's Lafarge is found to be innocent. Lafe McKee was also suspected of being the Wolf Man, as was Pat O'Malley, playing the sheriff, and Frank Lanning, a white actor portraying a character called Indian George.

Kermit Maynard, Ken Maynard's younger brother who had been doubling Ken in Ken's series Westerns for Tiffany studios, was hired by Canutt to work in the second unit and to stand in for George Brent. A friend-ship between Canutt and Kermit Maynard began at this time which would last until Kermit's death; in subsequent years the men, who lived only a short distance from each other, would regularly meet with their wives to play cards.

To the grouping of a triad hero, Levine added a triad villain, at least in a sense. The Wolf Man was almost always flanked by his chief agents, played by Bob Kortman and Dick Dickinson. At all times the Wolf Man kept his face covered by means of his black cape and a high-peaked, broad-brimmed black sombrero with the brim slouched in front. He rode a white horse, called his "Indians" with the wail of a timber wolf, and was a human counterforce to Rinty.

Hayden Stevenson, a serial star at Universal in the twenties, was cast as Frankie Darro's screen father. Although he is killed off in the first chapter, he was still given second billing in the credits, Levine feeling that his popular status warranted it.

The sites were as carefully selected as was the cast. Bronson Canyon, then located a short distance from Hollywood was well known for its "Indian Caves." These were indentations and passages in the canyon walls, running clear through the mountain in some cases, originally carved out while the canyon was being used as a quarry supplying stone for the bricks employed in the construction of the Los Angeles streetcar system. It was here that Levine located the Wolf Cave, the hideout for the Wolf Man where he meets occasionally with Kortman and Dickinson, filled with an empty, lonely, wailing howl as the wind rushes through it, obviously suggested by "Oldring's knell" in Zane Grey's *Riders of the Purple Sage* which, the reader may recall, also may have contributed to the Mystery Riders notion in *Phantom of the West*. William Colt MacDonald, screen-writer and author of Western fiction, subsequently borrowed the idea for his Three Mesquiteer book, *Riders of the Whistling Skull* (Crown, 1934), and naturally it showed up in Oliver Drake's screen adaptation for the Three Mesquiteer feature film, *Riders of the Whistling Skull* (Republic, 1937), produced by Nat Levine, and therefore reappearing as late as *The Feathered Serpent* (Monogram, 1948), a Charlie Chan low budget picture for which Drake reworked his old Western script, flanking Roland Winters' Chan with Keye Luke and Victor Sen Young to retain a triad hero.

The Prudential studio lot outside Kernville on the Kern River was frequently employed in the twenties and thirties in the production of Westerns. It had a town, a series of isolated shacks, and an arroyo used in Hal Roach's production of *The King of the Wild Horses* (Pathé, 1924) and therefore again in *The Vanishing Legion* so Canutt could match more shots with Rex, an extremely rough and undulating terrain for chases, and a high cliff overlooking a lagoon for dangerous jumps that Canutt had used for stunts as far back as his starring silent Western *White Thunder* (FBO, 1925). The town was named Sainte Suzanne for purposes of *The Lightning Warrior* and nearly all the exteriors were shot at the Prudential lot. The minimal interior sets were located at the Tec-Art studio in North Hollywood and at the Universal City studio.

Lee Zahler composed the opening theme, with a credit roll super-imposed over a visual of Rin Tin Tin atop a high rock. Levine had been so taken by the beginning credits to *Trader Horn,* inspired in turn by the effec-tive stage production of Eugene O'Neill's *Emperor Jones,* that he made use of the beating drums motif M-G-M had used for *Horn* throughout most of chapters one and four and periodically in the remaining episodes of *The Lightning Warrior.* The idea of an African ju-ju was transposed to become ominous Indian tom-toms. The demoralizing effect of continually thumping drums was part of the Wolf Man's campaign to drive the settlers from a mining district. A series of vignettes occur in the first chapter showing families brought to the edge of terror by these drums and the ultimatum from a tribe of Indians, apparently sequestered for some twenty years in a hidden valley, demanding that all white men leave the area before the new moon. "I have frequently observed in the analysis of Americans," Jung wrote in *Symbols of Transformation,* "that the inferior side of the per-sonality, the 'shadow,' is represented by a Negro or an Indian, whereas in the dream of a European it would be represented by a somewhat shady in-dividual of his own kind." The "shadow" in *The Lightning Warrior* is represented by Indian George, the only "real" Indian seen in the first eleven chapters since the Indians fighting for the Wolf Man are all white men disguised as Indians. It is also Indian George who brings about the final reckoning with the Wolf Man when he leads the tribe of actual Indians from their hidden valley to save the white men. Of course, these actual Indians have only a shadowy existence at best because they have fallen victims to the white man's mythology which holds that when a white man meets a Native American, the Native American vanishes. After battling against the Wolf Man's forces successfully, the tribe again vanishes to its hidden retreat.

"To know the secret name of a person is to have power over him," Jung further noted. "A well-known example of this is the tale of Rumpel-stiltskin. In an Egyptian myth, Isis permanently robs the sun-god Ra of his power by compelling him to tell her his real name. Therefore, to give a name means to give power...." In *The Lightning Warrior,* the true name and therefore the identity of the Wolf Man is written on a shred of paper con-tained in a secret compartment of Rinty's collar and all through the serial the Wolf Man's agents are in pursuit of Rinty to prevent anyone from opening the collar and reading the name.

Interestingly also, just as Edwina Booth ended up sharing the wealth of her inherited oil field, so at the end of *Warrior* Frankie Darro inherits his deceased father's rich gold mine and it is discovered that all the settlers are rich because a large vein of subterranean gold runs throughout the district, the caves and underground passages only reinforcing the identification of gold, concealed wealth, with the belief that this will bring happiness.

The basic ritual in so many of the Mascot serials permitted young-sters to undergo initiation and adults a rebirth, quite the same as in those mysteries Jung noted, writing about the collective identification with a cult-hero in *The Archetypes of the Collective Unconscious* (Princeton University Press, 1959), Volume IX, Part I of his *Collected Works*, where "the individual undergoes an indirect transformation through his participation in the fate of the god. The transformation experience is also an indirect one in the Christian Church, inasmuch as it is brought about by participation in something acted or recited." The identification of the triad hero with a sun god, or the mask of Helios, occurs in the fifth chapter when the narrator's voice informs the viewer that the Indians have named Rinty "the lightning warrior," the chapter itself entitled "The Invisible Enemy," providing the audience with some idea of what it is this triad hero is battling against, an archetypal symbol for the shadow world of the unconscious.

Yakima Canutt's stunting in *The Lightning Warrior* was in top form. Typical of his stunts was his close for the first episode. The camera was mounted on the front of a runaway wagon with Canutt and Helen Gibson aboard, doubling George Brent and Georgia Hale. They are being pursued by hostile Indians. The camera tracks to where the wagon hits a stump, mounted on the driver's seat at the moment of impact. The horses pull forward, taking the lip and their harnesses with them, the wagon rolling back slowly and gaining momentum as it hurtles down the hillside.

Another perilous moment is when Frankie Darro is fighting with Canutt dressed as the Wolf Man in an ore car presumably suspended high above the ground. Rinty jumps from a jutting wooden beam as the car passes, landing on the cloaked mystery figure. Frankie is thrown from the car, catching on and hanging from below. Canutt as the Wolf Man sees Canutt as George Brent starting toward him, holding onto a hook attached to the suspension cable. The Wolf Man jumps across into an ore car going in the opposite direction. The loss of his weight causes the car to dump over. In the nick of time Frankie grabs onto Rinty. Now the two are dangling from the overturned ore car. Canutt as Brent jumps atop the car in the next installment, thus pulling both boy and dog to safety, whereas it was believed from the previous week's cliffhanger that they had plunged to their deaths. All of this was accomplished only a few feet above the ground. But the illusion of its being hundreds of feet in the air is effectively maintained. When the ore car turned over, I am sure audiences gasped and screamed because I witnessed this reaction from college students at the University of Evansville in 1971.

Yak told me personally during one of our many conversations — when I lived in Los Angeles, I was within walking distance of Canutt's home — that he thought very little of Rin Tin Tin. He felt Rinty was at his best in close-ups, of which there were very few in *The Lightning Warrior*. Once Rinty bit him, missing entirely the protective pad Yak wore over his arm. Rinty's major double struck Yak as a better action player. Lee Duncan, according to Yak, would have to hit his dogs in order to get them to obey; on one occasion he used an iron chain. As far as Yak was concerned, Levine was buying the dog's name, not his ability.

Perhaps Yak's attitude was prompted somewhat by the run-in he had with Duncan which he wrote about in *Stunt Man*. "Another time," Yak recalled, "during the making of the serial, *The Lightning Warrior*, ... I was to do a jump from a rock ledge about eighteen feet high, onto a horse which was saddled and standing below. I had put blinders on the horse so that he would see out ahead, but not up. Lee Duncan ... was to have the dog follow me out of the scene. I got everything set so that I could make the takeoff noiselessly. I then asked everyone to keep quiet until I hit the saddle. I especially made it clear to Duncan, who had not been very co-operative.

"When all was ready, the director gave me a signal and, just as I took off, Duncan screamed at the top of his voice at his wonder dog. My horse jumped and took off and I landed in the rocks. I wasn't hurt, but I was mad. I got up and limped over to Duncan.

"'Mr. Duncan,' I said, angrily, 'I'm going to try this stunt again and if you holler before I hit the saddle, I'll whip you but good!'

"Duncan glared at me and walked away while we got the horse back in place. I made the jump, Duncan sent Rin Tin Tin in, and he followed me out of the scene the way the script called for.

"That night after dinner Nat Levine called me to his hotel room. 'Yak,' he said gravely, 'Lee Duncan said I would have to fire you or he would take his dog and go home. Let's hear your side of the story. What happened?'

"I told him exactly what occurred.

"'Well,' Nat said thoughtfully, 'if he meant what he said, I guess he'll just have to take his dog and go.'

"Duncan didn't leave, and from then on he was a little more co-operative. Nat Levine would back you if you were right."

The most disappointing aspect of *The Lightning Warrior*, as in many mysteries, is the explanation, when, in the final chapter, Indian George and his tribe finally rout the "phony" Indians. Such a denouement fails to take into account the fact that Frankie Darro once, to escape detection, trussed up an Indian boy and took his place in the circle of warriors performing a death dance around George Brent, tied to a stake. Was the Indian boy also an impostor?

Yet, no amount of carping as no amount of elucidation, anti-climactic or otherwise, can dull the thrill of the serial as a whole, the pace of its stunting with at least three remarkable feats in each chapter, or the charm of Frankie Darro and Rinty pitted against the powerful forces of a hostile world. The viewer believes for the moment because the characters themselves seem so surely to believe, so caught up are they apparently in the basic premises of this far-fetched and awesome spectacle. The over-whelming visual impact of the serial's images have almost an existence of their own and generate a psychic excitement rarely to be found in waking life, a dream-like quality that remains vivid and unassailable.

In a sense, therefore, Rinty's screen farewell was totally in keeping with his fabulous career. Duncan himself had long since "gone Hollywood," as the expression had it, and had built a magnificent mansion while otherwise unwisely investing Rinty's earnings. One afternoon, by then fourteen, the aged and now lame Rin Tin Tin jumped into his master's arms and died. He was first buried in the backyard in an unmarked grave, but was moved to a mausoleum when Duncan eventually sold the estate. In departing it should be said, the black-faced star had to his credit a serial that has impressed lastingly all who have seen it.

Five

Painted Faces

John Wayne had been convinced that his big chance had arrived when Fox Film Corporation starred him in their 55mm "widescreen" Western in 1930, *The Big Trail.* It died at the box office. Fox gave him such a fast shuffle that, by 1931, he was out looking for work and the best his agent could find for him was a slot as a contract player at Columbia Pictures where, among other things, he played second lead to Buck Jones and Tim McCoy in their series Westerns. Wayne was saucy, sullen, hard to get along with, and unhappy. He wanted to *star* in pictures. Nat Levine was prepared to give him that chance again.

"Nat Levine was a fat little man wearing thick glasses," Maurice Zolotow said in *Shooting Star: A Biography of John Wayne* (Simon & Schuster, 1974). "He looked like a wholesale butcher. He talked through a cigar. He looked like a caricature of a Hollywood tycoon. He made money on animal serials. He was the original producer of the Rin Tin Tin [serials]. Another one of his animal stars was Rex, the Wonder Horse. Rex played a brave kindly horse in pictures; in real life, as often happens with movie stars, he was a horse of another color. He was a vicious beast who loved to kick human actors and bite directors. He had bitten Levine often.

"'Shake hands with John Wayne,'" Al Kingston, Wayne's agent at the time, said to Levine.

"'It's a pleasure,' Levine said.

"'He was star of *The Big Trail* and he just finished out a contract with Columbia. He's got a little time between jobs while I'm firming up a deal with a major. So, Nat, you got a chance to grab a real talent before somebody else does.'

"'He looks younger than I expected,' Levine said.

"'You could age him,' the agent said.

"'We got a story here about a flier, a serial, you know, a Lindbergh type.'

"'Did you ever see anybody who was more the spit'n' image of Charles A. Lindbergh than this fellow here, Nat? He's an All-American type and you are a very fortunate man.'"

Lindbergh's historic solo flight in a monoplane had stirred the popular mind and filmmakers were anxious to exploit the public's interest and enthusiasm for aviation. William Wellman had directed *Wings* (Paramount, 1927), dedicated to "those young warriors of the sky whose wings are folded about them forever," and it had proved a sensation. Frank Capra devoted two of the films in his war trilogy to aspects of aerial drama, *Flight* (Columbia, 1929) and *Dirigible* (Columbia, 1931). Howard Hawks had directed *The Dawn Patrol* (Warner's, 1930), based on a story by John Monk Saunders who had also written the original story for *Wings*. And then there was the controversy around Howard Hughes' *Hell's Angels* (United Artists, 1930). Hughes in fact had instructed his writer on *Hell's Angels*, so fierce was the competition about aviation pictures, to inform Harry Cohn, head of Columbia Pictures, that he could have the props he wanted to borrow if Columbia would agree to hold up release of *Dirigible* until after *Hell's Angels* was released. The writer, Joseph Moncure March, not only did as he was bid with Cohn, but found himself in jail on a trumped up charge because Warner Bros. wanted to beat Hughes into release with their *The Dawn Patrol*.

Right in the midst of all this wrangling and back-stabbing, James Quirk, editor of *Photoplay*, remarked that "Lindbergh has put the cowboy into the discard ... [and] the Western novel and motion picture heroes have slunk away into the sagebrush never to return. The cow ponies have retired to the pasture with the old fire horses. Tom Mix, Hoot Gibson, and Ken Maynard must swap horses for airplanes or go to the old actor's home."

Levine wanted an aviation serial for Mascot. He offered John Wayne a contract that would pay him a total of $2,000 for three chapter plays to be filmed at the rate of a month each, although not successively. Sitting in Al Kingston's office with Wayne, he declared that it was his intention to start filming the first of the three serials, to be called *Shadow of the Eagle* (Mascot, 1932), the next day. Would Wayne be available, at that time and for that money? Wayne and his agent said okay. Levine responded that he would pick up Wayne the next morning at 4 o'clock and drive him out to location.

It was dark the next morning when Levine showed up in his chauffeur-driven Packard to collect Wayne. He had brought breakfast along with him for Wayne so they could save on time. Wayne busied himself with Danish pastry and coffee while Levine outlined the basic plot. The story was by Ford Beebe, Colbert Clark, and Wyndham Gittens, and Beebe was slated to direct, with Benjamin Kline in charge of photography and Yakima Canutt to double. This time, basically, Levine was going to try and see if he could manage with only one *principal* director.

It was a strong cast. Dorothy Gulliver was signed as the girl, Jean Gregory, and Edward Hearn was cast as her screen father. Among the suspects, one of whom is secretly the master criminal, known as The Eagle, were Walter Miller, Kenneth Harlan who the previous year, the reader will recall, had starred in two Universal chapter plays, and Pat O'Malley. Wayne would be helped out of various scrapes by Little Billy, whose character name on the credits was "The Midget."

After the establishing first chapter, a plot summary would be narrated as had been the custom for the 1931 serials, and it may well have been such a résumé that Levine read to Wayne as the car sped along. To the accompaniment of clips of visual action the narrator informs the audience in the final episode: "A mysterious criminal, who calls himself The Eagle, is plotting against the directors of an airplane factory, whom he has tried to frighten with warnings written on the sky in smoke and fire. The directors have reason to suspect that The Eagle is Nathan Gregory [Hearn], owner of a small carnival show, who has accused them of stealing from him an invention that is worth a fortune. Gregory's daughter, Jean, has found The Eagle's skywriting plane which she now discovers is operated by radio control. While Jean is in the plane, The Eagle sends it up into the air and telephones Craig McCoy [Wayne], Jean's friend, that he intends to crash the plane. Craig locates The Eagle's radio control room and makes a desperate effort to save the girl he loves."

I have forgotten to mention one of the character actors in this melodrama, Ernie S. Adams. Born June 18, 1885, in San Francisco, he worked in stage musicals before entering the motion picture industry. Until his death in 1947, if he had a speaking part he was generally a heavy, but throughout the thirties he was a very special kind of heavy. He was regularly typecast as a "stoolie," a role in which he excelled in a major production like *San Quentin* (Warner's, 1937) or in a low grade Western like *Bar Z Badmen* (Republic, 1937) with movie cowboy Johnny Mack Brown. Whenever a script writer got into trouble and could not figure out how it was possible to get the goods on a gang of villains, he would usually think of Ernie Adams and the scene would thenceforth write itself. Some of these screen confessions were actually quite elaborate, such as that in *Rollin' Plains* (Grand National, 1938) in which Tex Ritter holds a séance in a darkened room, reading from the *Bible* to an organ rendition of "Rock of Ages," and during which a supposedly murdered man appears as a spectre, Ernie reduced to gibbering terror before he gushes forth his confession. In a Western like *The Man from Tumbleweeds* (Columbia, 1940), when Bill Elliott organizes a group of state rangers made up of prison convicts, one needed only to see Ernie in the group to know that he would be squealing to the gang of villains he was sworn to capture. Ernie confesses in the final reel of *Shadow of the Eagle*. It is certainly not his most dramatic confession by far, but it is adequate to expose Kenneth Harlan as The Eagle. Harlan attempts to flee and is killed in an automobile accident.

Wayne had no idea what he was letting himself in for. His work week at Mascot would consist of six days, twelve hours a day. Once Ford Beebe kept going until midnight, getting 114 camera set-ups in one day.

Yakima Canutt and familiar heavy Bud Osborne were cast as two of The Eagle's henchmen. "I had never met John Wayne," Canutt wrote in his autobiography, "but Bud had worked with him a number of times. One day, when we were having lunch together, I asked Bud what kind of fellow Wayne was to work with.

"'Yak,' he said, 'you'll love him. He's really great. And when it comes to ribbing, he'll hold his own — even with you.'

"'If he likes to rib,' I said, 'let's start him off right. You tell him to be very careful about what he says or does around me, that I'm Nat Levine's stool pigeon, and that I report to Nat each night and tell him everything that happens during the day. But don't tell him this until he and I get acquainted.'

"The first day of shooting John arrived on the set and Bud introduced me to him. He was very friendly and said he was happy I was going to double him. He had heard a great deal about me and my rodeo achievements and was also familiar with my standing as a stunt man.

"The afternoon of the second day I told Bud to break the news to him about my being a stool pigeon. I stood off to one side making some notes in my little red book, and peeking out from under the brim of my John B. Stetson hat, when Bud walked over to Wayne and began giving him the lowdown on my spy activities. John looked at me in amazement, then turned back to Bud and shook his head in disbelief. A little later I walked up to him and asked: 'Well, how's everything going?'

"John just looked at me but said nothing. I took out a pack of cigarettes, lit one, and offered the pack to him. 'Have a smoke,' I said.

"He gave me a dirty look. 'No thanks,' he replied curtly, and walked away.

"I knew we had him hooked. John was ... a man who believe[d] in loyalty, whether ... to friend or country. One time I heard him say that there was only one thing worse than a stool pigeon and that was two stool pigeons.

"The rib had been going along for about a week when I had Bud and one of the other actors taking Wayne behind the set for a drink. I went around the opposite corner. John took a swig, and as he handed the bottle back to Bud, he saw me. I looked at my watch and then made a note in my little book. That did it. He blew his top and I made a hasty retreat. A little later I got to Bud and a couple of the fellows who were in on the gag, and told them that they had better straighten John out about me. I knew I couldn't out-run him and I wasn't about to fight him.

"When they told John it was all a joke, he laughed heartily, even though it was at his expense."

The night Ford Beebe kept cast and crew shooting until midnight, they were at the Bronson Canyon location. Beebe wanted them all to report back the next morning at 6:00. Wayne did not find the prospect of driving back to Los Angeles for a couple of hours very appealing, so he determined he would stay on location over night. Some of the crew had the same idea and they had built a fire as a shield against the late night cold. There was no place to stay, no cabins, no tents. A few had brought bed rolls. There were no commissary trucks. There was only bread and cheese and whiskey.

Wayne sat by the fire and pulled out a pint bottle of whiskey. He was cold and disgusted. His weary body ached. *[Continued on page 73.]*

Josephine Hill and Jack Hoxie, with treasure and a Hollywood "Indian," in Heroes of the Wild *(Mascot, 1927).*

Opposite, top: *Yakima Canutt diving with a blindfolded horse off a cliff into the Kern River.* **Bottom:** *Canutt jumping into the Kern River from a precipice.* **This page:** *Canutt, doubling George Brent in* The Lightning Warrior *(Mascot, 1931), leaping over a picket fence.*

Opposite: *A lobby card from* The King of the Kongo *(Mascot, 1929). Walter Miller is in the center and Boris Karloff is second from right.* **This page:** *Lucile Browne striking the pose typical of heroines in sound serials in the thirties and attired as heroines were typically attired.*

Opposite: *Publicity for* The Lightning Warrior *(Mascot, 1931). Note how Rinty's* vocal *qualities are emphasized. Courtesy of Bob Malcomson.* **This page, top:** *George Brent and Rin Tin Tin in Bronson Canyon on location for* The Lightning Warrior. **Bottom:** *Disney sound truck and engineers on location for* The Vanishing Legion *(Mascot, 1931); Mascot camera car at left.*

Opposite: *Edwina Booth holds The Vanishing Legion at bay in the 1931 Mascot film of that name. Joe Bonomo wears the large Stetson at center; Philo McCullough is hatless at right.* **This page, top:** *Rin Tin Tin the Indian fighter;* **bottom:** *The Wolf Man about to seize Georgia Hale while minions Dick Dickinson and Robert Kortman look elsewhere, in the Wolf Cave in Bronson Canyon; both shots are from* The Lightning Warrior *(Mascot, 1931).*

Opposite: *"Red" Grange, atop the taxicab, about to rescue heroine Dorothy Gulliver;* **this page:** *Grange, in the business suit; both shots are from* The Galloping Ghost *(Mascot, 1931).*

Opposite: *John Wayne taking The Eagle by surprise;* **this page:** *Wayne battling Roy D'Arcy as Dorothy Gulliver regains her feet; both shots are from* Shadow of the Eagle *(Mascot, 1932).*

Opposite: *Left to right, Walter Miller, Lucile Browne, Nelson McDowell, Edwina Booth, Harry Carey, Hobart Bosworth, and Junior Coughlan in* The Last of the Mohicans *(Mascot, 1932).* **This page, top:** *J. Paul Jones and Noah Beery, Sr. (with binoculars) at the race track in* The Devil Horse *(Mascot, 1932), one of many Mascot serials that stress horse racing.* **Bottom:** *Harry Carey and Frankie Darro try to make out the name of the man who murdered Carey's brother, scratched into the hoof of a horse, in* The Devil Horse.

Top: *A view of* The Whispering Shadow *never seen during the course of the film;* **bottom:** *his minions summoned to a meeting; both shots are from* The Whispering Shadow *(Mascot, 1933).*

Canutt sauntered over to the fire and crouched down. He did not speak. Wayne handed Canutt the bottle. Yak uncorked it and took a long pull. He wiped his mouth with the back of his hand.

"Well, Duke," he said — even then Wayne's nickname was used freely by his coworkers, "it don't take very long to spend the whole night here."

Wayne chuckled. He took a pull at the whiskey. "Sure don't," he said.

They both laughed. They had become friends and, indeed, Canutt would work with Wayne in more pictures than with any other star on the screen. The next day, when Canutt doubled him for a dangerous motorcycle stunt, Wayne marveled at his dexterity, the same way he admired his horsemanship. According to Maurice Zolotow in *Shooting Star*, Wayne even went so far as to understudy Canutt's loping walk, rolling back on the balls of his feet. However, when I once asked Wayne about this, he denied it. Yet he also denied that he mounted a horse the way Tom Mix did — Wayne had been employed as a prop boy with the Mix unit when he first starting working on the Fox lot — straight of back and limb, and this he very obviously did imitate.

The "high budget" entry that year, if such a term may be permitted, was Levine's next entry, *The Last of the Mohicans* (Mascot, 1932). This was the only literary "classic" Mascot would ever attempt to adapt for the screen and, in one sense, given the picaresque nature of the original novel, perhaps an episodic treatment worked best. However, before commenting further on just what Mascot did to Cooper's work, it might be advisable to spend a moment on Cooper himself and his Leatherstocking Saga.

Adding the Fenimore to his name in 1826 as part of an unsuccessful ploy to inherit some land, James Kent Cooper was born at Burlington, New Jersey, on September 15, 1789. Cooper's father was a judge and later a member of the New York state legislature who moved, when his son was but a year old, to the wilderness region of Otsego Lake where he assumed large land holdings which in time came to be known as Cooperstown. From earliest childhood, therefore, Cooper was surrounded by the forests and even some members of the Indian nations which would later figure significantly in his fiction. Cooper was educated privately by a clergyman and, in 1802, he entered Yale, only to be expelled two years later because of a prank. After living for two years at Cooperstown, Cooper's father decided that he should go to sea and the youngster signed on as a seaman on a vessel sailing from Maine to England. A year later, upon his return, Cooper received a commission in the U.S. Navy. When, after two years, Cooper's assignment was to assist in establishing a freshwater navy on the Great Lakes, he chaffed under the tedium but had no choice in the matter, since he was otherwise without a means of making a living.

When Cooper's father died, Cooper joined with his brothers in dissipating the large estate. He also married a very proper woman who insisted he resign his commission. Together the couple settled down on a farm owned by Cooper's wife and Cooper, other than siring five daughters and two sons, busied himself as a country squire, his only other interest being a part ownership in a whaling vessel. In 1819, reading aloud to his wife from a recently published English romance, Cooper announced he could write a better book himself. Since he was known to detest writing so much as a letter, Cooper's wife, Susan Augusta DeLancey Cooper, laughed; but Cooper was adamant and *Precaution* (1820), published anonymously, was the result.

It proved a turning point for him. Cooper found he could write with some facility by the standards of that day and he followed with *The Spy* (1821), a sea story, a genre at which he was far more talented and informed than with the life of the forests, despite his childhood, but in which, perhaps for that reason, he was less prone to indulge his fantasies or to create what would in time become national myths. This was clearly shown when he produced *The Pioneers* (1823). Originally intended to tell the story of his father and Cooperstown, Cooper included among his characters his most memorable literary creation, Natty Bumppo, who would henceforth be variously known by the names given him by the people of the forest, Hawk-eye, Deerslayer, Pathfinder. In *The Pioneers* Bumppo was a man no longer young and he was alone save for his friend, the Indian known as John Mohegan, who was a drunk.

Cooper, flush with his literary success, both in the United States and in Europe, left in 1826 to live abroad with his family, which he did for the next seven years. It was also in this same year that he published *The Last of the Mohicans* (1826), a novel set during the French and Indian War and featuring both Bumppo, called Hawk-eye, and Mohegan, referred to by his Indian name, Chingachgook, the great serpent, in the prime of their manhood, roaming freely through the parlous wild forests of the New World. The novel was in many ways a landmark.

First, it established as an accepted literary convention the division of Native Americans into two groups, those who, like Chingachgook and his son, Uncas, were allies of the white man, and those like Magua, chief of the Mingos, who was a savage identified with the Devil incarnate. Chingachgook was the embodiment of what the French encyclopedists referred to as a "noble savage." But Cooper was anticipating the peculiar American twist this notion had to be given. Land could not be stolen from noble savages, so not the nobility of the Native American had to be emphasized so much as his savagery. Against the savagery of the forest, Cooper pitted civilization, which meant white dominion. Cooper played upon the terror evoked by the forest dwellers and made it seem both by divine decree and by human justice inevitable that the white man take the Indians' lands in exchange for giving them the "blessing" of Christianity with its white god, along with many things Cooper either did not or would not mention such as venereal and other diseases, alcoholism, and despair.

The Last of the Mohicans was a romance, an American version of the kind of fiction Sir Walter Scott was writing in Great Britain about medieval times. There was no accuracy in it, nor any effort to be accurate.

That wasn't Cooper's purpose, nor was it what his readers wanted. Mark Twain in his satirical essay, "Fenimore Cooper's Literary Offenses," cites *The Last of the Mohicans* and comments that when Hawk-eye, Chingachgook, Uncas, and company are searching for the Munro sisters, the "trail is hopelessly lost." Calling Chingachgook by the name Chicago for short, Twain remarks "neither you nor I could ever have guessed out the way to find it. It was very different with Chicago. Chicago was not stumped for long. He turned a running stream out of its course, and there, in the slush of its old bed, were that person's moccasin tracks. The current did not wash them away, as it would have done in all other like cases — no, even the eternal laws of Nature have to vacate when Cooper wants to put up a delicate job of woodcraft on the reader." Nor is the aptness of this criticism lessened by the fact that in Cooper's novel it is Uncas, and not his father, Chingachgook, who diverts the water and is the first to see the footprints on the stream's bottom.

Cooper took numerous pains to fit his Indians into popular Christian mythology. When an Indian yells, "his cry was answered by a yell and a laugh from the woods, as tauntingly exulting as if fifty demons were uttering their blasphemies at the fall of some Christian soul." Even excusing his racial bias, Cooper personally knew nothing of Native American tribal history and he hopelessly confused in *The Last of the Mohicans*, and treated as interchangeable, the Maquas, Hurons, Iroquois, indeed the five nations of the Iroquois Confederacy; he could see none of their unique civilization nor the fact that the American form of government strongly paralleled the Iroquois' own articles of confederation. All he could say, at his most benevolent, was that "in a short time there will be no remains of these extraordinary people." And it was this book and the subsequent novels in the Leatherstocking Saga that white men were reading in Kentucky when all Native Americans in that state were banished to the Plains by President Andrew Jackson and given blankets infected with smallpox to accompany them on their journey; it was these books that the pioneers had read or were reading when they pushed forth to those very Plains and set about duplicating in the West what had already been accomplished in the East: making the Native American *vanish*.

"It is hard — and a little discomfiting — for critics," Leslie Fiedler wrote in *Love and Death in the American Novel* (Stein & Day, 1960), "to remember that the novel may function on the level of myth as well as that of literature." He added: "It no longer really matters whether one has actually read Cooper's books or not; he is possessed by them all the same, and just as [Alexandre] Dumas in Nineteenth-century France could call a work *Les Mohicans de Paris*, Bernard Malamud in Twentieth-century America can entitle a story 'The Last Mohican.' Neither has to doubt that he will be understood, for the title of Cooper's romance has become a part of the common symbolic language of the Western world."

The Munro daughters in *Mohicans* established another venerable — or, in retrospect, not venerable at all — stereotype. The one, the elder, Cora

Munro, the dark hair, with her dusky complexion come of Negro blood in her heritage, is passionate and vibrant; both Uncas, from among the noble savages, and Magua, from among the infernal savages, covet her; but neither can possess her because Cooper himself had a horror of miscegenation. For Uncas and Cora, it could only end one way, given this ingredient: they are united in death. It is the other, the younger, Alice Munro, the yellow hair, with her light complexion and trembling ways who is considered fit for life and a legitimate marriage to Major Duncan Heyward, the American colonial in service with the Royal Army. The image of Alice would persist in American literature, and by extension in Western fiction for nearly a century and a half, "the girl" who needs saving and male protection in literally thousands of melodramas, adventure stories, and ranch romances.

Stephen Crane, however, was not any more impressed with Cooper's fantasies than Mark Twain had been. "When you tell them," he wrote about the residents of Sullivan County in a sketch titled "The Last of the Mohicans," "about the noble savage of Cooper's fiction, they shake 'metaphorical fists' at Cooper's *The Last of the Mohicans* and scornfully sneer. The old storytellers of Sullivan County insist that the original for Cooper's fictionalized bronze god Uncas ended his life there not as a noble warrior who had yearned after the blood of his enemies, but as a derelict begging from house to house a drink of the white man's rum. ... He dragged through his wretched life in helpless misery."

D.H. Lawrence, whose *Studies in Classic American Literature* has already been referred to, called Natty Bumppo "a saint with a gun," and so it was that at the very advent of American literature and frontier fiction the hero was cast in the mold of a man who resolves human predicaments through the violent use of firearms, as in *The Last of the Mohicans* when Hawk-eye shoots and kills Magua. "...You have there the myth of the essential white America," Lawrence wrote. "All the other stuff, the love, the democracy, the floundering into lust, is a sort of by-play. The essential American soul is hard, isolate, stoic, and a killer. It has never yet melted."

It might be possible to agree at least in part with James Grossman, in his book *James Fenimore Cooper* (Sloane, 1949), that "it is true, as Mark Twain complains in his witty but parochial essay, 'Fenimore Cooper's Literary Offenses,' that Natty at times 'talks like an illustrated, gilt-edged, tree-calf, hand-tooled, seven-dollar Friendship's Offering in the beginning of a paragraph ... [and] like a Negro minstrel in the end of it.' But this misses completely how much Natty's few and rather limited ideas are enriched by the careless profusion of his means of expression. It is in fact Natty's inconsistency — his facility in turning from flights of formal rhetoric to such incisive statements as 'I peppered the blackguards intrinsically like,' his mixture of superhuman skill in shooting and disregard of elementary precautions, his fluctuations between philosophic indifference and childish showing off — that makes him emerge from the series a magnificent whole, one of the great rounded characters of American literature."

Cooper was living in Paris when he wrote *The Prairie* (1827), which told of the death of Natty Bumppo. It was the end of the Leatherstocking Saga in chronological order, if not in the order of composition. "By the end of *The Prairie*," Donald A. Ringe wrote in *James Fenimore Cooper* (Twayne Publishers, 1962), "the problem that Leatherstocking has had to face is abundantly clear. ... He has achieved the self-discipline he needs to lead a free and asocial life, but he has also learned that few others can attain by themselves the same desirable end. He has sought the woods to practice the kind of life he loves, but every step he takes Westward opens a path for the exploiters who follow him. At last, driven to the Great Plains 'by a species of desperate resignation,' he dies physically defeated; but intellectually and morally he still maintains his deeply felt philosophy." It is perhaps ironic to reflect that Cooper brought his hero to this pass only when he, Cooper, was about as far removed from the Plains as he could be, fêted and celebrated in France as America's foremost man of letters.

Leaving Paris, Cooper sojourned for a while with his family in Italy. By the time he returned to the United States in 1833, he found that everything had changed so much he had difficulty bringing himself to write historical romances. Although his books earned him what was literally a fortune for that time — as much as $20,000 a year — he was also heavily in debt because of his brothers' extravagance and his own penchant for living by the grand gesture, much after the fashion of his father, the squire and judge. Settling in Cooperstown, he turned to writing history as well as fiction, producing *The History of the Navy of the United States* (1839), which, upon publication, exposed him to a great deal of criticism in the press, all of which he fought, some of it through litigation. He also wrote *The Pathfinder* (1840), another Leatherstocking book, this time about Natty Bumppo in middle age enjoying his one serious flirtation and then rejecting it. Feeling out of sorts with the United States of his day and its obsession with raping the wilderness and its overwhelming greed, Cooper moved further and further back in the chronology of his Saga, concluding it with the book in which it actually began, *The Deerslayer* (1841), set in the very area where he was living, around Cooperstown, long before of course there ever was a Cooperstown. It was this last book that was Cooper's own personal favorite and, while Leatherstocking is as insistent in it as throughout the Saga that he is totally without Indian blood, we are told of him that "he had caught the stoicism of the Indians, well knowing there was no more certain mode of securing their respect than by imitating their self-command." Perhaps in this book, more than in any other, Leatherstocking is in deeper sympathy with the Indian cause and comments at one point that he is pleased that the white man has been compelled to retain the Indian names for places "for it would be too hard to rob them of both land and name!"

But Cooper remained ambivalent. In *The Oak Openings* (1848), one of his very last books, he not only decided to write a book without a romance, he chose as a hero a man who subdues the Indians and the wilderness, rising to a position of influence in his community, even becoming a state senator. Cooper had made his peace, it would appear, with the inevitable, shortly before, in 1851, he died at Cooperstown of sclerosis of the liver, but his peace diminished him as a creative and moral force. Probably it is for this reason that Henry Nash Smith wrote of him in *Virgin Land: The American West as Symbol and Myth* (Harvard University Press, 1950) that "Cooper was able to speak for his people on this theme because the forces at work within him closely reproduced the patterns of thought and feeling that prevailed in the society at large. But he felt the problem more deeply than his contemporaries: he was at once more strongly devoted to the principle of social order and more vividly responsive to the idea of nature and freedom in the Western forest than they were. His conflict of allegiances was truly ironic, and if he had been able — as he was not — to explore to the end the contradictions in his ideas and emotions, the Leatherstocking series might have become a major work of art."

Nat Levine was certainly not the first one to attempt to bring *The Last of the Mohicans* to the screen, nor would he be the last. As early as 1909 D.W. Griffith directed a film in one reel titled *Leatherstocking* (Biograph, 1909), and two years later two films appeared bearing the title *The Last of the Mohicans*, one produced by Pat Powers and one by Thanhouser. *Lederstrumpf* (German, 1920) was directed by Arthur Wellin and was released in two parts, *Der Wildtoter [The Deerslayer]* and *Der Letzte der Mohikaner*. But perhaps the most impressive of these very early versions was *The Last of the Mohicans* (Associated Exhibitors, 1920) directed by Maurice Tourneur. According to what Clarence Brown told Kevin Brownlow in an interview recorded in Brownlow's *The Parade's Gone By* (Knopf, 1968), Tourneur had only been working on *The Last of the Mohicans* two weeks before he "fell off a parallel and was in bed for three months. I made the whole picture after that." It may be academic whether Tourneur or Brown was principally responsible for the final product, but one thing is of importance: this version stresses the romance between Uncas and Cora and the triangle formed when Magua would have Cora for his wife.

In the film Wallace Beery was cast as Magua. While in the novel, Magua is driven equally by a desire for vengeance against Cora's father, Colonel Munro, who once had him whipped, in the Tourneur/Brown film the emphasis is almost entirely on his attraction to Cora. Tourneur/Brown, however, do retain Cooper's dichotomy in the contrast between Magua and Uncas, the former representing a demonic savage, the latter a noble savage living in complete harmony with his wilderness environment. Uncas was played by Albert Roscoe, an actor who in the early sound era would generally be cast in heavy roles, while Chingachgook, interestingly, was played by Theodore Lorch, the "mysterious cripple" from Levine's *The Galloping Ghost*. Hawk-eye was played by Henry Lorraine, Cora Munro by Barbara Bedford, and the music teacher, David Gamut, was played by Nelson McDowell. The Tourneur/Brown film, in its sentiments, supported Cooper's horror of miscegenation, despite the fact that it played up the romance between Cora and Uncas, and apparently would indicate that, as Cooper believed, the color line is divine in origin and eternal.

Levine kept one bit of casting the same as in the Tourneur/Brown film. At Mascot, David Gamut was again portrayed by Nelson McDowell. For the role of Hawk-eye, Levine cast Harry Carey in his second serial for Mascot. In many ways, Carey was perfect for the part, with just the right balance of philosophic self-understanding and quiet heroics, gentle concern for every one with whom he comes into contact and a subdued but determined sense of justice. Indeed, with the exception of Carey's starring role in the feature Western *The Last Outlaw* (RKO, 1936) and his work in his third and last Mascot serial, *The Devil Horse*, his work in *The Last of the Mohicans* was clearly on a par with his role in *Trader Horn*.

Having had a somewhat less than satisfying experience with Edwina Booth on *The Vanishing Legion*, the plot of Cooper's novel permitted Levine to hedge his bet by casting a second, supporting female lead, which he did with Lucile Browne, the heroine of *Danger Island* as well as *Battling with Buffalo Bill* and *The Air Mail Mystery* (Universal, 1932). This last would be playing in many theatres at the time *The Last of the Mohicans* went into release and it was on this serial that Lucile Browne met James Flavin, its star. Shortly thereafter they were married. The Flavins enjoyed one of the few successful and enduring marriages in Hollywood; they died within a few weeks of each other in 1976.

"I remember that Edwina Booth was very temperamental," Lucile Browne Flavin once wrote in a letter to me. "She was very demanding — always late on the set — had to have a car for her use only. I never thought of Edwina as an actress — an attractive woman but as I remember self-centered and shallow. I never thought Bob Kortman could act — he had an unusual face. The picture was shot at various locations in the San Fernando Valley — the Iverson Ranch was used — that was near Calabassas — some shots were only a few minutes from the studio off Laurel Canyon Boulevard. Harry Carey was a fine actor — a gentleman and a joy to work with. He was most helpful to young actors. I do remember that the exteriors were shot with no lights. When the sun went down, flares would be lighted and held by members of the crew so close-ups could be shot."

Lucile Browne played Alice Munro, Edwina Booth her sister, Cora. Since Edwina as well as Lucile was a blonde, Edwina had to dye her hair so as to meet Cooper's description of her as the dark hair. For the role of Magua, Levine chose Bob Kortman. Perhaps his acting left something to be desired, but he passed muster as a vicious Indian. Walter Miller was back, this time as Major Duncan Heyward. Mischa Auer was given the role of the French General Montcalm and Edward Hearn was cast as British General Munro. For the role of Chingachgook, Levine selected Hobart Bosworth and for his son, Uncas, juvenile actor Junior Coughlan. Both wore body paint, as did Kortman. The screenwriters felt it necessary to alter Chingachgook's screen name from this to a term Hawk-eye occasionally uses for him in the novel, the Sagamore.

After the problems Levine had encountered using only one principal director with assistants, he agreed to hire back Breezy Eason. Ford Beebe and Eason split the directorial load between themselves, with Canutt handling all the stunts as usual. In addition, Canutt played the role of an Indian named Black Fox, with John Big Tree, a Native American actor, portraying simply a nameless Indian. Joan Gale, who would eventually play an Indian maiden opposite Tom Mix in *The Miracle Rider* (Mascot, 1935), played Red Wing in *Mohicans*.

On the whole, however unlikely this casting may seem on paper, *Mohicans* proved to be superior cinematically and dramatically to *The Lightning Warrior* and maybe, when all is said and done, it remains the best all around chapter play Mascot produced. The tension and suspense of the last five chapters are unparalleled in any of the studio's other efforts and the constant action format blended uniformly with the episodic story line.

Edwina Booth had lost her lawsuit against M-G-M and she was so deeply in debt from legal fees that both Harry and Olive Carey were helping out by getting their friends to contribute money to aid her in her plight. Perhaps for this reason Booth's performance deteriorated even more from her woodenness in *The Vanishing Legion*; the rest of the cast and the story had to serve as a compensation. Levine determined that he would not exercise the option he had for Booth to do a third serial for Mascot and Edwina retired from the screen, only to marry a Mormon and take up homemaking.

With all the outdoor shooting demanded by the script, *Mohicans* required twenty-eight days to complete and to recoup rapidly on his investment Levine put it into release in May, 1932, the very month it was completed. Although the principal action is the chase back and forth after Colonel Munro's daughters, there are some brilliantly staged battle sequences and the story has a coherence and logic usually lacking in chapter plays of any kind. Hobart Bosworth, who had originally left the legitimate stage in the East and come to California for reasons of health in the teens, was an old man by the time he appeared here, but his fine physical condition belied his years and much of the running and jumping asked of him he did himself. Only a short segment of the first episode was shot high up in the mountains, namely the waterfall sequence and the shots of the canoes in the rapids with which it concludes. All of the other water battles and races were filmed at Sherwood Lake or on the Kern River. All of this, however, drove up the cost, when combined with Harry Carey's star cost of $10,000.

"In men," Jung wrote in *The Archetypes and the Collective Unconscious*, "a positive father-complex very often produces a certain credulity with regard to authority and a distinct willingness to bow down before all spiritual dogmas and values.... In dreams, it is always the father-figure from whom the decisive convictions, prohibitions, and wise counsels emanate. The invisibility of this source is frequently emphasized by the fact that it consists simply of an authoritative voice which passes final judgments. Mostly, therefore, it is the figure of a 'wise old man' who symbolizes the spiritual factor." I think a parallel can be drawn between a negative father-figure and old, venerable-appearing Lafe McKee in *The Vanishing Legion*, who is the invisible, whispering master villain known only as The Voice. But the archetype of the wise old man, being two-sided, might have a beneficial aspect as well, as Jung pointed out in *Psychologie und Alchemie* (Rascher Verlag, 1944; revised 1952). "That the father leads him to the source of life is easily understandable," Jung pointed out in connection with interpreting the fourteenth dream of a series of them, "for every father is the natural generating agency of his son's life. The father represents so to speak the land or the ground out of which the source of life springs. He is however figuratively the 'educating spirit' who introduces him to the meaning of life and who clarifies the secrets of ancient teachings. He is the go-between of traditional wisdom. The fatherly educator fulfills this practice in our time certainly only in the son's dreams through an archetypal image of the father as the 'wise old man'." For Uncas, in the Mascot serial, because of Harry Carey's age and performance and that of Hobart Bosworth, it is found that he has not one but two father-figures, both of whom teach him the traditional wisdom of the forest and, more, the values and traditions of two widely diverse cultures. In fact, Carey's characterization here, as in *The Vanishing Legion* with Frankie Darro and again in *The Devil Horse* with Darro later that same year, is more that of a father-figure, a wise old man, than a super hero.

Moreover, the Mascot story department made some important changes in the story line. Magua is attracted to Cora and much of the tension is established by his lust for her. In the final chapter, Magua goes so far as to take Cora to a high cliff. Trying to escape his grasp, she slips over the edge. Holding Cora by one hand, Magua bargains for his life with Hawk-eye, the Sagamore, and Uncas who have been in pursuit. In Cooper's novel, Magua never commits any villainy without being surrounded by other of his tribesmen. In the Mascot version, he is often alone. In addition he is only one part of a villainous triad comprised of Magua and his Hurons, a white man named Dulac and his henchmen in the employ of General Montcalm, and General Montcalm and his French Army regulars. After Magua is promised his freedom, Cora is helped to safety by Hawk-eye and the Mohicans. Magua then turns on the Sagamore and they fight, Magua plunging over the cliff to his death. Dulac, who has also been in pursuit, then shoots the Sagamore and wounds Hawk-eye. Avoiding completely the issue of miscegenation, it is Dulac who now covets Cora and tries to carry her off with him. Uncas, because he is presumably no older than twelve-year-old Junior Coughlan, is never romantically implicated. It is the wounded Hawk-eye who shoots Dulac. Cora races to where Heyward and Alice have been watching all that has happened. Hawk-eye and Uncas congregate over the body of the Sagamore, Uncas performing a Hollywood notion of an Indian ritual befitting the last surviving member of the tribe. Yet, even with the incongruities and historical inaccuracy of this ritual, the conclusion is in a sense far more reassuring than that of the novel, since in Uncas is embodied not only the end of his tribe but the hope for a new beginning and, unifying all the images, the idea of friendship between a Native American and a white American before there is as yet an independent America, when the emerging nation is as yet unrealized in fact, an idea nearly sacred if only in fantasy.

Six

Shieks in Bedlam

Using a railroad setting for an adventure film dates as far back as the very first narrative film itself, *The Great Train Robbery* (Edison, 1903). Frank H. Spearman, a novelist infatuated with railroads and the men who worked on them, published his best-selling novel *Whispering Smith* (Scribner's, 1906) three years later. In 1914 Kalem began its series of *The Hazards of Helen* which ran to 119 episodes before its completion; the episodes were related one to another by the fact that each had the same central character, played by Helen Holmes in the early entries and by Helen Gibson later on, and a preponderance of railroad action. In the wake of the popularity of this series, Spearman was retained to script a chapter play with a railroad background titled *The Girl and the Game* (Mutual, 1915), which starred Helen Holmes, and the next year his *Whispering Smith* (Mutual, 1916) was brought to the screen for the first time. The director on these two vehicles was the same as on the *Hazards* series, J.P. McGowan, Helen Holmes' husband at the time.

Levine followed *The Last of the Mohicans* with *Hurricane Express* (Mascot, 1932), the second of the projected John Wayne serials, this one with a railroad setting and J.P. McGowan was engaged to codirect it with Armand Schaefer. McGowan also received coauthor credit for the screenplay. *Hurricane Express* further elaborated the policy of cheating as to the identity of the mystery master villain already so true of the Mascot serials. In this case, The Wrecker, as the master villain was called, adopted a set of fiendishly deceptive rubber masks, each of which permitted him to look like one or another of the suspects in the cast.

Tully Marshall, who like Harry Carey had gotten his start with D.W. Griffith, got top billing and played the manager of a beleaguered railroad, while Conway Tearle, the railroad's attorney, got second billing. Shirley Grey, who earlier that year had played opposite Tim McCoy and John Wayne in *The Texas Cyclone* (Columbia, 1932), was the principal love interest. Levine had originally hoped to cut expenses on the Wayne serials so he could afford more expensive productions like *Mohicans*, but to his dismay Wayne's name had no drawing power at all as *Shadow of the Eagle* had demonstrated. For this reason, on the publicity Levine played up Tully Marshall and Conway Tearle as well as J. Farrell MacDonald who had given a memorable performance in John Ford's silent epic *The Iron Horse* (Fox, 1924).

The plot told of how J. Farrell MacDonald is murdered by The Wrecker, who is taking advantage of the competition between the L&R Railroad and an air transport company to engineer a number of train crashes. Wayne, as MacDonald's screen son, portraying an airplane pilot, swears to track down the master villain and destroy him. Shirley Grey joins forces with him. Among the potential suspects is the by now familiar figure of a man falsely convicted of a crime, in this instance Mathew Betz, playing a railroad engineer accused of embezzlement.

The final entry for the year was *The Devil Horse*. It was to be Harry Carey's third and last serial for Mascot. To replace Edwina Booth, Levine chose Greta Granstedt, a virtual unknown, and kept her part to an absolute minimum, playing up instead the relationship between the man, portrayed by Harry Carey, the Wild Boy, portrayed by Frankie Darro, and the wild stallion — the components of the triad hero. It had been Levine's intention to cast Rex in the role of the devil horse, "Diablo," as he had been in the silent feature of the same title, but with Harry Carey costing him $10,000 and Frankie Darro raised to $3,000, Levine decided to develop a new equestrian star, a three-year-old black stallion purchased from Tracy Layne, a stunt man and horse breeder, a wild mustang with an unbroken spirit. To direct, Levine selected Otto Brower. Years before Brower had been assistant director to Richard Rosson at Paramount engaged in the production of their Zane Grey Western series. While making *Shootin' Irons* (Paramount, 1927), far away from the studio on location at Lone Pine, California, Rosson fell ill and Brower, rather than hold up production, finished the picture himself. Brower had gone on to work with Harry Carey in the silent era, had directed the sound Hoot Gibson series for M.H. Hoffman, Jr., and had directed with the Tim McCoy unit at Columbia Pictures. Part of *The Devil Horse* was slated to be shot on location in Arizona and Levine, based on Brower's conduct on *Shootin' Irons*, was confident he could be trusted to handle the job. However, to keep costs well in hand, Brower was the sole director on the chapter play. To assist Canutt with the stunts, Levine permitted Yak to engage Richard Talmadge who had doubled for Douglas Fairbanks, Sr., during the twenties.

Several cast members accompanied Brower and Canutt to Arizona, with Canutt standing in for Carey, who refused to go unless he was paid more. They were supposed to get all the animal footage they needed, which included stampede shots of a herd of wild horses, sequences with Frankie Darro atop "Diablo," and horse action in general. The location shooting, however, took much longer than anticipated, although much of the animal footage was indeed spectacular. By the time the troupe returned to California Levine was confronted with a financial emergency. He had allocated $60,000 for production of the serial with Noah Beery, Sr., signed as the principal heavy. Yet, by all indications, were production to continue as scheduled, the serial would significantly exceed its budget. Levine decided therefore to drastically cut corners. With *The Devil Horse* this was done out of necessity. In the subsequent five serials Levine produced in 1933, he did it so as to stretch his budgets even further, convinced that he had discovered a new angle.

Corner cutting for Levine consisted of introducing what since have become known as "cheat" episodes, where one of the characters undertakes to recount previously shown action to some other person in the cast who is supposedly unfamiliar with what had occurred. As this narration begins, the film cuts to the former footage and, frequently in *The Devil Horse* and later, an entire reel might be consumed in this fashion. Corner cutting made five serials possible in 1933, for the price of four, but exhibitors complained so vehemently that the practice was halted by 1934. As a result, *The Devil Horse* contains only nine full episodes of action, interspersed with lengthy repetitions. This is sad because the story itself is quite engaging and the serial, in terms of the dramatic portrayal by Noah Beery and the interaction between Harry Carey and Frankie Darro, is superior to many that Mascot would produce. Noah Beery was one of the finest villains of the silent screen who, in the sound era, was adding notably to the Paramount Zane Grey series, most of these feature Westerns being directed by the young Henry Hathaway. He had just completed a commendable performance in a Tim McCoy Western titled *Cornered* (Columbia, 1932), directed by Reeves Eason, and the next year Mae West would cast him as Gus in *She Done Him Wrong* (Paramount, 1933). Levine would cast Beery again in *Fighting with Kit Carson* (Mascot, 1933) and in that serial he created the one and only notable scene, wherein he viciously poisoned Edmund Breese.

One of the reasons Brower ended up taking so long in Arizona was Apache, the horse playing "Diablo." The stallion, however inexpensive initially, was unaccustomed to motion picture work and sequences which had been planned with Rex in mind had to be shot and reshot repeatedly before they were right. Levine did not go to Arizona personally to supervise production or perhaps there would have been fewer retakes than there were—retakes were against Mascot policy. When outdoor recording failed, as it often did, dubbing was resorted to once back at the studio working with the exposed footage, inserting spoken lines often by actors other than those pictured. Apache was frightened and dangerous. Before Brower left location, he wired Levine and confirmed instructions to give the horse as a gift to the University of Arizona, which had been kind enough to allow the Mascot group to work with a large herd of horses it owned. The gift was short-lived and the University ended up selling the animal to a private interest.

For the first episode cliffhanger, Canutt devised one of his most harrowing stunts. Doubling for Harry Carey, he was supposed to grab hold of the bucking Apache's mane with his hands, clamping his legs around the animal's neck from the front, as Apache continually tried to shake him off and dash him with his hoofs. A pit shot was arranged, placing a camera in an indentation in the ground with boards over the top of it with only enough room for the lens to be exposed to the light. This camera would capture the hoofs rearing and stamping on the earth. Another camera with a long-range lens focused on the action was set up in front and a third was placed off to one side.

"This stunt was rough," Canutt recalled in his autobiography. "... We used a trained horse for the first part of the scene where he charges Carey. After Carey got hold of the trained horse's ears, I took over. Then we substituted the trained horse with [Apache].... I rigged a strong strap around the horse's neck so that I could hang on at either ear. Then, with three cameras set and ready to shoot, we put a blindfold over [Apache's] eyes and got him quieted down with the help of a couple of cowboys. I got a good hold of the strap and ears and, as the cameras started turning, the two helpers eased off the blindfold and dashed out of the scene. The horse stood for a second or two, then, as he started to rear, I swung my body under his neck and hooked my spurs over the top of his withers. He reared high and spun around trying to strike me with his front hoofs but, because of the position I was in, he could only hit me with the forward part of his front legs. Those spurs tickling his withers sure set him in motion — he practically exploded, rearing, spinning, and doing everything he could to shake me loose. I was able to hang on, but with my two hundred pounds hanging on his head, he was thrown off balance and he finally fell hard to the ground."

Yak was knocked unconscious and taken to a hospital. While Canutt recorded the incident accurately in his autobiography, he attributed it to another Mascot serial rather than *The Devil Horse*, but it was on *The Devil Horse* that Levine, once he heard of the mishap, asked first if the crew had got the shot and then, despite Canutt's incapacitation, agreed to pay him his run-of-the-serial contract salary of $1,000. Canutt would later use this same footage for the Gene Autry Western *Comin' Round the Mountain* (Republic, 1936), with Autry dressed as Harry Carey had been in order to match shots. Canutt did, however, have sufficient opportunity to play two small parts in *The Devil Horse*: in the early chapters as one of "Diablo's" victims and near the end playing a different character entirely. Evidently the incongruity of this dual appearance was accepted with equanimity by audiences of chapter plays.

Much of the burden of stunting for the serial fell upon Richard Talmadge. It was Talmadge who in the opening chapter, doubling Frankie Darro as the Wild Boy, according to the script a youth abandoned while still a child and raised by the beasts of the forest, jumped from a sixty-foot cliff into the branches of a tall conifer, bending it by his weight down to the ground; he incurred numerous scratches in the process, but no serious injury.

Lee Zahler did not compose a score for *The Devil Horse*. Levine cut another corner by using "canned" classical music under the main titles, the *written* synopses, which practice began with this serial, and as background accompaniment during the first episode. The thunder storm from Rossini's Overture to *William Tell* was used for the credit crawl. This choice would have long-lasting effects. The visual was of Apache racing toward the camera with hoofbeats and the Overture on the track. It inspired George W. Trendle to employ the same theme and hoofbeat sound effects when in December of 1932 *The Lone Ranger* made his debut on WXYZ radio in Detroit. An excerpt from Harold's Overture to *Zampa* was used consistently beneath the synopses and the conclusion of Wagner's "Ride of the Valkyries" from *Die Walküre* was used when Harry Carey was first introduced.

The screenplay was credited in part to Barney Sarecky who was then working in the Mascot story department. Sarecky would eventually become an associate producer under Henry MacRae at Universal where, among other serials, he would work on *Buck Rogers* (Universal, 1939), starring Buster Crabbe. The story had it that Darro, abandoned as I have said at a tender age, abandoned as a matter of fact after Noah Beery cruelly murders his father, is found and educated in the rudiments of speech and the communication of feelings by Harry Carey. Hence, in a psychological sense, once the real father has been killed, he is replaced by the loving wise old man. The first episode is broken down into individual sections subtitled "The Boy," "The Horse," and finally "The Man." Carey's brother in the film is also murdered by Beery and therefore, once Beery is done in, Darro finds in Carey the father Beery denied him and Carey finds a younger brother in Darro.

The Devil Horse, despite its production problems, is the first Mascot serial which, at times, slows the hysterical pacing to include tender human interludes, as Carey teaches the Wild Boy the ways of men, or when Darro responds to the new clothes Carey buys for him, or when Darro struggles to remember how to use a knife and a fork. These moments should be credited to Brower for their moving direction. The imparting of a name, Jung once said, is the equivalent of creating a soul, and *this* is the miracle that Harry Carey performs in *The Devil Horse,* a miracle which surpasses all the heroics, hard riding, and occasionally hectic action.

As already remarked, in 1933 Mascot increased production to five serials, each twelve chapters in length. The market was wide open. RKO Radio Pictures made a one-time effort to see if there was any sense in resuming serial production profitably as once had been true for their Pathé division, by this time limited to the production of newsreels, but the effort, titled *The Last Frontier* (RKO, 1932) and starring Creighton Chaney, Lon Chaney's son, was mediocre and was not followed by another. Universal remained Mascot's strongest competitor, but Mascot was steadily edging ahead in total number of bookings for its chapter plays. A Mascot serial might play in more than ten thousand theatres. At a flat booking rate of $5.00 per episode, a twelve chapter serial could easily earn $600,000 in gross film rental, and cost only a tenth of that to produce. Had Levine owned his own exchange network, as Universal did, his profit margin on his individual productions would have exceeded that averaged by the major producing companies on the majority of their feature films which, if profitable, ranged between $100,000 and $200,000 above negative cost; and this, in many cases, was true because they owned their own theatres and could guarantee their pictures a given number of play-offs. But to compete with a major producing company, even with Universal, which did not own a theatre chain, Levine had to do more than merely acquire an exchange network: he would have to increase production to support his own exchange network. Expanding serial production was one way in which to do this. The previous year Mascot had also produced its first feature film, *Pride of the Legion* (Mascot, 1932) with Rin Tin Tin, Jr., and Sally Blane. In 1933 Mascot would produce a second feature. However, it was not until 1934 that the firm seriously entered the field of feature production, and for that reason I have decided to devote an entire chapter to the Mascot features. For now, what should be stressed is the drive toward greater productivity.

Yet increased production, even with corner-cutting devices like "cheat" episodes, was an expensive proposition as long as Levine continued to rent space on sound stages from other studios. Therefore Levine decided to take a chance. The Mack Sennett studio located in North Hollywood was up for sale by the trustees, the Sennett company having been forced into receivership. Levine was not prepared to commit capital he needed for new production to an outright purchase, at least not right off, so instead he leased the Sennett studio from the trustees, with an option to buy. Mack Sennett in his book *King of Comedy* (Doubleday, 1954) recalled when he originally left his Edendale studio. "A group of enterprising real-estate operators in the San Fernando Valley thought it would be a fine thing if they could lure a motion picture studio into their community," he told his amanuensis, Cameron Shipp. "They offered me a gift of twenty acres of land near the trickle known as the Los Angeles River. I spent $500,000 in cash building a brand-new, equipped-with-everything motion picture factory and was ready for sound and talk on film when they came along a few years later." By the time Levine came along, the asking price of the trustees was $190,000 for everything, including all equipment and real estate. In the final analysis, had Levine purchased the studio in 1933, he would ultimately have made more on the real estate than he was to make as a result of his eventual merger into Republic Pictures combined with the sale of all of his negatives and rights. The real estate he finally did buy for a quarter of a million dollars was Jean Harlow's mansion, after her death. "That studio stands," Mack Sennett went on. "It is known as Republic." After he said that, the property changed hands again, and became known as CBS Television City. The mansion cost Levine more and profited him less — as it turned out, much less.

But definite changes were coming over Levine. He was making a small fortune by producing a certain kind of picture for a specific audience and sticking to it. He had learned serial production well. Yet Levine's business acumen, not inconsiderable in his area of expertise, was nonetheless somewhat limited in its scope. He had been, as the saying goes, in the right place at the right time. Everything had gone without a real setback and, possibly for this reason, he could never be quite certain as to the mechanics behind his success. Levine was no thinker but, then, neither was he only a calculating businessman at heart. He was above all a gambler to whom it meant a great deal to have moved in so short a span of years from a $5.00 a week job to that of overseer and owner of a producing company. Consistent with his temperament as a gambler, Levine strove to push his luck as far as it would go. He did not know how far this would be, and for this he cannot be blamed; but for the first time in his life he was not at all certain just *where* he wanted to go and, for this apparently, he tended to hold himself responsible years later when he looked back. Facing the prospect of becoming installed as the head of his own studio — until now the writing department was on the second floor above a cement factory on Santa Monica Boulevard in Hollywood — and potentially acquiring his own exchange network, he was too reserved and cautious to make any of it permanent. His rent was $12,000 a month.

The Whispering Shadow (Mascot, 1933) was the first of his five entries for 1933. Boris Karloff had had his start at Mascot. Bela Lugosi, who had created quite a controversial sensation in *Dracula* (Universal, 1931), pursued a career with almost opposite results. However circumscribed Karloff's dramatic talent might be, Lugosi's was even more limited. He did not act; he almost invariably overacted. His sense of melodrama predominated. While Karloff chose his scripts with some circumspection, including *The Black Cat* (Universal, 1934) with Lugosi, Lugosi would apparently take any role, simply for the money, and ended up in six serials, of which *The Whispering Shadow* was the first and probably one of his best. He was cast as Professor Strang, an eccentric whose wax museum is filled with curious, lifelike figures that appear nearly human in their movements. The written plot résumé at the beginning of one of the episodes informed the viewer: "The Whispering Shadow is a mysterious criminal, a scientific genius, who directs his agents by television and uses a radio 'death ray' to kill. Several persons are suspected of being the Shadow — notably Professor Strang, a sinister being whose wax work museum is known as the House of Mystery. In a sensational attack by the Shadow on the warehouse of the Empire Transport and Storage Company, Vera Strang, the professor's daughter, is captured by detectives but freed by the Shadow's agents. Jack Foster [Malcolm MacGregor], whose brother was murdered by the Shadow, goes to the House of Mystery to check up on Vera [Viva Tattersall], and is attacked by the Shadow's men."

Barney Sarecky, George Morgan, Norman Hall, Colbert Clark, and Wyndham Gittens were all credited for the screenplay. They improved on the notion of an invisible master villain from *The Vanishing Legion*. The Shadow speaks in a whisper to his minions, as did The Voice, but he has also invented a diabolical device which permits him to render a person invisible. The Shadow appears only as a dark silhouette — an outline somewhat ineptly created by cartoon animators drawing directly on the positively exposed frame — moving along walls or appearing outside moving vehicles. The Shadow also forces his men to wear a radio disc, which permits him to strike them dead whenever he pleases, a further perfection of the kinds of radio control employed by both The Voice and The Wrecker.

I think it is possible to agree with Jim Harmon and Donald F. Glut in *The Great Movie Serials: Their Sound and Fury* (Doubleday, 1972), that Lugosi, in his portrayal, was consistently menacing. "From his sinister, almost carved profile," they wrote, "to his apparently diabolical laboratory with its array of superscience apparatus and his private museum of wax figures that occasionally moved just a bit to assure that actors hired to stand around motionless all day were cheaper than making up statues. That, plus the fact that the unseen menace did sound like Lugosi, made it even more difficult to grasp that in the final episode it was revealed that Bela Lugosi was *not* the Whispering Shadow! Incredibly enough, Bela Lugosi, who rarely played anything *but* a villain, turned out to be only a 'red herring' — an overtly sinister-looking character to throw suspicion away from the real master criminal — in this case, a janitor who throughout the chapter play seemed no more than a harmless, bumbling idiot. Attempts to mislead viewers transpired as Lugosi, a mad look in his power-filled eyes, operated his humming, glowing laboratory devices, followed by a cut to the sibilant Shadow appearing on the side of a truck with the eerie, whispered warning promising destruction."

Albert Herman, a "B" Western director, shared directorial credit with Colbert Clark on *The Whispering Shadow*. This serial marked Colbert Clark's debut as a contract director for Mascot, promoting him from the writing department where he had been working. He had learned the techniques of serial production while working for Pathé. Clark did so well, in fact, on his portions of *The Whispering Shadow* that Levine teamed him with Armand Schaefer to codirect the next serial into production, *The Three Musketeers* (Mascot, 1933).

John Wayne's exposure in his two Mascot entries so far had been sufficient that he had been hired by Warner Bros. to star in a series of six remakes of Ken Maynard silent Westerns. The idea for this series was generated by Sid Rogell, who had worked as business manager on the Maynard Western series for First National, a company since merged with Warner Bros., and the idea was the same as that used by Paramount in its sound remakes of silent Westerns based on Zane Grey's novels. Wayne would attire himself exactly as Maynard had and the Maynard action footage would be intercut with closeups of Wayne. Wayne's leading lady in the first of these remakes, *Ride Him Cowboy* (Warner's, 1932), was Ruth Hall, originally a Paramount ingénue who had appeared with the Marx Brothers in *Monkey Business* (Paramount, 1931). Levine signed her for the feminine lead in *The Three Musketeers* and for an additional Mascot feature.

However, even with the Warner Bros. series going for him, Levine placed Wayne's name fourth in the credits. Credited first was Jack Mulhall who had appeared in chapter plays as early as *The Brass Bullet* (Universal,

1918), directed by Ben Wilson in eighteen chapters, and *The Social Buc-
caneer* (Universal, 1923), directed by Robert F. Hill in ten chapters. Billed
second was Raymond Hatton, a character actor who would have a long
career ahead of him in Westerns and who was currently appearing regularly
in the Paramount Zane Grey series. Francis X. Bushman, Jr., who had been
cast in *The Galloping Ghost,* was credited third. Creighton Chaney, billed
sixth after Ruth Hall, had of course recently starred in RKO's sole serial entry in the sound era.

The most extraordinary thing about *The Three Musketeers* was its
sizeable cast of villains, all veteran Western players got up in bed sheets to
simulate Arabs. Hooper Atchley, who made nearly a career in the early
thirties out of playing slick, well-dressed, fashionable villains, showed up
unexpectedly as El Kadur, suspected for a time of being the mysterious
master villain, El Shaitan. Hooper, because he was so typecast, was incredibly offbeat in his turban, as certainly was Al Fergusson, another heavy
from Westerns, as Ruth Hall's house servant, Ali. But then the entire
production was filled with the wildest incongruities.

Levine was personally fond of the Alexadre Dumas classic, *Les Trois
Mousquetaires,* which became a series of books, but he wanted to bring the
characters up to date. All that was really retained from the book was the
cry, "One for All — All for One!" used at the beginning of each episode and
occasionally in a sequence or two. Jack Mulhall, Raymond Hatton, Francis
X. Bushman, Jr., and John Wayne, although they were given different
character names — Levine assuaged Wayne's irritation at his billing by
assigning him the character name of Michael Wayne — were in a way supposed to represent Athos, Porthos, Aramis, and D'Artagnan. There was an
even greater force at work here, however, beyond Mascot's penchant for
triad heroes, or in this case a quaternity of heroes. The spirit of the United
States at the time, as the spirit of Franklin D. Roosevelt's administration,
was one of unity and collectivism. The theme was realized in motion pictures by an increasing preponderance of triads and collectivities of heroes.
One man alone was no longer expected to stand off a pack of thieves and
killers. Fighting villainy was now a *collective* effort. This feeling would persist through the Second World War and would only subside in the after-
math of President Roosevelt's death and the paranoia about Communism.

Levine would persist in this multiple hero approach even at Republic
when he bought screen rights to William Colt MacDonald's triad heroes, the
Three Mesquiteers, after RKO had made a single Western based on one of
MacDonald's novels. It was consistent of Levine — in part, I suppose,
because he had long become accustomed to balancing an unexceptional cast
and even an indifferent story with several strong personalities when a single
star did not avail himself, primarily because of low pay. The practice
proved a success and many youngsters, seeing first these Mascot serials and
then the later triad Western series, could identify with more than one hero,
further solidifying the idea of collectivism.

The physical ardors on this serial were acute insofar as Levine decided to shoot the desert footage on location on the Mojave outside Yuma, Arizona. "Ray Hatton helped me work out many of my scenes," Ruth Hall once told me, "especially when I had only one half hour a day to prepare. He would sit down with me and help me plan my movements. In Westerns I was not given very much direction and so I planned, timed, and thought through my own movements. The rule of thumb was, so long as one did not upset the direction for the star one was given one's own head. Acting to me is like a tennis game, the stronger your opposition is the better your game becomes. *The Three Musketeers* was shot in Yuma. We were there when Roosevelt closed the banks. However, the show went on. I did not have a double. I was exposed to the sun so much that I developed sun blisters which became pretty badly swollen, so much so that most of the latter scenes had to be shot from my back." Perhaps this is also why Ruth Hall was kept in tight riding breeches, to take out of necessity yet another step in the increasing awareness of the female body in Mascot productions. This tendency reached its highest expression in *Mystery Mountain* (Mascot, 1934), when heroine Verna Hillie went through her paces without aid of a support garment and Evalyn Knapp appeared naked beneath her close-fitting gowns in *In Old Santa Fe* (Mascot, 1934). And, even so, the feeling persists that the Mascot chapter plays, as serials and "B" Westerns in general, were intended only for the very young!

"The usual workin' day was twelve to twenty hours," John Wayne told Maurice Zolotow for Zolotow's book *Shooting Star*. "Mascot used two shifts of directors and two writers. We didn't have a hell of a lot of dialogue. And we didn't fool around with retakes. The first take was usually the one we printed. ... And you learned never to give in to the elements. We shot *The Three Musketeers* ... with the temperature hitting 120 degrees during the day. Now when you shoot on location in the desert you usually film early in the morning and late in the afternoon, when the sun isn't too murderous. Levine would get goin' at sunup and we didn't knock off until it was dark and we were about ready to drop dead from exhaustion. Levine was too much of a piker to bring properly trained horses, used to workin' in movies. Would have cost him a few dollars to get 'em shipped from Hollywood with a ramrod. He didn't. He found some tired beasts in Yuma. Well, they were ready for the glue factory. Now there is this scene where I ride up on my horse through a crowd . I grab hold of a rope and haul myself hand over hand to the second story of this North African fort. We were usin' the local jail as a fort. Now I didn't use doubles much in those days, but I couldn't climb a rope fast enough, so ole Yak was doublin' me in this scene. Now the poor horse, he was scared of the light reflectors which are focusin' the sun on him, and he was jumpy with all these extras standin' around in their long Arab robes. So the horse was paralyzed. Would not budge one inch. He just stood there. Yak was spurrin' it and cursin' it and it still wouldn't move and the camera was goin', so Yak asked me to get him a club, which I did, and then he started beatin' that horse without mercy, usin' this big hunk of wood, until finally the nag is trotting and the scene is over.

Later, I said to him, 'Yak, what will my fans think? They know that John Wayne is too decent a guy to ever beat a horse like that.

"He looked at me and grinned and said, 'You just tell them that John Wayne just had to beat the horse that one time and will never do it again'."

In addition to the location sequences, Bronson Canyon was back, here as a secret repository for illegal arms, and some action sequences were shot just north of Hollywood. Noah Beery, Jr., had a small part in the first installment, and was promptly killed off, but it might well be considered his Mascot screen test for a more substantial part in the forthcoming *Fighting with Kit Carson* (Mascot, 1933). Lee Zahler translated a French Legion song to be sung beneath the opening credits crawl.

In view of the tensions between the Arab nations and the United States ever since the Second World War ended, the political content of *The Three Musketeers* is perhaps even more interesting than any reflections on its making or the psychological content of its story line. It embodied that very strong impulse in Hollywood films from the thirties to support European control over underdeveloped countries. A fear of revolutions and underground movements, most aptly fictionalized by the late Sax Rohmer in his numerous tales about the evil archfiend Dr. Fu Manchu and the Si-Fan, was a commonplace theme and in *The Three Musketeers* three Legionnaires and one American flyer—this last, naturally, John Wayne—enthusiastically campaign to maintain French suzerainty over their North African colonies. It may also be worthwhile observing that the master villain, El Shaitan, is in fact a European, exploiting the Arabs for his own ends, although this is not known until the last chapter and what is seen of him prior to this is his usual meetings with his minions at which time he announces, "The Devil's Circle is complete ... El Shaitan is here." It would have to be a Devil's Circle to oppose the rule of the Establishment.

That the French had poorly governed colonies is not even hinted at in the screenplay. The Foreign Legion is conceived romantically, a popular and persistent Hollywood cliché still in effect as recently as Dick Richards' *March or Die* (Columbia, 1976) and Marty Feldman's *The Last Remake of Beau Geste* (Universal, 1976). Beyond the collectivism, youngsters, and those not so young, viewing *The Three Musketeers* were imbued with a sense of the white man's burden" and not surprisingly were reinforced in the belief widely held then, as now, that without proper occidental management the world would be doomed to hopeless dissension. That this posture might account for the primary ingredient of this dissension, namely antioccidentalism, apparently occurred to no one working in Hollywood, or at least it never found its way to the screen.

By 1933, since the Disney Company had increased production to such a degree it could no longer rent its sound equipment to Levine, Levine made a deal with the International Film Recording Company and, for *The Three Musketeers*, George Lowerre, the Disney sound man, was replaced by Homer Ackerman as principal sound engineer. This new equipment was actually an improvement and dubbing became less commonplace and certainly less inept. In fact, the dubbing was so much improved, it was used to further obfuscate the real identity of El Shaitan. Although in the final episode, storekeeper Edward Peil, Sr., is unmasked, Wilfred Lucas, not listed on the credits, played him when he addressed the Devil's Circle, while Yakima Canutt portrayed him for many of the exteriors, only occasionally using his own voice in place of expert dubbing of Lucas' voice, which was somewhat more feasible with the Hollywood-based footage. Robert Frazer, who played Major Booth in the cast, posed for all the lobby cards in the El Shaitan outfit and in the course of the serial both Frazer and Gordon DeMain, portraying Colonel Duval, would occasionally disguise themselves as El Shaitan. If there is one image from this serial which remains in my mind, it is the first time the viewer sees John Wayne. The Musketeers, greatly outnumbered, are about to be finished off by an attacking band of marauding Arabs. Out of the sky, to their rescue, flies John Wayne in his biplane, armed with a machine gun, and dozens of extras bite the dust. This was not only to become John Wayne's persona for most Americans; sadly, it was the way a great many Third World people came to regard Americans, dropping fire and bullets from the skies. It is to the nation's shame that no country in history has dropped more bombs on noncombatant civilian populations than the United States.

I visited Ruth Hall in June, 1976. She had married cinematographer Lee Garmes shortly after completing work on *The Three Musketeers*. The night I stopped at the Garmes' apartment, Lee was not home, but Ruth, still very much the enthusiast she had been when she worked in pictures, had invited the film director Edward Ludwig. During his active career, Ludwig had directed all manner of pictures, at studios as diverse as Republic and Metro-Goldwyn-Mayer. Ruth had shown Eddie a copy of my book *The Filming of the West*.

"I see," he said to me, his curly hair iron gray, his mustache snow white and without a part in the center, "that you've spent a lot of time in this book on Duke Wayne. I'm a shorty. Five feet five. I'll never forget the first picture I had to direct Wayne in. It was *The Fighting Seabees* [Republic, 1944]. Wayne, he's six four. He comes up to me and picks me up by the collar. '"Okay, coach,' he says, 'what is it you want me to do in this picture?!

"We had to shoot some of the picture on location in the South Pacific, where the Japanese had vacated. There was a saloon near our location frequented by servicemen and every time Wayne would go in there, some guy would pick a fight with him, wondering why he wasn't in uniform and instead only play-acting that he was in military service for his country. Wayne would lose more fights than he won and I had to forbid him going there if I expected to get him through the picture in one piece. Now he's a national hero."

"John Wayne was always on the set for *The Three Musketeers*," Ruth interrupted, smiling, ever the diplomat, "and he was a great man to be with. He is just as charming today as he was then."

Perhaps in this context it is interesting to recall the obituary devoted to John Wayne in *Newsweek* in which a Vietnam veteran reported that he had been inspired to enlist in the Marine Corps because he had seen John Wayne in *Sands of Iwo Jima* (Republic, 1950). He had had his penis shot off in action and lamented how he had given up his organ for the United States, but most of all for John Wayne.

Wayne, after finishing his third serial for Mascot, continued in his Warner Bros. series until September, 1933 when he signed a contract with Trem Carr of Monogram Pictures to make an undetermined number of Western feature films. The principal heavy in most of these films, and Wayne's double in all of them, was Yakima Canutt. Levine, after taking over the Sennett studio, offered to sublet lot and office space to Trem Carr, but Carr refused. Levine then extended a similar offer to two other small producing companies, Majestic and Chesterfield, and both accepted, somewhat easing Mascot's financial burden.

Laughing at Life (Mascot, 1933) was Levine's feature entry for the year, filmed in May, directly following release of *The Three Musketeers*. It was "old home week" in that J. Farrell MacDonald and Tully Marshall from *Hurricane Express*, Noah Beery, Sr., who was the first choice at Mascot when there was no need of a mystery villain for the role of principal heavy, and Ruth Hall were all in the cast. In a manner to be explained presently, feature production influenced the way in which the Mascot chapter plays were produced and distributed. For example, both *The Lost Jungle* (Mascot, 1934) and *Burn 'em Up Barnes* (Mascot, 1934), the first two serial entries for 1934, were released in feature as well as serial versions. These feature versions were issued under the Majestic logo, one of the two independent companies subleasing space from Levine.

Armand Schaefer and Colbert Clark codirected *Fighting with Kit Carson* (Mascot, 1933), which starred Johnny Mack Brown in the role of Carson. Brown had appeared as Billy in King Vidor's *Billy the Kid* (M-G-M, 1930) and he had also been cast in high budget society dramas. The next year he would appear opposite Mae West in *Belle of the 'Nineties* (Paramount, 1934). But *Fighting with Kit Carson* was the beginning of typecasting for him. By the middle of the decade he would replace Buck Jones as the frontliner in Universal's Western chapter plays and throughout the mid thirties and into the fifties he would regularly appear in one series after another of "B" Westerns of varying quality. Noah Beery, Sr., was cast as Kraft, the crooked white trader behind all the trouble and the secret leader — secret to the "good guys" including and above all Carson, but not to the audience — of the Mystery Riders. As in *Phantom of the West*, these Mystery Riders wore black capes and black sombreros and were heard to sing upon occasion; in fact, Lee Zahler translated from the Russian into English a Cossack legionnaire song for them to sing which was used beneath the opening credits. However, they were not vigilantes, but minions in Kraft's employ. Beery's son Noah, Jr., on behalf of whose health Beery himself had originally come to Hollywood, wanted to act in pictures and Levine cast him as an Indian — a "Hollywood" Indian — named Nakomas, who is a staunch friend of Carson's. Betsy King Ross, a young rodeo performer, had been cast earlier that year in *Smoke Lightning* (Fox, 1933) opposite Western player George O'Brien, a film based on a short novel by Zane Grey. Ross spent much of her time in the serial dressed as a boy to conceal her identity as a girl — her cast name was Joan Fargo, but, when disguised, she was called "Johnny" Fargo.

The "weenie" in this case was a shipment of government gold lost when a pack train headed by Carson is attacked. The gold is hidden and Beery and the Mystery Riders cause all manner of deviltry in their efforts to lay hold of it. This plot, as it stands, was weak enough. Noah Beery, Jr., was anything but convincing as an Indian. Johnny Mack Brown's performance was, at best, merely competent. But when to this is added the fact that Levine stretched footage through corner-cutting, the serial became, after a time, tedious. Worse, and hitherto unique in a Mascot chapter play, it became painfully predictable.

Nor did matters pick up appreciably with the next entry, *The Wolf Dog* (Mascot, 1933). Frankie Darro was back, raised to $4,000, playing Frank Courtney. His sister, Irene Courtney, was played by "Boots" Mallory, an ingénue who would go on for the next several years playing "the girl" in budget Westerns, while her father, Jim Courtney, was played by Henry B. Walthall, an actor who first came to prominence as a result of his role as the "Little Colonel" in D.W. Griffith's *Birth of a Nation* (Epoch, 1915), a player truly never appreciated by Hollywood. The "Wolf Dog" of the title was, of course, Rin Tin Tin, Jr., one of Lee Duncan's standins for the original Rinty and the dog Yakima Canutt considered the better actor. George Lewis, a character actor, was assigned the lead, portraying Bob Whitlock, and Hale Hamilton was cast as Frankie Darro's guardian. The title card résumé for the serial informed the viewer coming in on the final episode that "the Wolf Dog was found leading a pack of wolves in the Northern wilds. His young master, Frank Courtney, is the heir to a large fortune. Norman Bryan [Hamilton], Frank's guardian, is secretly trying to rob the boy of his inheritance. Bob Whitlock, a radio operator, has reason to suspect Bryan. Irene Courtney, working with Bob, has made a Dictaphone record of Bryan's conversation with his agents. At the home of Jim Courtney, Bryan's agents make a desperate attempt to regain possession of the record."

Again, it was a very thin plotline with very little going for it. At the beginning of the last episode, Rinty did manage to jump through a glass window in order to maul Hale Hamilton, but, as so many of the episodes, Chapter Twelve relied heavily on flashbacks. Harking back to *The Devil Horse*, title cards told the viewer that this was a story of a boy, a wolf dog, and a man, and so the triad hero was maintained, but the implementation of this plot was simply too conventional to sustain close scrutiny, much less retain interest week after week.

Mystery Squadron (Mascot, 1933) was obviously an effort to restore the heretofore high quality of the Mascot serials and it was definitely on a par with *The Three Musketeers*. Bob Steele, who had been playing Western heroes in "B" pictures since the late twenties, including a series for Trem Carr in 1930, was cast against type as an expert flyer, as was Guinn "Big Boy" Williams, a regularly featured character actor in Westerns and even star of a few very low budget entries. On the surface, *Mystery Squadron* was Mascot's answer to *The Phantom of the Air* (Universal, 1933) which starred Tom Tyler, again a movie cowboy cast as an aviator; but it went Universal one better. In addition to casting against type, all the traditional Mascot ingredients were varied in a new fashion. For a band of Mystery Riders, there was the Mystery Squadron itself, decked out in silver-colored flight suits and aviators' caps with goggles. For a mystery villain, there was the Black Ace, the sinister leader of the Squadron who has made it his personal mission to destroy the construction of a dam. Instead of warnings sent by darts as in *Phantom of the West* or by arrows as in *The Lightning Warrior*, the Black Ace issues his demands via a miniature aircraft.

There was a triad hero, of sorts. Jack Mulhall, who had played one of the Three Musketeers, was cast as Hank Davis, a foreman on the dam project. It is Davis who enlists Steele and Williams to assist him in tracking down the Black Ace. However, Davis is promptly kidnapped and is not seen again until much later. It, therefore, comes as quite a shock—provided you are *not* employing serial logic—when the Black Ace is unmasked and proves to be none other than Jack Mulhall.

Joining Colbert Clark on the direction of *Mystery Squadron* was David Howard, once an assistant director to King Vidor. Howard continued working on and off for Mascot on a nonexclusive contract for the next year before becoming a fulltime contract director for RKO Radio Pictures. Lucile Browne was cast as the feminine lead. And it was because of David Howard that the Mascot serials, as well as subsequently the Mascot features he directed, attained a new look. The viewer was aware of Lucile Browne's figure, yes, but because Howard, who had been directing the George O'Brien series at Fox, including *Smoke Lightning*, was aware of the creative uses to be made of the close-up, beginning with *Mystery Squadron* viewers became aware of what the heroine looked like, the play of emotions and emotional subtlety on her face, as well as on the faces of other cast members. I cannot recall any other chapter play, and certainly no Mascot chapter play, prior to this time which relied for dramatic effect as much on the use of close-ups as this and henceforth the other serials on which David Howard worked. According to Colbert Clark in conversation, he was so impressed with the effects Howard achieved through close-ups in the serials on which they collaborated that he tended to continue the practice later on when working with others as a codirector. At all events, it was a breakthrough and when combined, as it was in 1934, with a cessation of the cornercutting techniques Levine had adopted to save on expenses, the Mascot product again resumed its position of leadership in its field.

Seven

The Lost Jungle

The Big Cage (Universal, 1933) was a feature film which starred Clyde Beatty, an animal trainer and top attraction with the Hagenbeck-Wallace circus. The Hagenbeck-Wallace animals were also included, Beatty's most sensational act being when he entered a cage occupied by lions and tigers, males and females of both species, and put the beasts through their paces. Levine saw the film and knew at once he wanted Beatty and, of course, the Hagenbeck-Wallace animals for a chapter play. By releasing *The Lost Jungle*, as Levine's production was titled, as both a feature and as a serial, he felt, and rightly, that he would get twice the mileage that Universal had gotten out of its feature.

There was, according to the Mascot screenplay, an isthmus that once joined Africa with India but which subsequently sank beneath the ocean save for one, isolated island. The action takes place on this island with Beatty battling lions, tigers, panthers, bears, and other assorted inhabitants. The credit crawl of *The Lost Jungle* began with a close-up of a tiger prowling the vine-clung wilds of a sound stage. Levine was so taken with this opening that he chose to use a variation of it for the new Mascot Pictures logo. Always in the past the chapter plays had begun "Nat Levine Presents." Now, wholly in the spirit of M-G-M's Leo the Lion, Mascot Pictures were announced by a shot of a tiger perched on a ball painted to resemble the Earth. The tiger would let out two roars and the Mascot Pictures title would whirl into view, rather like the airplane that circled the globe in Universal Pictures' logo.

The plot of *The Lost Jungle* began with Beatty putting together tigers, lions, panthers, and bears in the same cage for his circus act. Presently he embarks on a safari aboard the dirigible *Victory* which crashes, after a storm, onto this unknown and so far unnamed island—incidentally, it is never explained how the brown bears got onto this island, but no matter.... Cecilia Parker, whose name was misspelled on the credits, had the feminine lead. She had been raised in a convent and her delicate screen image and what photographed to be obvious innocence had been so appealing to Ken Maynard that, after working with her in *Tombstone Canyon* (Worldwide, 1932), at KBS Productions, he had her cast in three of his Universal Westerns, *The Trail Drive* (Universal, 1933), *Gun Justice* (Universal, 1933), and

Honor of the Range (Universal, 1934). Since serials were not subject to cen-
sorship review boards and the Hays Office, which, in large measure, Mae
West's films had brought into existence, Mascot's wardrobe department
decked Parker out in a tight-fitting sweater with a plunging neckline and no
support garment beneath it and skin-tight slacks.

Mickey Rooney, who appeared briefly in the initial episode, was
working for Larry Darmour in the Mickey McGuire short comedies.
Majestic Pictures released Darmour's productions and so Mickey was on the
lot. In 1935 he would be placed under long-term contract to Metro-
Goldwyn-Mayer as a result of David O. Selznick's use of him playing Clark
Gable as a kid in *Manhattan Melodrama* (M-G-M, 1934). In 1938, when M-
G-M began production on the successful Andy Hardy series, Louis B.
Mayer's pet project, Cecilia Parker was added to the cast to play Andy's
older sister. Mayer, like Ken Maynard before him, emphasized Parker's
vestal purity. Levine, quite obviously, perceived something else in her.

The plot synopsis told all: "Clyde Beatty, famous animal trainer, is
on his way through 'the Lost Jungle' to recover a stolen treasure chest. The
safety of Ruth Robinson [Cecilia Parker] and her father [Edward LeSaint],
whose crew have mutinied, depends on Clyde's success. Kirby [Wheeler
Oakman] and Flynn [Lou Meehan], two members of the crew, are ahead of
Clyde, bent on obtaining the treasure for themselves. The Mystery Man
[Warner Richmond], who lives in the buried city of Kamor, has the
treasure. Clyde's pal, Larry Henderson [Syd Saylor], arriving at Kamor, has
been attacked by a fierce gorilla." On second thought, maybe the synopsis
doesn't tell *quite* all. The plot, unquestionably, owed more than a little to
The King of the Kongo and *King of the Wild.* Warner Richmond, a regular
heavy in "B" pictures in the thirties, might be the Mystery Man, but he was
not the only villain, however much his identity may have been concealed
from the audience. Syd Saylor's comic antics, which held some attraction
for Levine, were not at all appealing in the serial; he was , in short, not funny. But worst of all was Beatty's appallingly poor delivery of his dialogue.
Not even his fantastic work with the animals could compensate for this.

Credit for the screenplay was given to Barney Sarecky, David
Howard, Armand Schaefer, and Wyndham Gittens, while Armand
Schaefer and David Howard functioned as the codirectors. Note should also
be made of Terry Kellum, who took over as chief sound engineer with this
serial, and further improved the sound recording; Earl Turner, who had
begun editing the Mascot chapter plays in 1933, and who managed to build
tension through adroit cutting, which augmented the action being
photographed; and William Nobles who had been third cinematographer
under Harry Neumann on *The Wolf Dog* and now was promoted to second
cinematographer working closely with David Howard. The technical
proficiency of these men provided *The Lost Jungle*, at least visually, with a
sophistication that Beatty's ineptitude as an actor might otherwise have
caused one to overlook and forget in retrospect.

At the conclusion of Chapter Twelve, the audience was told that so ended the adventure in the Lost Jungle and this was followed by an exciting trailer for *Burn 'em Up Barnes*, filled with the thunder of roaring engines and the excitement of the speedway.

The silent feature film *Burn 'em Up Barnes* (Affiliated Distributors, 1921) had little in common with the Mascot chapter play other than the name of the protagonist. In the silent feature Barnes was played by Johnny Hines, a race car enthusiast sneered at by his father who is a manufacturing magnate. Barnes sets out on his own, is waylaid and robbed, and finds himself adopted by a group of tramps. Barnes becomes a tramp himself and leads a life of carefree adventure until he finds himself in a small town, offering assistance to a pretty girl.

In the chapter play, *Burn 'em Up Barnes* retained a race track setting, but in terms of plot it was as much a feature as it was a serial — indeed, it was written with the feature version in mind. It possessed a story quite similar to the race car setting of *Straightaway* (Columbia, 1933), a modest budget programmer starring Tim McCoy. Another Columbia action drama with Tim McCoy that comes to mind is *Speed Wings* (Columbia, 1934), which opens to a close-up of a spinning propeller of an airplane and Richard Wagner's music from the Prelude to Act III of *Lohengrin*. Likewise, *Burn 'em Up Barnes* begins with a close-up of a spinning wheel of a race car, with an overlay of cabaret music performed by a small-sounding orchestra characteristic of the credit crawls of many low budget features in the mid thirties, and even some from the major studios.

Jack Mulhall would have been a far wiser choice than McCoy for the Columbia films; he had all the youthful *savoir-faire*, zest for life, gameness, tendency to form sudden loyalties, and engaging charm which McCoy's rather austere screen presence lacked. In a word, Mulhall was precisely right for the role of Barnes. Lola Lane was cast as Marjorie Temple, owner of a financially troubled bus line as well as a seemingly worthless piece of property. Edwin Maxwell, often cast in the role of a ruthless business tycoon in the thirties, and Jason Robards, Sr., know of course that, far from being worthless, there is a rich oil deposit on this land — a plot ingredient so commonplace to programmers, Westerns, *and* chapter plays it is almost embarrassing to mention it! What consistently prevents the villains from coercing Lola into selling her property is the necessity of their having first to remove Barnes from the scene. This easily occupies twelve chapters. Who else but Jack Mulhall could have made credible the phenomenon of Barnes, motoring along one day, seeing Lola driving her school bus in front of him, her business near bankruptcy, and, learning of her circumstances, would chance everything, putting what money he has and what ingenuity and enterprise are his to command into making the bus line a thriving business for no other reason than he likes her, and because Barnes is supposedly that kind of guy? Frankie Darro, raised now to $5,000, was back, this time as the younger brother of one of Barnes' friends killed accidentally in the first episode. Mulhall again makes it believable that he would see to it that Frankie gets a college education, for that was the way his friend wanted it.

One of the more exciting aspects of the serial was the particularly vicious schemes of the heavies, including Edward Hearn, Lou Meehan, and Francis McDonald. Meehan starts off the action by ramming a hefty dump truck into Lola's school bus, demolishing it, missing the children being transported by only seconds. Next the villains frame Barnes for murder in a grisly fashion, so effectively carried off that momentarily the viewer forgets how frequently this has been done since movies began and is outraged as if seeing it for the first time. The direction by Colbert Clark and Armand Schaefer and the camera work by Ernest Miller and William Nobles sensuously concentrate in the initial scenes on the contours of Lola's anatomy decked out in close-fitting white coveralls, establishing an obvious love interest. Julian Rivero, one of the few Spanish-American actors working in Hollywood at the time, albeit in limited roles, was cast as an Italian and Lola's general handyman. Jack Mulhall, Lola, Frankie, and Julian form an heroic quartet, joining forces to overcome the machinations of the dishonest capitalists.

There is no series of sequences in any sound serial I have seen that can quite equal the madcap chase in the third and fourth episodes. Frankie has a reel of film exposed at the scene of the murder for which Barnes has been framed; the film proves Barnes' innocence. At the beginning of the third chapter, the heavies take it from Frankie, or think they do. Actually, Frankie has hidden the real film and the heavies have only an empty film case. Well, that's the plot. From the moment Barnes walks out of Consolidated Film Industries with the developed film, either the heavies have it, or Barnes has gotten it back, or the heavies succeed in taking it away from him again. In one scene, Frankie and Julian are cornered in the bus company garage, with Lola in a closet. Stanley Blystone and Al Bridge, for the heavies, chase Frankie all over the place, Frankie tossing the film to Julian. Julian is rushed and pitches the film back to Frankie. The heavies finally grab it and jump into their car, only to have Barnes show up in a race car, hot on their trail. Speeding around Van Nuys, California, taking corners on two wheels, narrowly missing cars, running through fences, crashing into boxes — you name it. There is nothing the serial calls to mind at this point so much as the zany chases in the old Mack Sennett comedies. Armand Schaefer had worked for Mack Sennett in the twenties and his apprenticeship there may well have contributed significantly to these episodes.

Later on in the action, several sight gags are introduced by Julian Rivero, and a number of other comic routines from the Sennett days. They fill up time because there is a sagging in the middle chapters containing material extraneous to the feature version but vital to twelve chapters of a serial. Somewhat incredibly, Burn 'em Up is hired as a motion picture stuntman. The ending to the eighth episode shows Barnes on the top wing of a biplane about to perform a stunt when the rudder cable breaks. The biplane crashes in a stock footage shot taken from Ken Maynard's *King of the Arena* (Universal, 1933). The next chapter begins with the crash and, although the biplane goes into a direct nose-dive, Barnes is not even scratched. Apparently, lacking a parachute, Barnes has no alternative but to cling tightly to the upper wing right through the crash and still is able to walk away unharmed!

The movie company next enlists Barnes to stunt in a sequence which was actually used as a cliffhanger in *The Vanishing Legion*. He is supposed to be driving a truck on which the brake rods have been cut, only to have it go out of control while on a steep grade. The footage of Barnes in the truck is cleverly interpolated with footage previously used in the earlier chapter play, and even some out-footage not used. Tom London, a heavy hoping to get rid of Barnes once and for all, really does cut the brake rods. The truck skids down the steep grade, via a stock shot, but Barnes jumps free just as, originally, Harry Carey did in *The Vanishing Legion*.

Moreover, the incident does raise a somewhat interesting question. In an essay titled "Vom Wesen der Träume" ["On the Nature of Dreams"] contained in Volume VIII of his *Gesammelte Werke; Die Dynamik des Unbewussten [The Dynamics of the Unconscious]* (Rascher Verlag, 1967), after stressing that words and images in a dream can *never* be reduced to a single meaning, Jung pointed out that dreams very often do have a definite dramatic structure. "The dream begins for example," he wrote, "with a *statement of place*, like: 'I am on a street, it is a broad thoroughfare.' ... I designate this phase of dreams as the *exposition*. The second phase is that of the *entanglement*. For example: 'I am on a street, it is a broad thoroughfare. In the distance an automobile appears, that is rushing closer. It moves in a strangely uncertain fashion, and I think that the driver is possibly drunk.' ... The situation becomes somehow complicated, and it introduces a certain tension that one doesn't quite know where it will all lead. The third phase is that of the *culmination*, or of the *peripatetic*. Here something decisive occurs, or something suddenly changes, as for example: 'Suddenly *I* am in the vehicle and apparently am myself the drunken driver. I am certainly not drunk, but rather strangely uncertain and rudderless. I can no longer manage the rapidly moving vehicle and collide with a crash into a stone wall.' ... The fourth and final phase is the *lysis*, the *solution* or the *result* generated through the dream work ... for example: 'I see that the forepart of the vehicle is smashed. It is a foreign vehicle that I do not recognize. I myself am uninjured. I reflect with some trepidation about my accountability.' ... The final phase yields a balanced laying out of the facts of the case which at the same time is the 'sought after' result. In the ... dream obviously a certain rudderless confusion is provided a new significance, that is, it ought to be regarded in such terms that the dream itself is seen as a compensation for such a state of rudderless confusion. ... The ... dreamer is a man who because of difficult family circumstances lost his head and didn't want to let it come to extremes."

Jung first published this essay in 1945. Nearly twenty-five years prior to that German novelist and poet Hermann Hesse had consulted Jung, in part, to be sure, about the marital difficulties Hesse was then having and the decision he was about to make to abandon his children so he could do justice to his career as an author. In the short novel titled "Klein und Wagner," which Hesse included in the volume *Klingsors letzter Sommer* he published in 1920, Hesse narrated one of Klein's dreams. "He awoke," he wrote, "from a dream the last part of which remained in his memory. He sat — so he dreamt — in the front seat of an automobile that was moving swiftly and fairly hazardously through a street, uphill and down. Near him sat someone who was driving the vehicle. In the dream he gave this person a punch in the stomach, tore the steering wheel from his hands [the sex of the person is left ambiguous in the German text], and steered now himself, wildly and anxiously, uphill and down, narrowly past horses and toward a show window, grazing trees that flashed fleetingly before his eyes."

I would not venture to guess that Jung derived the dream he made mention of from Hesse, but it would seem probable that Hesse discussed such a dream with Jung, since Hesse's interpretation of the dream in the story is the same as Jung's interpretation of a very similar dream: namely, being in a vehicle that is out of control represents a personal life situation where one feels his life is out of control. Assuming control over the vehicle means that one is regaining control over the situation. The dream acts both as a compensation for the feeling of being out of control and an anticipation of regaining control. Given the fact that not only this situation, but numerous similar situations occur in chapter plays with great regularity, it is perhaps likely that the cliffhanger in a serial served an identical psychological function. By placing the hero, or heroes, or heroine in a tense situation and then, at the last minute, extricating one or another of them from it, in the mind of the viewer it was much the same as being confronted by an apparently insoluable personal dilemma beyond one's control only to have control restored and a balance regained. In this light, a chapter play is and was a prolonged and repeated effort to affirm in fantasy what is and was often impossible to achieve in real life: a painless assertion of personal control over a situation which appears for the moment to have been carried to hopeless extremes.

Although several days presumably pass during the course of *Burn 'em Up Barnes*, and most of the heavies change clothes, as do Barnes and Julian, Lola invariably wears either the same print dress or her white coveralls; this is not totally sexist, though, since Frankie Darro never so much as changes his trousers. The concluding chapters return to the wild antics of the opening episodes and Barnes captures Edwin Maxwell by means of a ruse, with Lloyd Whitlock as the District Attorney recording the evidence on a Dictaphone. In the closing sequence an oil gusher is brought in. Lola in a sparkling white outfit is embraced by Barnes who is covered head to foot with oil, an embrace that is all hands and which leaves Lola, by the fade, almost as black as he is. The lack of logic — but not serial logic — in some of the middle chapters and a few sequences which even with serial logic still unduly stretch the viewer's credulity flaw *Barnes*, but on the whole it was an entertaining enough chapter play. Wyndham Gittens, although he was not listed among those who worked on the screenplay, nonetheless always counted it among his credits and this may well have reflected the feelings of the entire company toward the serial.

The Law of the Wild (Mascot, 1934) was the third entry for 1934. Reeves Eason, whom the reader may recall Levine fired the first time during production of *The Galloping Ghost* and who was fired a second time on *The Last of the Mohicans* simply because he arrived at the studio three hours late after working until three o'clock in the morning, was again rehired. There was a very good reason for this. Eason was a very capable and not expensive action director. He was teamed with codirector Armand Schaefer.

Bob Custer, who was assigned the male lead in *The Law of the Wild*, had been a rodeo champion in the early twenties and had been hired to star in a series of independently produced low budget Westerns for release by Film Booking Office. The first of these was *Trigger Finger* (FBO, 1924) and it was directed by Reeves Eason. Throughout the late twenties, Custer had continued starring in Westerns, even heading up his own production company for a brief period in 1927, his films still being released by Film Booking Office. The transition to sound was particularly arduous for Custer, first because he was basically inept as an actor, but second, and more importantly, no matter how he might try, he could not deliver his lines with even a modicum of conviction. Custer's *The Fighting Boob* (FBO, 1926) was, as far as its title went (and not the character he played in the film, which was called The Tiger), all too typical of his screen work.

Custer, in fact, languishes in such obscurity that film historians have on occasion even resorted to ascribing to him appearances in wholly fictitious films. The late Ernest N. Corneau in *The Hall of Fame of Western Film Stars* (Christopher Publishing, 1969) wrote that Custer went on "to make two chapter plays for Mascot. These turned out to be his best work on the screen. The serials were called *The Adventures of Rin Tin Tin* and *Law of the Wild* and featured the dog star, Rin Tin Tin, Jr. and Rex, King of the Wild Horses. The productions were smash hits and gave Bob's career a much-needed boost." Arthur F. McClure and Ken D. Jones in *Heroes, Heavies, and Sagebrush: A Pictorial History of the "B" Western Players* (A.S. Barnes, 1972) made a similar claim. "In 1934," they wrote, "he made several serials for Mascot, *The Adventures of Rin Tin Tin* and *Law of the Wild.*" Perhaps McClure and Jones read Corneau. At any rate, they are collectively in error in attributing *The Adventures of Rin Tin Tin* to Custer, since Mascot never made a serial by this title and Custer's only work for Mascot was *The Law of the Wild. The Adventures of Rex and Rinty* (Mascot, 1935), starred Kane Richmond as the human male lead.

Prior to *The Law of the Wild,* Custer had been off the screen for over a year, his last series of Westerns having been produced by Big Four Productions on the very lowest of low budgets and of which *Mark of the Spur* (Big Four, 1932) is at once the best and the worst. Kalton C. Lahue was scarcely always accurate himself in *Winners of the West: The Sagebrush Heroes of the Silent Screen* (A.S. Barnes, 1970), but his assessment of Custer and his problems as a screen cowboy is probably worthy of mention, simply because most of it is born out by watching Custer's films. "...Custer began to put on weight," Lahue wrote. "His features fleshed out sufficiently to destroy any notion that he was photogenic and soon his 6-foot frame was distorted enough to destroy even the illusion of height on-camera, an unfortunate circumstance that also overtook Jack Hoxie. Custer's stern, relentless visage never changed its expression; he marched through film after film like a wooden soldier. Leading ladies were present only for motivation — that is, their ranch had been stolen or they were in other danger from the villainy he had sworn to eradicate. Love interest was nothing more than a pretense and I suspect that even his horse chuckled now and then as Bob peered under his huge Stetson at the palpitating heroine with something less than interest. Occasionally, he showed a gleam of his acting range by cracking a half-smile, but woe to the viewer who sat through a Bob Custer Western watching for it — one yawn and all of his waiting might well have been wasted." Another point needs making. *The Law of the Wild* was not a smash hit. What popularity it had in theatres was due principally to Rex and Rin Tin Tin, Jr. Lucile Browne was the heroine and she was given most of the action sequences, rather than Custer, when the action called for was *human* action. Richard Cramer was given the role of the principal heavy and, although Ernie Adams was in the cast, Edmund Cobb delivers the confession which exonerates Custer, who is falsely accused of murder. For comic relief, silent screen personality Ben Turpin, as cross-eyed as ever, something I for one have never found particularly amusing, was included.

According to the plot résumé at the beginning of the last chapter, "Rex, a wild stallion, and Rinty, a police dog, are pals. Their master, John Sheldon [Bob Custer], falsely accused of murder, has been arrested by the sheriff [Jack Rockwell]. His accuser is Frank Nolan [Richard Cramer], leader of a band of crooks who have succeeded in stealing Rex. Alice Ingram [Lucile Browne] and her hired man, Henry [Ben Turpin], who believe that Sheldon is innocent, have located Rex in the barn of the horse doctor at Boulder Creek." In order to raise money for Custer's defense, Lucile Browne decides to race Rex, riding him herself. It proved to be one of the few exciting moments in an otherwise mundane effort.

Once Mascot was merged into Republic Pictures, Rin Tin Tin, Jr.'s career as a serial star came to an abrupt end. The dog fell on hard times, as hard as were the times for Bob Custer. Under the circumstances it was perhaps only to be expected that they should be costarred together in the wholly unremarkable and even atrocious low budget feature, *Vengeance of Rannah* (Reliable, 1936), in which the camera-work was so shoddy that at one point Lee Duncan was identifiable in the frame giving instructions to his dog and the film was kept rolling. I would like to say that this never could have happened in a Mascot serial, no matter how slap-dash they were filmed, and I would be justified in doing so. However it could, and did, happen in a Mascot *feature*, *Harmony Lane* (Mascot, 1935), where a grip was clearly visible in the lower part of the frame — and here, as in *Vengeance of Rannah*, a retake was not deemed necessary.

Eight

Laughing at Life

Mascot Pictures commenced feature film production with a picture originally titled *Pride of the Legion*, as stated in an earlier chapter. The picture was first released on October 18, 1932. It did such poor business that Levine withdrew it, blaming its title, and it was reissued for its New York City première under the title *The Big Payoff*. This titled was at least somewhat more appropriate since the basic plot of the picture had to do with the underworld and it was quite obviously an imitation of the cycle of gangster films which were then popular, beginning with *Little Caesar* (First National, 1931) directed by Mervyn LeRoy, *Public Enemy* (Warner's, 1931) directed by William Wellman, and, finest of all three, *Scarface: Shame of a Nation* (United Artists, 1932) directed by Howard Hawks.

The Big Payoff was directed by veteran low budget Western director Ford Beebe. Not only was Beebe no LeRoy, Wellman, or Hawks, he was not even one of the better directors who worked for Mascot. His direction, when it came to action, was acceptable, but he was totally incapable of directing dramatic interplay and unfortunately for him *The Big Payoff* did have its dramatic moments as well as even one or two delicate and difficult scenes. Heading up the cast was Barbara Kent, a character actress whose roles in the silent era had been mostly confined to playing sweet, innocent girls virtuously in love in what was then termed society dramas. J. Farrell MacDonald, as a police chief, was billed second, but his billing was misleading since he was on screen for a minute at best—Levine paid him by the day, mostly for the use of his name. Way down in the credits was the actual leading man in the film, Victor Jory, whose role consisted of playing a policeman who is discharged from the force for cowardice. After a pistol duel, Jory finds that he cannot even hold a gun without going to pieces. He drifts into drink and, in a fit of despondency, tries to commit suicide by jumping into a river. It is at this point that Rin Tin Tin, Jr., makes his dramatic entrance, rescuing Jory. Lucien Littlefield portrayed an old shoemaker who specializes in befriending human derelicts, for which Jory qualifies, and it is out of gratitude to Littlefield and love for Littlefield's daughter that Jory undergoes a reclamation that in due and predictable course sees him saving Littlefield's son from the electric chair for a crime he did not commit and bringing to justice bootlegger Ralph Ince and his gang.

The upshot of all this is that Jory regains his place on the force and marries Littlefield's daughter.

What might have worked in a chapter play just could not work in a feature film of this kind, although Ford Beebe, who adapted the original Peter B. Kyne story, apparently did not foresee that. In the opening sequence, he shows a police officer shot three times at close range and then blown up with nitroglycerine, only to have a fade to black and then a fade to a new scene where the same officer is observed leaving a hospital in perfect health. The sense of time elapsing is something that can be ignored in a serial, but never in a feature film intended to be taken seriously. Yet before I leave the reader with a wholly one-sided view of the film, the *New York Times* in its review had this to say: "After the title is flashed on the screen, there is a dedication: 'To the bravest of the brave.' That must mean policemen. ... As a 1932 urban version of the old Westerns, *The Big Payoff* has a lot to be said for it. The action is plentiful, the crooks are wicked, the policemen are brave, the hero is good looking and the heroine is wistful. Ralph Ince contributes as formidable a portrait of a gang leader as a connoisseur in these matters could ask for."

Laughing at Life (Mascot, 1933) was Mascot's second feature film. Evidently Levine had few reservations about Ford Beebe's ability as a director, since Beebe was not only given the direction again but was also credited with the story. Victor McLaglen was the star, supported by an extremely strong cast. The *New York Times* in its review commented that "the producers seem to have pounced upon most of Hollywood's free-lance actors, giving them parts usually meted out to extras. But it is all a waste of talent and, possibly, plot." The review was, therefore, not exactly complimentary, but it was a review in a major circulation newspaper, something that never happened with Mascot chapter plays because serials were reviewed, if at all, primarily in the trades.

McLaglen's role was strictly derivative. John Ford had filmed a somewhat similar picture in making *Mother Machree* (Fox, 1928), which told of a mother's losing her son and then regaining him. McLaglen's role in *Mother Machree* was convincing the mother to take a job in a sideshow as a "half-woman" to earn enough money to send her son to an exclusive school only to have the principal of the school, once the mother's profession is discovered, force her to surrender her son to him. In *Laughing at Life*, McLaglen is a gunrunner working in Panama who is forced to desert his wife and son when his dishonest activities are uncovered. Because it was Mascot, however, and Ford Beebe, this part of the story lets off for a while during which time we follow McLaglen's adventures in Singapore, Tahiti, China, and as a soldier in the Great War. When in China, McLaglen learns of his wife's death, but it is not until after the war, once McLaglen is working as a revolutionary in South America, that fortuitously he encounters his son. Both are living under assumed names, so this chance meeting begs for credibility. The son was played by Regis Toomey. Toomey's fiancée was portrayed by Ruth Hall, the picture following right after *The Three Musketeers.* It is Ruth who persuades McLaglen that he must not permit his son's life to become the waste his has been — though filled with climbing up cornices, mad equestrian rides, brilliant military campaigns — and, regretting himself, McLaglen works it so that Toomey can go forward to an illustrious engineering career happily married to Ruth.

Whatever the *Times* had to say, the cast was the most positive aspect about the entire enterprise. Lois Wilson, in one of her last motion picture appearances — she had been the heroine in the silent epic *The Covered Wagon* (Paramount, 1923) and had appeared the previous year opposite Tom Mix in *Rider of Death Valley* (Universal, 1932) — played McLaglen's wife. Henry B. Walthall was cast as President Valenzuela. Also included were Noah Beery, Sr., Tully Marshall, J. Farrell MacDonald, "Big Boy" Williams, Frankie Darro, William Desmond, Lloyd Whitlock, Conchita Montenegro, and, as a detective on McLaglen's trail, William "Stage" Boyd who would work anywhere, any time, and not much at that, since he had recently been involved in a notorious scandal. Of course, the *Times* was right to this extent: most of these players had time remaining on their serial contracts with Mascot and so Levine decided to use up that time in this fashion. It did not cost him any more and he had what he felt to be a much stronger theatrical drawing card with such a variegated cast.

It was not until 1934 that Levine turned his attention to a concerted release schedule of feature offerings. The year began with the feature version of *The Lost Jungle* and concluded with the feature version of *Burn 'em Up Barnes*, but between these two Mascot produced and released five bonafide feature films. The first of them, *Young and Beautiful* (Mascot, 1934), was directed by Joseph Santley from a story and adaptation by Joseph Santley and Milton Krims, but the screenplay was by Dore Schary, the man who would eventually replace Louis B. Mayer as head of production at M-G-M. It was to some extent a sexual exploitation film, opening as it did to a musical number during which the Wampus Babies of 1934 came out on stage and paraded their wares. Some were later to become minor actresses, like June Gale. Although her relationship with Hoot Gibson would lead to her costarring in a few of his low-grade Westerns in the mid thirties, it was not until Gale married Oscar Levant and went on television in Los Angeles that she won at least local recognition. Jean Carmen was another who would carve out a minor career for herself.

Judith Allen was the heroine, according to Schary's screenplay the thirteenth Wampus Baby. When photographed at John Miljan's swimming pool, with all the other Wampus Babies clad in bathing suits, the camera actually had to avoid Allen's body because, by comparison, she was rather plump. Obviously she was cast because of her facial resemblance to Joan Crawford — she alone among the girls was not *really* a Wampus Baby. She is supposedly secretly engaged to William Haines, playing her press agent. He does not want their romance publicized, although they have a few sickly sentimental scenes together to assure the viewer that they are truly in love as couples truly in love were portrayed in programmer pictures in the thirties. The Sennett lot was made over by means of a sign to read Superba Pictures and Edward Hearn was cast as Allen's director. Allen becomes increasingly disgusted with all the publicity gimmicks Haines keeps dreaming up for her and finally leaves him for Miljan.

The credits noted that additional dialogue and construction were contributed by Al Martin and Colbert Clark, but no matter what they did, apparently they could not prevent the picture from falling apart in the middle. A series of disconnected vaudeville skits were strung together to get the plot from this point to where Haines, realizing the error of his ways, fakes a suicide and finally gets Allen back by the fade. *Young and Beautiful* was supposed to be a sophisticated Hollywood comedy, but, failing that, at least it had a typical social message from that day: a woman would rather be a loving housewife and mother than an exhausted celebrity. As trite as this may sound, I do not doubt for one minute this was a belief held by the audience for which Levine intended the picture. It was not, however, quite true of Judith Allen, since she had divorced her husband, Jack Doyle, who was a character actor, and had appeared in a number of Paramount films prior to *Young and Beautiful*, and would continue throughout the decade working in films made by minor studios like Monogram, Grand National, and Republic, as well as returning the next year in a film produced by Mascot.

After several less than wholly successful efforts at making a serial with a suitable aerial backdrop, Levine came much closer to the mark in *Crimson Romance* (Mascot, 1934), undoubtedly the best of the Mascot features for the year and in many ways superior to all of the Mascot chapter plays in 1934. Ben Lyon, who had appeared in Howard Hughes' *Hell's Angels* (United Artists, 1930), was given the lead, but the most surprising performance of all came from Erich von Stroheim as Captain Wolters, a commander in the German air force during the Great War. In a chilling scene, von Stroheim comments that commanding air squadrons is an exercise in subtraction, that when an even number of planes are sent out, an odd number are sure to return.

The plot, if curious, is nonetheless worth retelling. Lyon and his best friend, James Bush, the latter from a German immigrant family, are working in an American airplane factory when the war breaks out. When Bush is forced out of his job because of American war hysteria and prejudice, the two friends decide to join the German air force. Von Stroheim is their commander. Sari Maritza is an ambulance driver and both men fall in love with her. When the United States enters the conflict on the side of the Allies, Lyon is torn between his essential loyalty to his country and the threat of being shot for treason by the Germans. Bush engineers Lyon's escape. When Lyon returns leading an American squadron to bomb a German ammunition dump, von Stroheim personally leads the German defense. At one point it seems that von Stroheim will destroy Lyon's plane, so in a frenzy of desperation Bush crashes into von Stroheim's aircraft. The final scene shows Lyon, with Sari Maritza, visiting Bush's German mother in the United States, played by Bodil Rosing, and Rosing is given a moving antiwar soliloquy with which to end the film. Generally reviewers singled out David Howard's skillful direction and Ernest Miller's splendid photography, particularly during the aerial combat sequences. "A revival of the air fighting during the World War," *Film Daily* reported, "is ushered in with this picture, but with the horror of war stressed rather than the alleged glory, so that it really becomes a preachment against war." The review added: "On this angle it should be sold, for that is the only way to sell the femmes this type of picture with the present feeling against armaments and war propaganda. The direction is very commendable, the story is intelligently developed with some good dialogue and a grown-up philosophy about life and things in general."

I have little doubt that it was on the basis of his acting in this film that von Stroheim especially appealed to Jean Renoir who, it will be recalled, went on to cast him in his own classic war film, *La Grande Illusion* (France, 1937), some three years later. Obviously, too, the film came at a time when the United States was firmly entrenched in its feelings of isolationism, with little concern about the dangerous course events were again taking in Europe. For this reason, *Crimson Romance* stirred up some adverse criticism, as well as invoking advice to exhibitors that the romance — which was definitely low-keyed — be played up rather than the true import of the film.

In Old Santa Fe (Mascot, 1934), directed by David Howard, starring Ken Maynard, and introducing Gene Autry and Smiley Burnette, was next in order of production and release, but since I intend to discuss this film in connection with Maynard's serial *Mystery Mountain* (Mascot, 1934) in the next chapter, I will pass over it for the moment. It was followed by *The Marines Are Coming* (Mascot, 1934) starring William Haines, who gave no better an account of himself here than he had in *Young and Beautiful*, namely a wiseacre who painfully laughs at his own not very funny jokes and who refuses ever to take his roles seriously. But David Howard was directing and the performances of the supporting cast, especially Esther Ralston, Conrad Nagel, and Edgar Kennedy, somewhat compensated for Haines.

The film producer, Walter Wanger, when he was an executive at Paramount originally "discovered" Esther Ralston and gave her the role of Mrs. Darling in the silent production of *Peter Pan* (Paramount, 1924). In 1934, now working for M-G-M, Wanger again "discovered" Ralston, this time as a result of watching her in *To the Last Man* (Paramount, 1933) directed by Henry Hathaway. Wanger wanted Ralston for an important role in a new Joan Crawford vehicle, *Sadie McKee* (M-G-M, 1934). "The events of my present screen comeback duplicate those of my earlier career so exactly that I keep thinking, 'I've done all this before'!" Ralston told Mark Dowling for an article in the June, 1934 issue of *Movie Classic*. "Ten years ago, for instance, I started in horse operas — Westerns — at Universal. Just recently, as my first picture on returning to the American screen, I played in a Zane Grey Western, *To the Last Man*. I did the same stunts I had done before; I wore the same kind of costumes. It may have been the same white horse! I even got out pictures of myself in the old Western make-up and compared them with the new ones. I could not tell the difference!" And maybe she couldn't. But one thing was different about *To the Last Man*. Esther Ralston had an all-nude bathing scene, hardly standard fare for Westerns at that time. Ralston's work in *Sadie McKee* did not lead to an M-G-M contract, but it garnered her much publicity and it did result in several other roles, some for major studios, and a number of character roles for Mascot, the most substantial being that in *The Marines Are Coming*.

In the film, Ralston is engaged to Conrad Nagel. She is, however, attracted to Haines and finally decides to marry him. Haines, for his part, is being pursued by Armida, a Spanish singer and dancer who performs a well-choreographed song for the picture, "My Brazilian Baby," and follows it with a Spanish dance. From this point on, the picture becomes both predictable and bad. Haines is drummed out of the Marine Corps — he has been a lieutenant — but reenlists as a private, goes to Latin America with a detachment of Marines to battle the forces of renegade revolutionary George Regas, called The Torch, and ends up saving Conrad Nagel's life. This action footage, in the best Mascot serial tradition, helps the picture, but not sufficiently, and the ending is a double clinch, Ralston and Nagel reunited, while Haines pairs off with Armida.

In comparison to David Howard, Phil Rosen was an indifferent, unimaginative, and mediocre director, and it was Rosen who was assigned direction of *Little Men* (Mascot, 1934). Ostensibly it was based on the story by Louisa May Alcott, insofar as she received screen credit, but in some ways the film was more an elaboration of the prepubescent antics of Hal Roach's Little Rascals. One thing is certain. It contained none of the stark realism except for its conclusion of William Wellman's *Wild Boys of the Road* (First National, 1933) from the previous year which, incidentally, as *Little Men*, starred Frankie Darro.

In fact, it may well be that *Little Men* was only a sentimental fantasy made in direct contrast to the Wellman film. *Wild Boys of the Road* told of youngsters forced by the Great Depression to leave home because their parents could no longer afford to support them and it recounted how these youngsters, boys and girls, were riding the freight trains from city to city looking for work and founding their own shantytowns at trackside. *Little Men*, on the other hand, showed an idealized way of life for homeless youngsters. Ralph Morgan played Professor Bhaer and Erin O'Brien-Moore was cast as his wife. When David Durand, at the beginning of the picture, playing an orphan, first comes to the school populated by child actors like Dickie Moore, Dickie Jones, and Tommy Bupp, he comments: "This is not like a school at all. It's like heaven."

It is not too long before Durand meets Frankie Darro, who is a homeless paper boy. Durand talks him into coming to the school. Darro, of course, is street smart, even if completely virtuous. He fights for what he believes in and before long he is framed by another boy for supposedly stealing Tommy Bupp's four quarters. Darro is banished as a trouble-maker, although Erin O'Brien-Moore never doubts him for a minute and refers to him as her eldest "son." By the last reel, the culprit confesses to Ralph Morgan and Morgan goes off to seek Darro. He finds him and brings him back to the school and to general rejoicing. The ending is so sentimental it easily borders on the maudlin.

Evaluating the entire year, both *Young and Beautiful* and *The Marines Are Coming* were flawed because of their star, William Haines. Reputedly, Haines had retired from the screen for a time to pursue a career as an interior decorator, and these films in tandem were to constitute a comeback for him. That did not happen and, viewing them, the reason is obvious. However, *Crimson Romance* was an amazingly well-made economy film and *In Old Santa Fe* was a better Western than Ken Maynard would ever make again over the next ten years of his screen career. *Little Men*, whatever its overall tone, had its engaging moments and *The Lost Jungle* and *Burn 'em Up Barnes* very nearly were better feature films than they were chapter plays. Much of the action in these features, especially those not edited from serials, had the Mascot chapter play look, in the breathless pacing, in the sometimes incredible contrivance and coincidence, and in their ingenuous super-heroics. But taken as a whole, Mascot's feature productions all made money and some of them demonstrated unmistakable promise.

For the 1935 season, Levine increased feature production from five features and two feature versions of serials to a full complement of eight features, none of them edited from chapter plays. *Behind the Green Lights* (Mascot, 1935) led the release schedule. It was inspired by an incident sup-plied by Captain Cornelius W. Willemse, once head of the Homicide Squad of the New York Police Department, and for the New York première at the Criterion Levine had Willemse make a personal appearance on stage to in-troduce the film. Judith Allen, who had appeared in *Young and Beautiful*, was back, this time as an ambitious young attorney who goes to work for Sidney Blackmer, a high-priced mouthpiece whose objective it is to get criminals out of jeopardy in exchange for most of their loot. Allen was not a highly capable actress but her performance was made more arduous by the fact that she had to remain an innocent all the time she worked for Black-mer, enthusiastically defending the men her fiancé Norman Foster, a detec-tive, arrests, and despite a growing estrangement from her father who is a sergeant on the local police force and Foster's superior. Not until Allen gets Theodore von Eltz acquitted on a murder charge through befuddling the district attorney's prime witness by referring to an almanac and claiming that the night, far from moonlit, was dark, and von Eltz shoots and wounds her father during commission of a robbery, does Allen come to see the wrong she has done. Blackmer is finally arrested and Allen is accepted back into her father's good graces, chastened and thus deserving of Foster's love.

In retrospect, *Behind the Green Lights* was not a very good picture, but it was the equal of most of the programmers being turned out by studios like Columbia and Warner Bros. and it was a cut above most of the independent product against which it competed. The same cannot be said for the next entry, *One Frightened Night* (Mascot, 1935), which, like *Behind the Green Lights*, was directed by Christy Cabanne. Cabanne, who had been under contract to RKO at the beginning of the decade before freelancing with a number of independent producing companies only to return to RKO by the middle of the decade for which studio he would do his best work in the thirties, was a director who could manage to achieve a surprisingly polished and sophisticated product on a limited budget. Cabanne had entered the industry in 1910 directing Douglas Fairbanks, Sr., and for five years was an assistant to D.W. Griffith.

Stuart Palmer, creator of the detective fiction team of Hildegarde Withers and Inspector Piper, which had been brought to the screen as early as *The Penguin Pool Murder* (RKO, 1932) with Edna May Oliver and James Gleason playing the principals and which was in 1935 still an ongoing series at RKO, wrote the original story for *One Frightened Night*. But even with Palmer to recommend it, the plot was strictly derivative. One of the central ingredients of *The Greene Murder Case* (Paramount, 1929), directed by Frank Tuttle and based on a Philo Vance mystery by S.S. Van Dine, pseudonym for art critic Willard Huntington Wright, was the Greene library, which had been sealed for almost twenty years. In *One Frightened Night*, there was likewise a room that had been locked for twenty years; the difference was that this room had modern — circa 1935 — light fixtures. Another production ineptitude was the capricious rain. One minute it would be raining a torrent, the next the suspects would be wandering through garden shrubbery, both the shubbery and the suspects as dry as if they were in the midst of a drought.

Of what were these wandering suspects suspected? Well, as Palmer's plot had it, Charles Grapewin, cast as a crusty and eccentric millionaire, decides to leave his fortune to an assortment of people around him because he cannot find his granddaughter. This group consists of Regis Toomey, a nephew, Hedda Hopper (in one of her last acting roles), his niece, Lucien Littlefield, his physician, Clarence Wilson, his attorney, and Rafaelo Ottiano, his housekeeper. What ruins it for all of them is the sudden appearance of Evalyn Knapp, claiming to be Grapewin's granddaughter. The situation is further complicated when Mary Carlisle turns up, also claiming to be Grapewin's granddaughter, accompanied by Wallace Ford, her boy friend and a performing magician. Clarence Wilson was responsible for producing Knapp and pleading her claim. It looks very bad for him when Grapewin finds Knapp's body and it proves that she was an impostor. But then, however avaricious Wilson might be, all the others, who stand to be disinherited, have equally strong motives.

The Laurel and Hardy Murder Case (M-G-M, 1930) was intended as a spoof on the S.S. Van Dine Philo Vance films — each Vance novel and each film was referred to as a particular murder case — and in that comedy

Fred Kelsey was cast as an investigating policeman. It was the typical dark house drama turned into a farce. In *One Frightened Night* Fred Kelsey, an actor given primarily to low comedy, was cast as the sheriff. Without Wallace Ford's assistance, solution of the case would have been hopeless, thus reinforcing a notion rife in much detective fiction at the time, to wit, that the police are made up largely of buffoons and imbeciles hopelessly at sea were it not for the brilliant amateurs who come to their rescue. The screenplay by Wellyn Totman and Cabanne's direction could never make up their collective mind, it would appear, whether this was supposed to be a genuine mystery or a comedy, and so it became both, and not with the happiest results, since most of the eeriness and terrors of an old, dark house were dissipated by the absurd antics of the characters. As if in final testament to this contradiction, it is Charles Grapewin himself, with clues not available to the viewer, who beats both Kelsey and Ford to the identity of the murderer, Lucien Littlefield, as outrageous and as illogical a happenstance as the unmasking of any of the mystery men in the Mascot chapter plays.

When it comes to *The Headline Woman* (Mascot, 1935), if you are one to put much stock in film reviewers, you can choose between the *Chicago Tribune*, which headed its review "a poor story stumps cast and director," or the *Film Daily*, which summed up its opinion "an outstanding independent production. Good newspaper yarn well handled all around." The truth may lie somewhere between these two. The screenplay by Jack Natteford and Claire Church owed something to both *Front Page* (United Artists, 1931) and *It Happened One Night* (Columbia, 1934). Conway Tearle was cast as a police commissioner who, dissatisfied with the way the press is dealing with the police department, cuts off all news. This leads the reporters to try an alternative source, picking Ford Sterling, a flatfoot, to act as their "leak" in the department. Just as Syd Saylor, who was in the cast here, could ruin every scene he was in when cast in a serial like *The Lost Jungle* or *Mystery Mountain*, Sterling is so ridiculously and heavy-handedly playing his role for laughs the credibility of the plot is utterly destroyed. The persistent presence of a stooge in so many Mascot films must be attributed to Levine who seemed to like this kind of comedy. He would do the same thing when he became head of production at Republic so that in a serial like *Dick Tracy* (Republic, 1937) the viewer is supposed to accept with equanimity the casting of Smiley Burnette, playing the same stooge character he did in Gene Autry's Western features, as an agent for the Federal Bureau of Investigation. Ward Bond, as an alcoholic reporter not fond of leg work, is far more believable in *The Headline Woman*, but unfortunately he has to take a back seat to Ford Sterling.

The serious, or at least melodramatic, part of the plot had to do with Heather Angel, daughter of the publisher of the newspaper for which hero Roger Pryor works as a reporter. She is implicated in a night club murder while in the company of shady Jack LaRue (who turns out to be the guilty party) and Pryor hides her, first to get the exclusive story, and second to prevent her being railroaded by the police. Inevitably, as with Clark Gable and Claudette Colbert in a similar situation in *It Happened One Night*, the two fall in love and all ends happily. The really positive aspects of the picture—and story *was not* one of them!—were Roger Pryor's performance and the fast, clever dialogue in the scenes with the reporters played by Franklin Pangborn, Russell Hopton, George Lewis, Harry Bowen, in addition to Ward Bond. William Nigh, who directed, was certainly not the equal of Christy Cabanne, much less of David Howard, but he cannot be blamed either for the hackneyed screenplay nor the casting of Ford Sterling, although he might well have exerted some restraint on Sterling.

Norman Foster was back, as the male lead, for *Ladies Crave Excitement* (Mascot, 1935), as were Evalyn Knapp and Esther Ralston and Purnell Pratt—Pratt had played Judith Allen's father in *Behind the Green Lights*. More than perhaps any other Mascot feature hitherto, this one had nonstop action and slick production, which combined to keep the viewer's interest. Eric Linden runs a newsreel production company and Foster is one of his ace reporters. In a variation on *The Headline Woman*, Evalyn Knapp is the daughter of Purnell Pratt who owns a rival newsreel company. She wants a business career for herself, something Pratt definitely does not want. Foster meets Knapp at a race track. He does not know who she is and she tells him her name is McCloskey. In actual fact, Knapp owns the race horse Starling and Foster, by sheerest chance, photographs heavies Jason Robards, Sr., and Stanley Blystone drugging the animal.

When Linden's incompetent son loses the footage detailing the handicap race, Foster covers for him and is fired. Esther Ralston's part—scarcely major—was that of Linden's private secretary. Foster and Knapp then form their own newsreel production outfit. Once Foster dramatizes the race and the drugging, he takes the finished film to Linden, who likes it, agrees to buy it, and determines to start a new series to be titled *The March of Events*. There are a lot more incidents yet to go—the film is, if anything, extremely episodic—but in this instance the rapid pacing obscures all—well, almost all of the potential weaknesses, not the least of which is Syd Saylor's presence as a newsreel photographer. One of the more interesting innovations was the way in which the titles were presented, each time a camera car rushing toward the camera with the credits written on the side of it. Nick Grindé directed *Ladies Crave Excitement*.

For *Harmony Lane* (Mascot, 1935), a highly romanticized screen biography of Stephen Foster, Joseph Santley was back as the director and was also credited with being coauthor of the screenplay. It is because of the presence of the same structural flaws as in *Young and Beautiful* and a similar tendency toward the most vulgar sentimentality that I feel justified in placing most of the blame on Santley—the common factor in both films—rather than on Levine. I think Levine's parsimony was probably responsible for the niggardly sets—the dude ranch from *In Old Santa Fe* was here supposed to be a home in Kentucky (it was on the Mascot back lot) and the house/school set from *Little Men* was made to serve for Foster's home—but Santley alone has to answer for a camera so stationary as to make virtually every scene seem needlessly static and for so positioning his actors in front of the camera that even a photographed stage drama could reasonably excite more interest. To Joseph Lewis and Ray Curtis, the editors on the film, should go all the credit for getting as much as possible out of the few close-ups Santley permitted and the use of intercuts during rather lengthy conversations. But not even this could save the screenplay, which for the first half of the picture anyway seemed to indicate that for Stephen Foster life was nothing more than a series of song cues. When his fiancée Susan is about to leave, Douglass Montgomery, playing Foster, is suddenly struck with the lyrics for "Oh, Suzanna." When on a visit in Kentucky, he asks about the old black servant, Joe, and finds out he's dead, another song comes to him, after looking appropriately melancholy and then inspired, "Old Black Joe," sung in the film by a chorus of young black children but coming out on the soundtrack with an unmistakable bass figure.

Santley's plot would have the viewer believe that all his life Foster was in love with Susan Pentland, played by Evelyn Venable, who early rejects his suit for a man with better prospects, and that when Foster did marry Jane McDowell, played by Adrienne Ames, she proved a frightful shrew constantly urging and demanding he make more money because, as she tells him over and over again, she gave up everything for him. When Foster refuses to give up his friendship with William Frawley, cast as the minstrel entertainer Ed Christy, the scene, although played straight, resembles nothing so much as *Their First Mistake* (M-G-M, 1932), a Laurel and Hardy two-reeler in which Mae Bush, as Mrs. Hardy, threatens Mr. Hardy with divorce if he doesn't give up his friendship with Mr. Laurel, and when Mr. Hardy doesn't, sues Mr. Hardy for divorce and Mr. Laurel for alienation of affection, Mr. Hardy's affection. Foster, pining for Susan, separated from Jane, goes to live in New York and proceeds to drink himself to death. Problem drinking and acute alcoholism, when they have been dealt with at all in Hollywood films, somehow seem to inspire the most lachrymose of sermonizing or soap opera melodrama, with possible exceptions like Billy Wilder's *The Lost Weekend* (Paramount, 1945) and *Come Fill the Cup* (Warner's, 1951), the latter directed by Gordon Douglas and starring James Cagney. The montage of Foster's decline into drunkenness is effective, but not all of the editorial dialogue is. Yet, come to think of it, *Swanee River* (20th-Fox, 1939), directed by Sidney Lanfield and starring Don Ameche as Stephen Foster, does not handle this part of Foster's life any better than *Harmony Lane* does. What keeps both versions afloat, if not alive and enjoyable, are their respective medleys of Foster's songs, but here *Swanee River* has the edge because it had Al Jolson.

Streamline Express (Mascot, 1935) was not only a title but the name of a train, a futuristic train able to achieve 160 miles per hour. It can travel from California to New York in 20 hours. The plot, conversely, looked back to the previous year's *Twentieth Century* (Columbia, 1934) directed by Howard Hawks. Leonard Fields was Mascot's director, but given the players he had to work with—Victor Jory starring as a stage director,

Evelyn Venable as his capricious leading lady, Erin O'Brien-Moore whose husband is running away with Esther Ralston, Sidney Blackmer as the typical society roué putting the blackmail bite on Ralston, and Syd Saylor as a railroad steward — and the plot — how, when spanking Venable with her shoe, Jory discovers he loves her, and how Venable, when Jory is framed by Blackmer, discovers she loves him — perhaps it can be said that few directors, and probably not even Howard Hawks, could have managed to make a better job of it. Venable lacked the fire Carole Lombard brought to her similar role in *Twentieth Century*, and Jory was certainly no John Barrymore, the latter believable as a stage director simply, if for no other reason, because he managed to change his personality every minute he was on camera.

Nor was *Waterfront Lady* (Mascot, 1935) a significant improvement, although it was released through the Republic exchanges and, therefore, had an even greater popular exposure than the majority of the previous Mascot titles, which had still been marketed via state's rights. It was basically a Poverty Row version of *The Glass Key* (Paramount, 1935), which had been released earlier that year. The Paramount film was only a mediocre rendering of the Dashiell Hammett novel, despite the fact that Hammett preferred this novel among his works and even visited the set one day and spoke with George Raft who was portraying Ned Beaumont. In *Waterfront Lady*, Frank Albertson is cut into a partnership with his boss, Charles C. Wilson, in Wilson's gambling ship enterprise. When the police stage a raid on the boat and Wilson, in a scuffle, shoots and kills finger man Jack LaRue, Albertson takes the gun from Wilson and jumps overboard with it. Albertson is perfectly willing to go on the lamb, throwing suspicion of himself and away from Wilson. He hides on a houseboat, assuming the dress and occupation of a sailor, and meets J. Farrell MacDonald and Ann Rutherford. At this point, the film breaks down to an ordinary cliché-ridden romance, whereas it need not have — the friendship between Albertson and Wilson could have been emphasized and explored with insight. The reason — once more, without question — can no doubt be attributed to *Waterfront Lady's* director, Joseph Santley.

After the meeting between Albertson and Rutherford, the two begin to fall in love. This romance would still have been viable had Santley retained the focus on Albertson's dilemma and the relationship with Wilson; instead of that, Grant Withers is introduced into the scene as Rutherford's aggressive admirer. To press his suit, Withers must somehow expose Albertson and to this morbid melodrama Santley devoted most of the remaining screen time. While the overall production was slick and swift-moving, the film was nonetheless further marred through excessive use of process screen photography and, during a fight sequence, the presence of Smiley Burnette as a comic stooge who foolishly hits combatants over the head with a tambourine, thus destroying any semblance of reality the fight might have had.

Confidential (Mascot, 1935) directed by Edward L. Cahn and starring Donald Cook and Evalyn Knapp closed out the year. One of the standard plot ingredients of many of Tim McCoy's sound Western films, as well as other "B" Westerns, was for the hero to join a gang of thieves and murderers in an attempt to get evidence against them suitable for a conviction. The suspense was invariably generated by the fact that with regularity one member of the gang was either suspicious of the newcomer or, sometimes, was even aware of having seen him before, although he cannot quite place where. About two-thirds of the way through the film, of course, the wrongdoer *does* remember where and from that moment on the hero is in jeopardy until he is rescued by the arrival of the law at the last minute. *Confidential* merely upraded this formula to the contemporary scene, casting Donald Cook as a G-man who goes to work for Herbert Rawlinson's numbers racket. Of course, at the start Cook does not know that Rawlinson is the brains of the mob. He has to find this out just as he has to obligatorily fall in love with the innocent bookkeeper for the mob, Evalyn Knapp. J. Carrol Naish was assigned the role of the gun man who could recall having heard Cook's voice somewhere before, but not until well into the picture could he recall precisely where and under what circumstances. By which time there is only enough footage remaining for a moment of suspense, followed by the general clean-up.

The plot was not so dated in 1935 that it could not be used over and over again in the future, even notably by Anthony Mann in his pseudo-documentary *T-Men* (Eagle-Lion, 1947), which because of its lighting occupies a place of more than minor interest in the *film noir* canon — *film noir*, or dark cinema, being the term applied to those films which tend to emphasize the sense of being trapped, a situational drama that can be traced, in part, to films like *Confidential*. Mascot released *Confidential* on October 17, 1935. On April 18, 1935, Warner Bros. had released *G-Men*, directed by William Keighley and starring James Cagney. *G-Men* was responsible for two things. First, it introduced the term G-men into the American vernacular. Second, it initiated what the trade papers predicted would be a new cycle of films. *G-Men* told of how Cagney, in an effort to avenge the death of a friend, becomes involved with underworld mobsters, although he is secretly a government agent. In *Confidential*, Cook joins the gang primarily because a buddy of his has been viciously murdered by them. "One thing that *G-Men* demonstrates," *Variety* commented, "is that the new cycle which is causing so much chatter is not likely to last very long. This picture has about all the elements the type can be endowed with. It is red hot off the front page. But beyond that it has nothing but a weak scenario along hackneyed lines. The others in this line can't grab very much from the front page that isn't here, and can't, if playing the same or a similar line, get in any better story background."

Film Daily was enthusiastic in its review of *Confidential*. "One of the best G-man dramas," the review went. "This is devoid of the usual hoke, and is a very businesslike and realistic presentation of the work of the Federal men as they go about the job of tracking down a nation-wide racketeering gang putting over the number lottery game." *Film Daily* praised Edward L. Cahn's direction, as did *Variety*, which claimed for him "a bang-up job of direction, keeping up growing suspense, holding his characters straight, maintaining conviction throughout, and combing for all the inherent comedy." What was meant by "inherent comedy" was probably Warren Hymer as the stooge of the mob. To inject a very negative note amid all this praise, Hymer was unrealistic, but no more unrealistic than the entire view of organized crime projected by films like this. Not merely did *Confidential* and so many like it indulge in self-congratulatory fantasies about crime and law enforcement, which inspired in the public a totally false sense of security, but they succeeded only in adding to the already distorted conception of organized crime that had been put forth by the gangster film cycle begun in the early thirties which influenced films like *Pride of the Legion*. Mascot probably should not be singled out for blame, but neither should *Confidential* be classed as anything more than a fable, quite the same as a chapter play like *The Lightning Warrior*, and about as irrelevant to actual life.

In *Caught Short* (M-G-M, 1930), a society drama, Marie Dressler and Polly Moran played two friends who were landladies in boarding houses on the same side of a street. Polly plays the stock market, but she cannot convince Dressler to do so. Polly's son, Charles Morton, and Marie's daughter, Anita Page, are lovers, but their romance is interrupted when Marie decides to speculate in the stock market and, with her winnings, stages a society splurge for her daughter at a fashionable resort. By the end of the film, true love triumphs and the two landladies come to learn that very important lesson that money is not more important than friendship and happiness.

The last feature film Mascot produced was *Doughnuts and Society* (Mascot, 1936), released through the Republic exchanges some months after it was produced. Louise Fazenda and Maude Eburne were cast as joint owners in a coffee and doughnut shop. Fazenda's son, Eddie Nugent, is in love with Maude Eburne's daughter, Ann Rutherford. When Eburne comes into a gold mine, she determines on a society marriage for Rutherford. To counteract this, Fazenda invests in a five-story parking lot and she and her son also enter society. When the gold mine is found to be worthless, Rutherford's marriage to a prince is called off and the romance with Nugent is on again. Meanwhile, Fazenda and Eburne, both having fallen on hard times, end up once more at the coffee and doughnut shop.

Copying an old plot may not be that remarkable, but it is somewhat curious when you reflect that Karen DeWolf, Robert St. Clair, and Wallace MacDonald were credited by Mascot for the original story and screenplay and Gertrude Orr and Matt Brooks were cited for additional dialogue. William Berke, who would later become a prolific producer and director of Westerns, was the producer and Lewis D. Collins the director.

In 1940, after Nat Levine had left Republic, he had a feature version edited from *The Phantom Empire* (Mascot, 1935) released as *Radio Ranch* and sold on the state's rights market, as had been all of the Mascot features and serials until the Republic merger, but it was actually a film that had been edited at the time the serial was made and simply not previously released. Viewed as a group, although many of the Mascot features revealed the inevitable signs of haste in production and weakness in story-lines, on the whole they were capably cast and, with the exception of those directed by Joseph Santley, competently, and sometimes even adeptly, directed.

One aspect of the Mascot features, however, should be stressed. There was no indication of linear progression. They did not get better consistently, or even better on a hit and miss basis. Built into the very fabric, the very conception of these films was the guiding idea of low budget production. The best of them — like *Crimson Romance* — had moments, but none of them ever escaped the low budget look and low budget execution. Working with low budgets, after all, was Levine's peculiar métier and nothing he ever produced escaped from it entirely. This is an observation important to keep in mind when critically assessing Mascot productions. It was something perhaps Levine himself should have kept in mind, but did not, when he decided to work in production at Metro-Goldwyn-Mayer. A Mascot film, like *Doughnuts and Society*, might have the same plot-line as an M-G-M film, but that was all it would have in common. There were two very distinct ways of approaching a motion picture, one where all questions and problems and all energies answered first and last to the budget, the other where the final product itself, the motion picture, took precedence. Levine mastered only the first way. He never could, or would, master the second.

Nine

Mystery Mountain

Ken Maynard was born on July 21, 1895, at Vevay, Indiana. Later, studio biographers would feel impelled to change his birthplace to Mission, Texas. In addition to Ken, William H. Maynard and his wife, Emma May (née Stewart) Maynard, had three daughters, Trixie, Willa, and Bessie, and, on September 20, 1897, a second son whom they named Kermit. When he was twelve, Ken ran away from home to join a traveling Wild West show. His father, who was a building contractor by trade, caught up with the boy and made him return home. But Ken remained obsessed with the idea of becoming a circus performer. At sixteen he asked for and received permission to join a touring carnival. His formal education ended there, although studio biographers attributed to him, as to Tom Mix, attendance at the Virginia Military Institute.

In 1914 Maynard was the leading attraction with the Kit Carson Show, named after the frontier scout who had died in 1868. Moving from show to show and from job to job, Maynard perfected his horsemanship, learned to rope (largely from the famed Mexican rope artist, Oro Peso), to stunt, and to perform numerous riding tricks. Maynard joined the Hagenbeck-Wallace circus in 1915 — the same outfit that would later headline Clyde Beatty and whose animals would appear with Beatty in *The Lost Jungle*. When the Great War came, Maynard enlisted in the U.S. Army and was stationed at Camp Knox, Kentucky, as an engineer, and married a mountain girl. Once he was discharged, he left both Kentucky and the girl and rejoined the Hagenbeck-Wallace circus. In 1920 Maynard became a member of Pawnee Bill's troupe and, dressed as Buffalo Bill, rode in the Rose Bowl parade. At the insistence of friends, Maynard entered the Pendleton Rodeo that year and won a trophy as the All-Around Champion Cowboy. As a consequence, Ringling Brothers signed him as a center attraction in 1921.

In Hollywood, Maynard got to know Tom Mix and Mix helped him get a billed part in *The Man Who Won* (Fox, 1923), directed by William Wellman. On February 14, 1923, Maynard married Jeanne Knudsen in Los Angeles. The marriage was short-lived. In 1924 his break came when William Randolph Hearst's Cosmopolitan Pictures company went into production on a new Marion Davies film titled *Janice Meredith* (Metro-

Goldwyn, 1924), shot in and around New York at Hearst's International Studios. Maynard's role was that of Paul Revere, which he was given on the basis of his superior riding ability. Hearst paid Maynard $1,000 a week. If it had been for a year instead of four weeks, Maynard figured it would far outstrip the $40,000 a year he was making with the Ringling show.

When the Davis Distribution Division, a small, independent producing company, approached Maynard to make a series of eight Westerns, Ken jumped at the opportunity. Beginning with $50,000 *Reward* (Davis, 1924), these Westerns helped establish Maynard as a screen personality. They were entertaining, if cheaply made, and filled with plenty of horse action and stunting by Maynard; indeed, in *The Grey Vulture* (Davis, 1926) there were even some bathing beauties in relative distress. A publicity campaign was mounted to promote the new movie cowboy. The only objection the make-up people at Davis had to Maynard was the way he parted his hair; they claimed he looked like a barber and wanted to give him a permanent wave. This Maynard flatly rejected.

While still with Ringling Brothers, newspapers had carried stories of the death of Mazie, one of the performing horses Maynard had used. Photographs had been published of him with Brownie, a mare he had traveled twenty thousand miles with. But it was at Newhall, California, that Ken bought a golden three-year-old palomino for fifty dollars. He named him Tarzan, after Edgar Rice Burroughs' jungle hero. Tarzan began appearing with Maynard in the Davis Westerns. In 1925 Maynard was signed to do a non-Western called *North Star* (Associated Exhibitors, 1925) in which he costarred with Strongheart, still perhaps Rinty's strongest competition. Maynard got his name in the papers when he married Mary Leeper on the set, a girl from South Bend, Indiana. It was her first marriage, Maynard's third. Although in old age he said he had wanted them, Maynard never had any children from any of his marriages.

Charles R. Rogers then proposed to Maynard that he star in a high budget series of Westerns intended for First National release. The contract represented that First National would undertake to build Maynard into a familiar screen property and that Tarzan, like Tom Mix's horse Tony, would receive billing on the credits. First National hoped that Ken Maynard would be as successful for them as Hoot Gibson was at Universal or Tom Mix and Buck Jones were at Fox. Davis sought to take advantage of this new publicity effort by recutting Maynard's features for them into a pseudo-serial which they titled *The Range Fighter* (Davis, 1926). It was not wholly coherent and not really a chapter play, but it was episodic, to say the least.

In mid-1926 First National was definitely a studio on the rise. A group grew up around Maynard at First National, one member or another of which would be associated with him for all of his most bountiful years in the industry. Had he not abandoned the last of them, Sidney Rogell, his career would probably not have nosedived. Foremost was the producer of the series, Charles R. Rogers. He was a Ken Maynard fan personally and was resolved to fully exploit the young circus rider. Sid Rogell was the money manager. He was placed in charge of business affairs on the First National Westerns and many times proved his worth. When Maynard signed again with Universal in 1933-1934, Rogell was the man he called upon to act as his financial and production adviser. Harry Joe Brown, who was given credit on the eighteen Westerns Maynard made for First National as the production supervisor, was actually the associate producer for the series and worked closely with Rogers. Brown had earlier been affiliated with the Fred Thomson Westerns for FBO release; he brought the same expertise to the Maynard vehicles. He assigned Marion Jackson to the unit to write the screenplays, handled Maynard's screen image himself, and even, upon occasion, took over direction of the pictures. Albert S. Rogell, the unit's principal director, brought with him a wealth of silent Western action technique which he gained working with Jack Hoxie at Universal and Fred Thomson at FBO. When the advent of sound retarded Western film production in 1930, it was Al Rogell personally who engineered Maynard's contract with Tiffany Productions. It was to this group, therefore, and their astonishing collective ability that Maynard owed nearly all of his success and the success of his First National series and his first and second series for Universal. Maynard's only really notable Westerns separate from those somehow associated with this group were *Dynamite Ranch* (Worldwide, 1932) and *In Old Santa Fe.*

Senior Daredevil (First National, 1926), the initial entry, was budgeted at $75,000 and emphasized Maynard's fabulous horsemanship. The pacing was brisk, just at it was in the best Fox Westerns with Tom Mix, but to this was added the romance and good-natured humor — on screen! — which were Maynard's own unique contribution. The film was well received by the public and even the critics admired Maynard's dexterity and his good looks. *Photoplay*, however, felt the plot left much to be desired. *The Unknown Cavalier* (First National, 1926) was second with a story that stressed comedy and suspense. It was remade as *Ride Him Cowboy* (Warner's, 1932) in the series of John Wayne remakes already referred to.

Ralph Brauer in his book *The Horse, the Gun, and the Piece of Property: Changing Images of the TV Western* (Popular Press, 1975) finds the "horse" Western to be the first, and most primitive, form in the evolution of the television Western and, to an extent, this might also be found reflected in the development of the cinematic, or theatrical, Western. If so, among movie cowboys' horses, Tarzan may have been the most exceptional. Unlike Roy Rogers' Trigger, billed as the smartest, and Gene Autry's Champion, billed as a world wonder, Tarzan was not entirely the creation of studio publicity. His only real rival would be Tony, but Tony's supremacy was confined to his ability to direct horse action and to behave with almost human intelligence, and in this Tarzan equalled him in Maynard's films like *Come On, Tarzan* (Worldwide, 1932). Readily trained by means of one-syllable instructions, Tarzan was Maynard's costar in virtually every film. Scenes were constantly written into Ken's pictures calling for the horse to dance, to bow down, to roll over and play dead, to nod his head in response to questions, to ring a fire bell, to pull Ken from a turbulent river, to chase desperados by himself, to untie Ken, to jump from great heights or great distances, to plunge into burning buildings, to drag Ken hanging onto his tail on land or in the water, to rock a baby crib, or to cook a meal, as well as providing the reluctant hero with a push into the willing heroine's arms. While at First National, Maynard assembled an entire string of palomino horses to support Tarzan, one of which would buck or rear, one of which would run up to a certain mark and stop cold, one for pulling and tugging at objects like jail bars, but viewers always looked for the identifying black birthmark on Tarzan's rear flank and thereby could tell whether it was the original or a double.

In 1928 First National was bought by Warner Bros. and the companies combined facilities at the First National studio in Burbank. Jack L. Warner, who did not especially like Westerns, took over as head of production. Maynard finished his series and his contract with *The Royal Rider* (First National, 1929), which was released in a music and synchronized effects version. Charles R. Rogers and Sid Rogell associated themselves with the newly organized RKO-Pathé, while Harry Joe Brown and Maynard negotiated themselves a contract with Universal Pictures to make sound Western features.

Carl Laemmle, who had been to see *In Old Arizona* (Fox, 1929), an all-talking Western, felt that perhaps sound Westerns were possible. But he was very hesitant and cautious. He signed Maynard, but, as in the case of Henry MacRae and the chapter play unit, he held off and procrastinated in giving a green light to sound productions filmed outdoors. Maynard's first four Westerns for Universal, as a result, were completely silent, and the next two were only partly talking. Maynard, who had been at the screening of *In Old Arizona* at the Criterion Theatre, as had Laemmle, was personally intrigued with the songs and musical content in the picture and wanted to incorporate songs in his own Westerns. On April 1, 1930, Tiffany released one of its *Voice of Hollywood* filler shorts and in it Maynard was introduced. He brought Tarzan on stage with him, then took up a fiddle — Maynard played several instruments by ear; he could not read music — and proceeded to sing "The Drunken Hiccoughs." That same month Universal released *The Fighting Legion* (Universal, 1930) which, for the sound portion, had a male trio, billed as the Hook brothers, played by Les Bates, Bill Nestel, and Slim Whitaker, performing a saloon ditty. *Song of the Caballero* (Universal, 1930) and *Sons of the Saddle* (Universal, 1930) closed out Maynard's contract and, all-talking, had a substantial musical content. Maynard even went so far as to cut a number of discs for Columbia Records, of which, in later years, he was not particularly proud, asserting that he could not sing well and so compensated for this by singing *loud*.

When Maynard signed his contract with Tiffany Productions, after leaving Universal, Samuel Bischoff, who had collaborated with Nat Levine on *The Silent Flyer* (Universal, 1926), was the production manager. None of Maynard's Tiffany Westerns had a musical content, save for his humming in his first feature, *Fightin' Thru* (Tiffany, 1930), since Bischoff had little use for the notion of a "singing" cowboy. Oddly enough, the influence of Maynard's musical interludes for his Universal Westerns was to be seen in Trem Carr's independently produced Bob Steele Westerns for Tiffany release. In *Headin' North* (Tiffany, 1930) Steele and Perry Murdock disguised themselves as an English dance hall team and sang and danced through several arrangements. In *The Oklahoma Cyclone* (Tiffany, 1930), the action slowed down to a complete halt while Steele, who was an even worse singer than Maynard was, sang a song accompanying himself on a guitar. He then sang a second song, and a third. Then the heroine, Rita Rey, took the stage and sang a song!

Tiffany Productions and the Tiffany marketing force were a wholly owned subsidiary of E.W. Hammons' Educational Pictures by the time Bischoff joined it and the Tiffany product was released through the Educational exchange network supplying second and third run houses with a steady flow of cheaply produced features and short subjects. Educational maintained several distribution agreements with independent producers so as to provide a full release schedule. Most of the filming for these independently financed productions was done at the Tiffany California studio and, for interiors, at the Tec-Art studio where, for a time, Levine also rented sound stages. Space and equipment, as a matter of fact, were always leased out to nonaffiliated production groups when not in use so as to get maximum usage and income from the existing facilities.

Neither Trem Carr nor Samuel Bischoff were satisfied with the Educational setup. In 1932 Bischoff organized KBS Productions and in addition to his own product he agreed to distribute a new series of Bob Steele Westerns produced by Trem Carr. It was with the conclusion of this second series that Carr went into partnership with W. Ray Johnston of Monogram Pictures and continued to specialize in the production of Western series. More will be said about Monogram when I come to the Republic merger and more about Educational when Levine, after leaving Republic, was approached to join the Educational group in a new venture.

Maynard's Tiffany Westerns were neither good nor bad, merely adequate. His first Western for Bischoff's company, *Dynamite Ranch*, was filmed on a more elaborate budget than any of the previous Tiffany films and for location was shot on the Warner ranch. Maynard had seen John Wayne's remake of *The Unknown Cavalier* and importuned Bischoff to engage Wayne's leading lady in that film, Ruth Hall, to appear opposite him. Although light on action, *Dynamite Ranch* owed much to Ted McCord's expert photography. McCord had been Maynard's principal cinematographer during his first series for Universal and it was prudent of Maynard that, when he left Bischoff to return to Universal, he took McCord with him. Sid Rogell, who had produced the John Wayne/Ken Maynard remake series, had used McCord as his chief cinematographer.

"Ted McCord," Ruth Hall once told me, "gave me every break he could with camera angles and lighting. I was referred to as 'the girl.' The girl had to hit her marks, which were chalk marks on the floor or the dirt, in order to receive the best light. Ted took the effort to give me the best light he could. The girl had to play her scene right because there were no second takes and, horrors, of course no retakes. The main stars were coached but not the girls. Here Ted taught me how to use the light to my best advantage."

Maynard, who genuinely liked Ruth Hall, cast her again in *Between Fighting Men* (WorldWide, 1932) in which Wallace MacDonald, who would presently go to work in the Mascot writing department, played Ken's friend and sidekick. It was while at KBS that Maynard assembled a second group around him, sort of a repertory company. Ruth Hall, Cecilia Parker, and Dorothy Dix as his leading ladies, Frank Rice as his on-again, off-again sidekick, Kermit Maynard, who had started in low budget Westerns for W. Ray Johnston in the silent era under the name "Tex" Maynard but whose career was not flourishing, as his double and, in one film, *Drum Taps* (Worldwide, 1933), he was given a major speaking part.

I went to talk to Kermit Maynard for the first time in December, 1969, a guest at his North Hollywood home. Facially one could still see a strong resemblance between the two brothers, although Kermit's features were more austere, ascetic, and while he had the same thin lips Ken had, his jaw was not quite so pronounced. His hairline had receded more dramatically than had Ken's at a comparable age, and he made no effort to hide it. We met in his living room.

"Have you been out to see Ken?" he asked. At the time Ken was still living in a house trailer in the city of San Fernando.

"Yes," I replied. "I was just out there yesterday."

"Does Ken know you've come to see me?"

"I didn't tell him. Should I have?"

Kermit smiled. "I don't know how he would feel about it now, but for years anybody that had anything to do with me he wanted nothing to do with."

"Why the animosity?"

"I've never approved of his drinking." Kermit paused. "You see, I don't drink. Never have. And I don't smoke. I play nine holes of golf every day that I'm not working." (For years, since the late thirties in fact, Kermit's career had been limited to extra work and walk-ons, only infrequently a speaking part.) "All Ken has done for years is sit around in that trailer of his and drink."

"When did he start drinking?" I asked.

"That I can't tell you. We didn't see much of him after he left home to join a traveling show. It wasn't until I came out here to try my hand in the picture business that we saw each other very much, and then Ken was already a heavy drinker. He used to say it was a habit he picked up when on the road. I don't know if that was true or not."

"But you worked with him at KBS?"

"Yes. Samuel Bischoff asked me to. Ken drank especially hard when he would go out on location and once, in Kernville, he had ridden drunk through the town, his guns loaded with real bullets, shooting out street lamps and windows. Bischoff wanted me to kind of keep an eye on Ken, keep him out of trouble when they were in production. Ken used to listen to me somewhat in those days."

"Even at the very beginning of the sound era you could see Ken was putting on weight. Was that from the drinking?"

"I think it was. He kept getting fatter and fatter, up until last year, that is. Then a doctor told him that he would either have to lose weight or risk a heart attack. After that, Ken went on a diet."

"He still drinks."

"I wouldn't doubt that for an instant."

"Why didn't he at least curb it when he saw it was ruining his career?"

Kermit leaned back in his reclining chair and let out a sigh.

"I don't think he cared," he said.

"About his career?"

"I don't know what it was Ken wanted. I'm pretty sure, though, that he had trouble with what he was made to look like on the screen and the way he was off the screen."

"You mean he was world famous for being something he wasn't?"

"I don't know if I would put it just that way, but, yes, that's more or less how it was. On screen he was Ken Maynard, a hero who could outride, outshoot, outfight all the heavies. Off screen...." Kermit left the statement unfinished save for a shrug and then clamped his teeth together.

"What caused you two to have a falling out?"

"The way he treated Mary, his wife. They would be fighting almost all the time whenever they were together. Mary used to like to play bridge. Ken was working for Universal then, in 1933, and I had gone along with him, standing in for him, things like that. He had his own bungalow on the Universal lot and he used to do a lot of drinking there. When Ken drinks, he gets mean. When he had enough to drink, he'd get in his chauffeured limousine, be driven home, and then raise hell. Once he went home with his guns strapped on. He broke up Mary's bridge game, terrifying everybody, grabbing one of Mary's friends in his arms and carrying her upstairs, telling everyone they should leave. I got to the point where I couldn't take it any more. I told Ken I'd had enough. After that, we just didn't talk. Maybe it's better that way."

Kermit Maynard died on January 16, 1971, a full two years before Ken died. There are those who, remembering Ken as he appeared on the screen, would rather not know anything about his personal life. They want to believe in the screen image as if it were a reality. It never was. The Ken Maynard who appeared on the screen was a person who never existed. He was a fiction, an imaginative creation, a manufactured product, not a human being. Ken knew that, even if most of his admirers didn't. I have always felt — and Ken Maynard was not the only movie cowboy imprisoned by this contradiction — that the most interesting, and dangerous, aspect of the Western movie hero is the price exacted on the men who had to play these parts on screen, who had to identify with a personality and a character who could never exist in real life; that price, in almost every case, was misery, misery come of being known and highly regarded for being something you are not and could never be. The tragedy in the lives of these men, the former cowboy heroes of yesterday's movies, came about because, no matter how they might resist it, they began to believe in themselves as they *were supposed to be*, not as they were.

In his essay "Images of the Unconscious," published in 1950, Jung wrote that "the persona ... is that system of adjustment or that manner through which we deal with the world. Almost every occupation has its characteristic persona.... The danger is only that one might become identified with his persona, like somewhat the professor with his textbook or the tenor with his voice.... One could with some exaggeration say: the persona is that which a person essentially is not, but rather what he and other people want him to be."

In the instance of the movie cowboy, this is precisely what happened. He became identified with his screen image so thoroughly that for him, as for his public, he became his persona. To this, I would add one more observation.

In his book *Zwei Schriften über analytische Psychologie [Two Essays on Analytical Psychology]* (Rascher Verlag, 1967), Jung claimed that the *mana*-personality is an archetype of the collective unconscious, by which he meant, in his words, "a being filled with an occult, conjuring capacity, or mana, and endowed with magical skills or powers." Jung went on to remark that "the mana-personality manifests itself historically in hero figures and divine images." Maud Bodkin, applying this notion to imaginative literature in her book *Archetypal Patterns in Poetry* (Oxford University Press, 1963), commented that "if within the conscious life the personal self comes to be known only as 'an onlooker, an ineffective speechless man,' utterly insignificant; while yet, within the life that animates that particular brain, strong reactions are excited of sympathetic exultation and delight at imaginative representations of human achievement ... then there may arise, as compensatory to the belittled self, the figure of the self-hero, or mana-personality, fashioned as it were, from the stuff of these imaginative reactions; just as the figure of the hated father was fashioned from the energy of the repressed hostility, in compensation for the over-idealizing love."

In the chapter in *Zwei Schriften* that Jung devoted to the phenomenon of the mana-personality, he felt compelled to warn that "one can only alter his attitude in an effort to impede being naively possessed by an archetype that compels him to play a role at the cost of his humanity. Possession by an archetype makes a man into a purely collective figure, after the fashion of a mask, behind which his humanity can no longer develop, but rather increasingly atrophies. One must remain conscious of the danger of falling beneath the dominant of the mana-personality. The danger consists not merely in the fact that one person assumes the mask of a father figure but that that person can fall victim to the same mask when it's worn by another person. In this sense, master and pupil are one and the same."

I would not stress this notion of the archetype of the mana-personality if I personally had not been exposed to it and its effects repeatedly. Expressed in other words, by pretending to be cowboy heroes we can fall victim to believing in cowboy heroes. But cowboy heroes cannot really exist and, therefore, if modern psychology is correct, there may be a serious hazard to our mental health, both personally and collectively, caused by an uncritical acceptance of them. When I saw time after time what being a cowboy hero and believing in the reality of cowboy heroes had done to literally cripple, and in some cases totally destroy, the lives, and if not the lives, then the sense of humanity of almost every former movie cowboy with whom I became acquainted, the hazard seemed both very real and very concrete. Nor is it by accident that I introduce these reflections at this juncture of my history of Mascot Pictures or in telling of Ken Maynard's career before he came to Mascot, since Mascot's last year of corporate independence would be very much linked to the lives and fortunes of three movie cowboys, Ken Maynard, Gene Autry, and Tom Mix, and what proved to be true for Maynard, sadly, proved to be no less true for the others.

When Samuel Bischoff was offered a job in production supervision at Warner Bros., he pulled out of KBS Productions, which changed its name to Admiral Productions. This left Ken Maynard without a studio contract. As it happened, Tom Mix had just quit, right in the middle of a new series of highly successful Westerns at Universal, and Universal approached Maynard to be his replacement. Maynard had Sid Rogell negotiate the contract. In the interim, Max and Arthur Alexander, two Poverty Row producers, got in touch with Maynard and proposed to sign him for a series of six Westerns. Maynard informed them that a deal with Universal was imminent and that he would accept their offer only if the Universal deal fell through. The Alexander brothers ignored this and began preparing stories, casting, and arranging for crews and equipment. On the day they were set to commence shooting, Maynard telephoned them at their office in what was then called Gower Gulch, on Gower Street just off Sunset Boulevard, and told them that the contract with Universal had been signed.

Max Alexander was in a quandary. He had a director, cast, and crew standing on location expecting Maynard to show up momentarily. He ran out of his office and searched the Gulch for a suitable cowboy star. He found one having his boots shined. After a brief conversation, he brought him back to his office and signed him up. It was none other than Jack Hoxie, the same Jack Hoxie that Nat Levine had starred in *Heroes of the Wild* in 1927. Hoxie had not worked since in pictures, although he had been touring with some small circuses.

"It seemed like such a good idea," Arthur Alexander once recalled for me in conversation, "and, as Max pointed out, we were getting him so cheap. Just imagine how we felt when we rushed him out to location in a touring car, screeched to a halt, handed him a copy of the script, only to find out that Jack couldn't read!"

This notwithstanding, Jack Hoxie made the six films for them.

Maynard had been receiving $8,000 a picture from Bischoff and the KBS Westerns had had $75,000 budgets, with Maynard raised to $10,000 a picture near the end of the contract. At Universal, Maynard was to get $10,000 a week for each week shooting, $10,000 for the story if he wrote it himself, and a percentage of the profits from the pictures. He was also to have his own unit. The pictures were to be Ken Maynard Productions. Henry Henigson, the story editor at Universal, was to have script approval, but after that Maynard could make the films as he pleased. Maynard, of course, would eventually go to work for the Alexander brothers in 1938 and make six pictures for them, being paid $2,500 each; by that time, it was the best offer in town.

Universal needed a picture at once. Tom Mix's last Western had been released on March 16, 1933. Maynard commenced production with a film tentatively titled *King of the Range* although, upon release, this would be altered to *King of the Arena* (Universal, 1933). He built a substantial part of the Wild West show sequences from stock footage of both himself and his youthful child star Jackie Hanlon doing numerous stunts and tricks from Maynard's earlier Universal film, *Parade of the West* (Universal, 1930). The Coleman Bros. circus was playing in North Hollywood, and he arranged for the show to be included in *King of the Arena* as it had been in *Parade of the West*, so he could best match shots, something Sid Rogell, after his experience on the Wayne/Maynard remakes, taught him to do. Lucile Browne was cast as the girl.

Maynard had a penchant for outlandish and improbable plots, perhaps as a compensation for the hostility he felt toward the idealized character he was forced to play. In *King of the Arena* he featured his own airplane and added some unusual aerial stunts including the crash of an adroitly constructed model. Michael Visoroff, who had played a friendly if not very convincing Mexican bandit with an Italian accent in *Arizona Terror* (Tiffany, 1931) with Maynard, was cast here as a cruel border bandit in possession of a chemical pellet that, upon discharge, would char a man's face and was called the black death.

In *Fiddlin' Buckaroo* (Universal, 1933), next in the series, Maynard played a ventriloquist. Maynard pretends that Tarzan is capable of human speech and this so disconcerts jailer Bob McKenzie that Maynard and his sidekick Frank Rice are able to make good their escape. In this picture Maynard had an opening scene filmed on Mauser Street in the center of the Western town set on the Universal back lot performing a few musical numbers on the fiddle while the townsfolk danced. For *The Trail Drive* (Universal, 1933), Maynard both composed and performed the theme song, "The Trail Herd."

In the case of *The Strawberry Roan* (Universal, 1933), Maynard purchased screen rights from Curley Fletcher for his ballad "The Strawberry Roan," had music added, and worked out his own fiddle accompaniment. That year the Ralston Purina Co. had begun to sponsor a radio program titled *The Tom Mix Ralston Straight-Shooters*. Mix licensed the show to use his name in exchange for a royalty, although he himself was portrayed by someone else. In a few years Curley Fletcher would be one of the actors to portray him on the air. Maynard sang twice in *The Strawberry Roan* and the ballad completely dominated the film. Ruth Hall was his leading lady.

Cecilia Parker played opposite Ken in *Gun Justice* (Universal, 1933) and then, in an effort to keep his marriage together as well as to help promote his films in Europe, Maynard accompanied by his wife, Mary, embarked on a European trip. His first stop was in London where he was pleased to learn that Universal was advertising British release of *The Strawberry Roan* on the sides of trams. He was amazed at the size of the crowds that everywhere thronged him. Many Londoners were curious as to just what a strawberry roan was. It sounded more like a flavor of ice cream than a horse. Maynard had not screened the completed film at the studio. He saw it for the first time in Paris, dubbed into French.

There was a perverse streak in Maynard and it so happened that, for the moment, it worked in Nat Levine's favor. Levine, after seeing *The Strawberry Roan*, decided he wanted to make a series of musical Westerns, possibly as chapter plays with feature versions edited from them. He telephoned Maynard in London and asked him if he would be interested in starring in a musical Western chapter play, or if it would interfere with his Universal contract. Maynard responded that he would think the whole thing over and get back to Levine.

Maynard was ebullient upon his return to the home he had bought on Las Palmas Avenue in Los Angeles. He had installed a wooden front door he had brought back from Italy and at the piano in the sun room he set to music the words he had written while abroad which would constitute the theme song for his next film, *Wheels of Destiny* (Universal, 1934). The music and lyrics for both this song and for "The Trail Herd" were included in *Ken Maynard's Songs of the Trails* (M.M. Cole, 1935). In a brief afterword which Maynard wrote for the novelization of *Wheels of Destiny* (Engel-van Weisman Five Star Library, 1934), Ken commented that "the romance, the excitement, and the villainy of the early West provide the material for your entertainment. Most of it is from real life." Did he really believe this? I think he convinced himself he did. "Men and women and even children," he said, "lived dangerous lives in those pioneering years. When the frontier moved still further West there came the great ranches for cattle raising. The cowboys are the people who created the romance and the adventure that the Wild West has given you. Theirs is the story I like best to tell...."

In *The Pocatello Kid* (Tiffany, 1931), Maynard had played a dual role as the Kid and a lookalike crooked sheriff. In *Honor of the Range*

(Universal, 1934), Maynard revived a variation on this notion, playing Ken, an honest sheriff, and Clem, his twin brother, a crooked storekeeper. A high budget permitted a number of split-screen confrontations between the twins. The plot had it that Clem kidnaps Cecilia Parker, playing Ken's fiancée, and hides her out in the caves at Bronson Canyon. In his frustration and unhappiness, I suspect that Maynard felt at times that he had much in common with Clem. Yet, when it came to most fundamental emotions, Ken Maynard was wholly inarticulate.

Carl Laemmle, known popularly as Uncle Carl, was still titular head of Universal, but since his son's twenty-first birthday, Laemmle had put Junior in charge of production. Maynard's Westerns, while they were proving popular with exhibitors, were costing too much to produce. Out of seven feature Westerns, Maynard had not brought in a single film for less than the budgets he had drawn up, and most of them were requiring well over $100,000 to produce. One of Maynard's pictures would average 10,000 play-offs on a flat $30 one-to-seven-day exhibition contract. This figure, however, should be contrasted with the Westerns Buck Jones was then making for Columbia Pictures, which similarly averaged 10,000 play-offs at $25 flat rental, grossing upwards of $250,000 but costing no more than between $25,000 and $35,000 to produce. Uncle Carl thought Universal might be better off with Buck Jones working for them and when Jones came on the lot to film his summer chapter plays for Henry MacRae, Laemmle made it a point to hold a meeting with him.

Maynard knew that his budgets were excessive, but he closed his ears to all protests. Junior Laemmle would prance onto his set twirling his long gold watch chain. He would order Maynard to exercise caution. Maynard would thereupon fly into a rage. He'd yell aloud for anyone within earshot that his films were all Ken Maynard Productions and that he knew very well what he was doing. The clashes between Maynard and Junior became increasingly bitter, and matters were not helped when Kermit quit the unit.

In May, 1934, irked at all the pressure, Maynard began work on a film he titled *Doomed to Die*. It was Maynard's custom at the time to fly in his plane to Yucatan or South America and take home movies during his crocodile hunts. He made up a story that would permit him to work crocodiles into the script and thus charge off his whole trip to Yucatan to get additional footage. In the film, released as *Smoking Guns* (Universal, 1934), Maynard is falsely accused of murdering character actor William Gould—Maynard with his hair dyed blond—and disappears into a tropical jungle. Walter Miller, playing a lawman on Maynard's trail, pursues him—Miller is a Texas Ranger and Maynard is quite obviously outside his jurisdiction, but no matter—and, in trying to bring Ken back, gets mauled by a very fake crocodile in footage shot around a pool on the Universal back lot. Once Miller dies, Maynard, looking at the corpse, is no less amazed than the viewer—well, maybe a little less—to discover that he and Miller, beneath their beards, are exact lookalikes! Maynard returns to Texas and finally catches the guilty man, everyone accepting him as Walter Miller.

Maynard, in his chaotic fashion, intended the film as a parody, and a demonstration to the Universal management, and Junior in particular, that Ken Maynard would and could do any damned thing he wanted. Having an open offer from Nat Levine to come to Mascot and make an unlimited number of Westerns, both chapter plays and features, at a firm salary of $10,000 a week gave Maynard courage. Junior thought Maynard's film ridiculous and complained vehemently about it and about Maynard to his father. Uncle Carl, by this time, definitely wanted to replace Maynard with Buck Jones, so he acted promptly. Maynard was in Havana on a personal appearance. Uncle Carl summoned him back to the studio.

When Maynard entered Uncle Carl's office, Laemmle jumped up from his desk, shaking a rebuking forefinger.

"You have made me a very bad picture, Ken," he told him. "Why didn't you spend two or three thousand dollars more and make it a good picture?"

Maynard became irate at once. He referred to both his first Universal series and the present one.

"Mr. Laemmle," he said in rebuttal, "I have made sixteen very bad pictures."

"Change the picture, Ken," Laemmle insisted.

"This is Junior's doing," Maynard declared. "I'll quit first."

And quit he did. It was in this spirit that he met with Nat Levine to accept his offer. Levine felt he was getting a bargain and that Maynard was well worth, in box office appeal, the salary he had agreed to pay him. Production was scheduled to begin in September, 1934, on what would be Maynard's first musical Western feature for Mascot, tentatively titled *Down in Old Santa Fe*. Wallace MacDonald, by now in the Mascot writing department, contributed to the screenplay. Levine had purchased screen rights to the title song and he projected a musical interlude at a dude ranch for the song to be sung by Gene Autry, whom he had just signed, accompanied by Frank Marvin and Smiley Burnette, who had come along with Autry. Levine also had a serial script in preparation with a strictly action format titled *Mystery Mountain* and another serial in the writing stage called *The Phantom Empire*. This latter serial would again surround Maynard with a musical setting.

David Howard was set to direct *In Old Santa Fe*, as it was titled upon release on November 15, 1934, and he was taken with Evalyn Knapp, who was cast as the heroine, and her penchant for wearing no undergarments. One day on the set, when Maynard was scheduled for a noon call, Howard had Evalyn backed by a fireplace in which a fire was roaring. She was being photographed in such a way that the transparency of her clothing, aided by the lighting aft, left nothing of her flapper figure to the imagination. Maynard, arriving unexpectedly, stormed onto the set in a state of moral indignation.

Howard's contract expired before the film was completed. Levine was in a quandary. He did not want to renew Howard's contract, nor was he willing to pay Howard extra to finish the picture. So he assigned one of his film editors, Joe Kane, to finish the film. One sequence had Maynard in an exterior shot wearing a double-breasted suit coat over his Western outfit. The shot with which it had to be matched was an interior with Maynard simply in his dark blue outfit, without the suit coat. Kane shot a short interlinking scene in which Maynard, silhouetted against a curtained window, stripped off his suit coat before climbing inside through the window.

George Hayes was cast as Maynard's sidekick, Cactus. Hayes had been slowly transforming his screen image from parental roles to a sensitive combination of humor and pathos and it was on the basis of his performance in *In Old Santa Fe* that Harry Sherman, who was producing the Hopalong Cassidy/Bar 20 films for Paramount release, put Hayes under contract. Hayes remained with Sherman until 1938 at which time he returned to work regularly under contract to Republic, usually in their Roy Rogers series Westerns. H.B. Warner, who had been Cecil B. DeMille's Christ at Pathé during the silent era, portrayed Evalyn's father.

What was innovative about *In Old Santa Fe* was not the song Maynard sang at the beginning—his voice was dubbed because Levine felt he could not sing well; nor was it the musical interlude with Autry and Burnette—there had been such interludes in several of Maynard's Universal Westerns; what was innovative about *In Old Santa Fe* was the capricious and incongruous blending of the old West with the modern West. The plot found Maynard battling big city gangsters, Evalyn Knapp nearly running over Maynard and Hayes driving her high-powered sports car, and H.B. Warner sending a gold shipment aboard a stagecoach which, appropriately, is held up by desperados. Henceforth, Westerns at Republic would frequently employ such anachronistic ingredients, especially the Autry and later Rogers vehicles. Even the dress in *In Old Santa Fe*, a combination of Park Avenue styles with Western apparel, was made acceptable by the superabundant dreamlike quality which consistently had characterized the Mascot product. The fantasy content remained predominant at Mascot and during the dark Depression period accounted for much of Mascot's success. Indeed, without such a phantasmagoric orientation, it would have been inconceivable that of all people Gene Autry should be transformed, and successfully, into a movie cowboy.

Levine next went into production on the chapter play *Mystery Mountain*. It was based, at least as concerned the master villain and his schemes, on story ideas from *Hurricane Express*. A railroad was under siege from a phantom outlaw leader who, by means of a series of rubber masks, could assume the identity of anyone in the cast. To further confuse the viewer, Edmund Cobb was cast as The Rattler, as the master villain was called, in his phantom disguise, while Edward Earle was unmasked in the final episode. When The Rattler spoke, it was with Cobb's voice. Autry, who was under contract to Mascot, was being given riding lessons by Yakima Canutt, but was not very good as yet, so he was given a non-singing part as a wagon driver, as was Smiley Burnette. There was no musical content at all, as a matter of fact, save for the rousing theme, composed by Lee Zahler and played under the credits.

Maynard had been anything but pleased by what he considered Mascot's slap-dash production methods and he was determined to have more control over this production than he had had over *In Old Santa Fe*. First off, he insisted the picture be shot in part on the Universal lot so he could flaunt his resilience in front of Junior Laemmle. Maynard's agreement with Levine called for him to be paid $10,000 a week for each week that he worked. The schedule was four weeks. But Maynard back on the Universal lot spelled disaster. He began by changing the story to suit himself. As the shooting script had it, the first chapter was to conclude with Maynard being pursued by three of the Rattler's men and falling to his doom over a high grade. It didn't come out that way. The Rattler was supposed to be seen in the episode; he wasn't. Maynard had his own ideas. In the first reel, when the Corwin Transportation Company was introduced, Maynard used stock footage from his own *The Wagon Master* (Universal, 1929), showing a wagon train. Next he interpolated the exciting race between three stagecoaches from his *The California Mail* (First National, 1929), which was the highlight of that picture. The original script was further altered, inserting scenes intended for the second installment; namely bringing Bob Kortman to town only to have him escape through the office of the Corwin Transportation Company and leaving a gap of five minutes' shooting time for the second chapter. Syd Saylor, whom Levine continued to think funny, was told by Maynard to fill up this slot with a static, slow, labored, unfunny struggle to get the reins of a team of stage horses organized. Maynard then shot additional background footage for the stage race involving a coach in which Saylor was riding, followed by one in which The Rattler was supposed to be, with Maynard and Jane Corwin, played by Verna Hillie, in the third coach.

When the exposed film was edited into a chapter, the results were not altogether pleasant. Maynard, who had his guns on when the chase between himself and The Rattler's men began, lost them in the fracas, had them again when he brought Bob Kortman into town, and suddenly lost them for a second time when he disarmed Jane Corwin's coach by means of holding up her men with a stick. Moreover, the absence of The Rattler physically in the opening episode made his appearance on the title cards of the second chapter somewhat of a shock. However much Maynard personally might think he knew about filmmaking, he watched few films and virtually none of his own; hence, he really could not tell how an idea that appealed to him in front of the camera would look when projected on a thirty-foot screen.

Mystery Mountain was budgeted at $65,000 and ended up costing $80,000, with Maynard getting an extra $10,000 for an additional week's work. The added costs were due directly to Maynard's emendations and his truculence. Breezy Eason and Otto Brower were the codirectors and Armand Schaefer was in charge of supervision. If Schaefer or one of the directors did not like one of Maynard's changes, Ken would go into a paroxym of outrage. When they were on location, Maynard's drinking kept him permanently surly. Maynard would also, to the horror of the cast and crew, take out his frustrations by beating his palomino horses. One of his more violent sessions was recorded by the sound engineers and played back for Levine. How could this man, this cowboy hero who supposedly loves horses and Tarzan above all, whip his horses mercilessly, the animals screaming in torment? The answer, of course, was very simple. Hollywood had made Ken Maynard a movie hero. Those who were horrified were horrified because they were believing the illusion they themselves were responsible for creating.

Levine summoned Maynard to him and told him he would be finished at Mascot if he persisted in his behavior. Further, he counseled, the scenario was to be filmed as written and Maynard had better do as he was told. Levine should have consulted with Joe Kane. Kane had tried to kid with Ken when they were wrapping up *In Old Santa Fe.* "When I handed Ken the revised portion of the script," Kane recalled for me, "I said I understood he needed a few minutes to memorize that much. I started away but suddenly found myself facing a six-gun aimed at my middle. Ken decided I was being sarcastic. He had a violent temper and a low boiling point. At first I thought he must be putting on an act, but he wasn't. His eyes told me that. He invited me to take the other gun from his holster belt. I guess they were really loaded."

Gene Autry intervened. He got the fuming Maynard to one side. Autry idolized Maynard and sought to model himself on the way Ken appeared on screen. He watched all of Maynard's scenes during the making of *Mystery Mountain* and even after Maynard left Mascot and was working for Larry Darmour in a series for Columbia release, whenever Autry was not working in one of his own pictures he would be visiting the Maynard set and sitting quietly on the sidelines watching Ken. He wouldn't say anything, just watched.

Maynard admired Levine's forthrightness, but he decided on the spot that he was finished at Mascot and would therefore do things his way no matter what came. In this he was right. Levine, privately, had already made the decision to chuck Maynard after *Mystery Mountain*, but he intended to do what he could to get a finished picture out of Maynard. Autry was about to get his break. The publicity for *The Phantom Empire*, which pictured Maynard as the star, was junked. Levine apparently never had cause to regret this turn of events, even though, upon release, *Mystery Mountain* would prove the second highest money-maker in the entire history of the company, second only to *The Miracle Rider* (Mascot, 1935) with Tom Mix, which grossed a million dollars and, like *Mystery Mountain*, cost $80,000.

In the first act of Goethe's *Faust*, Part Two, Mephistopheles gives Faust a key when he is about to descend to the Mothers. Within that deepest of the deep, "deeper than did ever plummet sound" as Shakespeare once put it, Mephistopheles tells Faust he will find a glowing tripod: [cont. page 153]

Top: *John Wayne saving Rayond Hatton from an attack by an Arab in* The Three Musketeers *(Mascot, 1933).* **Bottom:** *A lobby card from that film — obviously a re-issue since Wayne has first billing.*

Opposite: *Betsy King Ross immediately flanked by, left to right, Johnny Mack Brown, Lane Chandler and Noah Beery, Jr., disguised as the Mystery Riders;* **this page:** *Beery as an Indian, Ross, and Brown as Kit Carson; both shots are from* Fighting with Kit Carson *(Mascot, 1933).*

This page: *Lucile Browne and Bob Steele in a romantic clinch in* Mystery Squadron *(Mascot, 1933).* **Opposite:** *A one sheet showing the principal cast members of the ambitious* Harmony Lane *(Mascot, 1935).*

NAT LEVINE PRESENTS

DOUGLASS MONTGOMERY

in Musical

"HARMONY LANE"

BASED ON THE LIFE OF
America's Great Composer
STEPHEN COLLINS FOSTER

with

EVELYN   ADRIENNE
VENABLE   AMES

WILLIAM FRAWLEY

JOSEPH   GILBERT
CAWTHORNE   EMERY

JAMES BUSH   LLOYD HUGHES
DAVID TORRENCE   CORA SUE COLLINS
FERDINAND MUNIER

CLARENCE MUSE

AND THE SHAW CHOIR OF TWO HUNDRED VOICES

AND ALSO

VICTOR DeCAMP · EDITH CRAIG · FLORENCE ROBERTS
JAMES CARSON · AL HERMAN · RODNEY HILDEBRAND
MARY McLAREN · WYNNE DAVIS · EARL HODGINS AND
MILDRED GOVER

Directed by JOSEPH SANTLEY · Supervised by COLBERT CLARK

NAT LEVINE presents
Frankie Darro
IN
"BURN 'EM UP BARNES"
with
JACK MU
LOLA
CHAPTER 2
THE NEWS REEL MURDER
MASCOT SERIALS
A Mascot Super-Serial in 12 Thrill-Inspiring Chapters!
Directed by COLBERT CLARK and ARMAND SCHAEFER

Opposite: *A lobby card from* Burn 'em Up Barnes *(Mascot, 1934).* **This page:** *Edmund Cobb, wearing The Rattler's get-up, talking to his gang in Bronson Caverns, in* Mystery Mountain *(Mascot, 1934).*

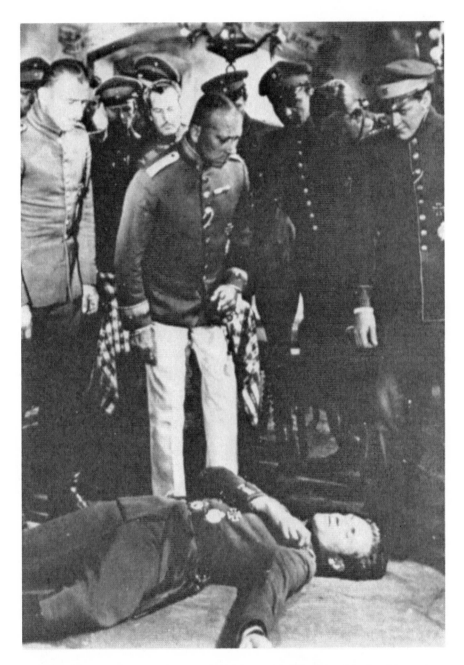

Opposite: *Tarzan, Verna Hillie, Ken Maynard, and Syd Saylor in* Mystery Mountain *(Mascot, 1934).* **This page:** *Erich von Stroheim, center, in* Crimson Romance *(Mascot, 1934).*

Opposite: *Gene Autry and the Junior Thunder Riders.* **This page:** *Griffith Park Observatory in the Hollywood Hills was one of the locations for the miraculous underworld kingdom of Murania; Autry is at top; both shots are from* The Phantom Empire *(Mascot, 1935).*

Opposite: *Warner Richmond is about to operate on Gene Autry's lungs, to see why he sings all the time, in* The Phantom Empire *(Mascot, 1935).* **This page:** *An older and sadder Tom Mix in* The Miracle Rider *(Mascot, 1935).*

Opposite: *Jim Thorpe, far left foreground, and Robert Frazer, center, as Black Wing, initiating Tom Mix into the Ravenhead tribe, surrounded by Hollywood "Indians" on the back lot of the Sennett studio at what was called the "Indian Village"—from* The Miracle Rider *(Mascot, 1935).* **This page:** *Tom Mix and his fifth wife, Mabel, upon their return from a trip to Europe in 1939, a few months before he died.*

The STUDIOS of MASCOT PICTURES CORPORATION North Hollywood, California

Photograph courtesy of Nat Levine.

Bei seinem Schein wirst du die Mütter sehn,
Die einen sitzen, andre stehn und gehn,
Wie's eben kommt. Gestaltung, Umgestaltung,
Des ewigen Sinnes ewige Unterhaltung.
Umschwebt von Bildern aller Kreatur;
Sie sehn dich nicht, denn Schemen sehn sie nur.

[You shall behold the Mothers by its light,
Some of them sit, some walk and stand upright,
As it happens. Formation, transformation,
The eternal organ of creation in eternal recreation.
By images of all creatures thronged;
They cannot see you; they see only shadows.]

The German word *Märchen* seems preferable for folk stories and not the English equivalent "fairy tales." Its meaning is closer to fables and from it comes *märchenhaft* ("fabulous"). The Mascot story lines, in their own inimitable way, had a fabulous quality about them. In *Mystery Mountain*, Verna Hillie's screen father is murdered in the first chapter. By 1934 so many Mascot productions had opened with the death of a father or a father-figure that it would be impossible to interpret this circumstance as coincidental. "The mountain," Jung wrote in *The Archetypes and the Collective Unconscious*, "... often has the psychological meaning of the self." He quoted Richard of St. Victor: "Do you wish to see the transfigured Christ? Ascend that mountain and learn to know yourself." The Rattler, who is disguised by a black cape, speaks in a deep voice, as if heard in a cavern. Only by battling successfully with this master villain at the summit of Mystery Mountain can the hero then plummet to the mountain's depths, where he finds not only the means of transformations – The Rattler's collection of rubber masks which permits him to assume other identities – but he also finds a rich gold mine, guarded by The Rattler's ally, an old man with a wooden leg. The third chapter is titled "The Eye That Never Sleeps," which here must be taken as a symbol of the unconscious and, significantly, it refers to nothing whatever that takes place in the chapter play. "It is thus possible," Jung continued in the same book, "that the old man is his own opposite, a life-bringer as well as a death-dealer," and perhaps it was therefore quite intentional that the old, peg-legged man brings about the destruction of the mountain and The Rattler with it. If all that I have said about this and other Mascot serials strikes the reader as somewhat whimsical or unduly complicated for a strictly low budget form of entertainment, I can only remind you of Thomas Mann's remark in *Die Entstehung des Doktor Faustus [The Genesis of Doktor Faustus]* (Bermann-Fischer Verlag, 1949) that the most unique aspect of the ravings of John of Patmos was that he raved in the same imagery as had every prophet before him. The plots of the Mascot chapter plays were contemporary fables for audiences in the thirties, but they called upon conventions which recur throughout the folk literature of many cultures and have for many centuries.

During his final years, Ken Maynard was intensely miserable, the years after his fourth wife, Bertha, was dead and when he himself wanted nothing more than to die. One day I stopped over to see him at his trailer and he had the door locked; he said he had a gun and that he would only let me in if I had brought him a bottle of whiskey. Fortunately I had a bottle of Jack Daniel's with me. He let me inside.

After several drinks, I suggested he let me take him out to dinner, to which proposal, to my surprise, he readily acquiesced. There was a restaurant nearby which Ken liked and I took him there. He ordered a large salad, garnished with thousand island dressing, and to this he added a half dozen tablespoons of sugar over the top, so dependent had he become on sugar. He had been drinking for so many years and so intensely that even when he was sober, which is to say even when he had not had a drink for a day or two, he still sounded as if he were drunk, talking most of the time in a high-pitched whine.

When we got back to his trailer that night, he showed me his secret treasure, as he referred to it. It was not his guns or gun belts; he had sold those many years before. All he had from his days as a star were a few old neckerchiefs, his circus scrapbooks, and, hidden, a box of movie stills. No, Ken Maynard's secret treasure was his notebook which he had been keeping on Mary, Our Lady of Fatima. Although a Baptist by birth, and practicing no religion, he was fascinated by what he believed was a mystical appearance by the Mother of God.

His condition deteriorated rapidly, but not rapidly enough; a lifetime of punishing his constitution had met with an heroic resistance. A hooker and her husband moved in on him, got hold of his box of stills, and tried to sell them at the cinema shops in Los Angeles dealing in memorabilia. The hooker claimed at times that she was married to Ken—she had prepared a phony marriage certificate and Ken was too drunk most of the time to know whether it was real or fake—and, at other times, she claimed to be his daughter. When Ken, covered with bed sores, became a virtual prisoner of these people, I pulled every string I could and undertook to have Ken moved to the Motion Picture Home in Woodland Hills.

It was there that I saw him for the last time, three weeks before he died. He was fond of telling visitors that I knew his pictures better than he did, and, although he had long refused to allow me to screen for him any of his films, he finally did ask me to screen *The Strawberry Roan*. The screening was held in what the nurses called the ding-a-ling room, a general screening for all the patients well enough or cognizant enough to attend.

Ken was wasting away, dying of stomach cancer, a frail, emaciated figure, sitting in a wheel chair at the front of the room. Larry Fine of the Three Stooges was there, and Frieda Inescourt. The previous year I had said farewell to "Broncho Billy" Anderson at the Motion Picture Home and a decade before to Hoot Gibson.

A nurse's aid, brought to tears by the contrast between Ken's robust form and good nature on the screen and the shriveled, dying man in the wheelchair sitting before the screen, fled the room. I have asked myself since, had Ken Maynard not been that man on the screen, or had he not pretended to be, would I have found myself there, or, later, sitting with him in his room? No, probably not. Because it was my work which had brought me to him.

Yet, I had become attached to him, as a human being, as a suffering mortal man. I still retained the hope that I might come to know the man who lived behind the bigger-than-life movie cowboy. He wanted to show his fellow patients *The Strawberry Roan* because he wanted to demonstrate somehow what he had done with his life. Or was it that? Could he just be showing off, being Ken Maynard movie cowboy one more time?

He was no longer that for me. I was uncomfortable facing the ravages of his disease, the harsh reminder of mortality. These were foolish feelings, but I was young. He sensed that. When I started to leave, he called me back to him, and he looked me straight in the face.

"Good-bye," he said. He extended a thin arm and hand, but the grip he gave me had strength.

Then his eyes seemed to cloud for a moment and were flickering suddenly with a harsh intensity. He wanted a cigar. He wanted to go back to his room. He was a movie cowboy again, being demanding of an admirer.

Ten

Miracles and Music

"I received a half dozen letters from Autry during 1933 asking for an opportunity to work for me in anything I would suggest in pictures," Nat Levine once told me. "Autry's name value at the time was limited to an independent radio station in Chicago, practically an unknown with questionable ability. On one of my trips East, I stopped off in Chicago, not to meet Autry, but for business I had with my distributor. But I did get to meet Autry and he virtually begged me for an opportunity to come to Hollywood and work in pictures. While he was nice looking, it seemed to me he lacked the commodity necessary to become a Western star: virility! I was not impressed and tried to give him a nice brush-off, telling him I would think about it. For a period of six months he wrote to me continually, conveying that he would do anything for the opportunity."

Levine finally did put Autry under a five-year contract, along with Smiley Burnette and Frank Marvin, who worked with Autry on the "National Barn Dance" broadcast on WLS, the Sears, Roebuck radio station in Chicago. "Autry was completely raw material," Levine went on, "knew nothing about acting, lacked poise, and was awkward. A couple of days after his arrival I had him at my home and invited my production staff to meet him. The next day all my associates questioned my judgment in putting him under contract. They thought I was slipping. But I persisted, and for the first four months he went through a learning period. We had at that time in our employ a professional dramatic and voice teacher, and Autry became one of her pupils. He wasn't much of a horseman either, so I had Tracy Layne and Yakima Canutt teach him how to ride."

The contract called for Autry to be paid $100 a week, Burnette and Marvin $75 a week each. "I don't believe he ever acknowledged my contribution to his career," Levine added about Autry, "nor did I ever receive thanks."

The first time I spoke to Autry, at his office at KTLA in Los Angeles, I asked him about his early work at Mascot. He was suddenly very vague. "Well," he said, "I sang a few songs in *In Old Santa Fe,* and then I made a serial for them." For whatever the reason at the time, Nat Levine appeared to be right: Autry had forgotten. But when I brought up the subject of *The Phantom Empire,* he wanted to know who was distributing it for television.

156

"I have a print of every picture I ever appeared in," he said, "except that one, and I would like to see it again."

I told him that Columbia Pictures Television was the distributor of record for *The Phantom Empire*. A few weeks later a friend of mine at Columbia informed me that Autry's secretary had called and requested a print and that they had had one struck for him. This conversation took place in February, 1970. It was my practice, then, when possible, to have screened for actors, actresses, writers, directors, or producers prints of their work so that they might serve to jog their memories and bring back associations long forgotten. I hoped that seeing *The Phantom Empire* might have a similar salutary effect on Autry.

The next time I encountered Autry was at the ceremonies at the National Cowboy Hall of Fame in Oklahoma City in 1973. "The Vanishing Legion" was then running in serial form in *Views & Reviews* and the issue with *The Phantom Empire* installment had just been published. I had heard from virtually everyone I talked to in the motion picture industry who knew Autry or who had worked with him that since the late thirties he had been a very heavy drinker, if anything more in recent years than ever before. The occasion, among others, at the Hall of Fame was to mark the unveiling of a painting of Gene Autry which would henceforth hang in the permanent collection of the Western Heritage Museum.

Mrs. Buck Jones, who was present with her daughter Maxine to witness her late husband Buck Jones being entered into the roles of the National Cowboy Hall of Fame, had flown over in the same plane with Joel McCrea, Barbara Stanwyck, and Autry, as well as other notables. Autry, according to Mrs. Jones, had been drinking quite a lot on the flight and thought it very amusing that he had accepted a free ticket rather than fly his own plane over, "and he," she said without amusement, "with all his millions."

At any rate, come the night of the awards, Autry, staggeringly drunk, inexplicably was permitted to be alone and unattended on stage. Off to stage left was the veiled portrait.

"I have asked to unveil my own portrait," Autry said into the microphone, and then proceeded rather uncertainly to make his way over to the easel on which the painting was set. He tugged at the draw strings but nothing happened. He staggered back to the microphone.

"You know," he told the audience of some three hundred people, "I feel like a man who is let loose in a harem for the first time. I know what to do, but I don't know where to begin."

The audience laughed and some people applauded. Autry, in the meantime, was again back at the easel unsuccessfully working the draw strings. This time when he came to the microphone he was obviously highly annoyed.

"I know that you folks want to see this painting of me as much as I do," he said, "and if those strings don't work this time, I'll just rip the curtain off."

Before he could make good on his threat, two ushers rushed onto the stage and, with alacrity, pulled the draw strings, and there, at last, fully revealed, was the painting, Autry's likeness all aglow in a fancy shirt, holding a guitar, with Champion behind him, the little six-guns attached to the sides of his bit.

"Back in the saddle again," Autry began to warble into the microphone, his whiskey voice terribly off key, "out where a friend is a friend." At this point he must have forgotten the rest of the words because he began humming the melody. No one cared. By ones, and then in groups, the entire audience began to rise, giving him a standing ovation, as he continued to hum.

I was seated at a table next to the president of a local bank and his wife. The wife, as she clapped enthusiastically, turned toward me, with tears in her eyes.

"Isn't it a shame," she said, "that young people today don't have heroes like this that they can look up to?"

Later, when the festivities were breaking up, I made my way over to Autry's table. His wife, Ina, was sitting next to him. I handed him the current issue of *Views & Reviews*, opened to the page which had publicity stills from *The Phantom Empire*.

"I thought," I said, "that you might be interested in reading this."

"My God," Autry said, looking at the stills, "where ever did you get hold of these?"

"Have you had a chance to look at the serial yet?" I asked.

"No," he said, and grinned. "But I'll give you a Gene Autry story for your researches, if you'd like. Being here at this hotel we're staying at reminded me of it. Do you know how I got into the hotel business? I once went on a short vacation with Ina and, once we were checked into a room, she complained to me about the lowness of the hangar bar in the closet. I went out and bought the hotel on the spot. 'There, Ina,' I said to her, 'now you can remodel it to suit yourself'."

Gene smiled and Ina smiled.

It was not really a story I thought I could use about his work in Western films, but I thanked him and took my leave.

I did not hear from Gene Autry again until some time in 1974, when I was completing work on *The Filming of the West*. I sent him the two chapters that were devoted to him. Not long after I received a copy of a telegram he had sent to my publisher threatening to sue them and me if they dared publish what I had written about him. The publisher, which at the time had sports writer Mickey Herskowitz and Autry both under contract to coauthor the official Gene Autry autobiography, was further threatened by Autry that, in addition, if they did not suppress those chapters, he would take his book elsewhere. The chapters were submitted to the legal department of the publisher for a careful scrutiny, after which Autry was told he *could* take his book elsewhere, if he so desired. Apparently he did not since, in due course, it appeared.

On page 172 of *Back in the Saddle Again* (Doubleday, 1978), by

Gene Autry with Mickey Herskowitz, the statement occurs: "A Western movie critic once wrote of me, 'Autry's role as an investor has permitted him to consume alcohol at a fantastic rate and never have it negatively influence the companies he financed.' I guess that is what you might call a left-handed compliment." The Western movie critic was I and the quotation was from "The Vanishing Legion" installment I had given Autry in Oklahoma City. "Drinking impairs your judgment and eventually your health," the coauthors remarked a few pages later. "I appeared on stage, a very few times, when I was less than cold sober. Socially, I said or did things that embarrassed me later. But I learned. I can't do much now about the rumors and exaggerations. I believe my success in business answers the worst of them."

While working on the book, Autry asked John Wayne to autograph a publicity photo of himself suitable for reproduction, and Wayne complied, inscribing it: "Gene — A lot of water has run under the bridge, whiskey too. Duke. 1976."

The public raised to believe in heroes will resist in every way being reminded that these men are *not* heroes, but only men. Autry, like Ken Maynard, Tom Mix, and so many movie cowboys, not least of all John Wayne, really came to believe that if he was not exactly like the hero image he projected on the screen, he ought to be, not only for his youthful public, but for himself and for his own sense of well being.

Autry put it best himself in *Back in the Saddle* when he explained why he did not go to Smiley Burnette's funeral. "Death, accidents, illnesses are just difficult for me to handle," he said. "I won't attempt to explain that or defend it. Maybe it is related in a sense to why I wanted my films to entertain the spirit, not challenge it. Why the endings were always happy and the plots often implausible. I felt that people saw enough unpleasantness in the normal turn of the wheel. I saw no need to force on them more of the hard reality that each of us comes to in our own time, in his own way."

What I have had to say about Ken Maynard, and what presently I will say about Gene Autry, comes about as a result of my separating their screen personas from them as human beings, something which I know, from experience, they were unable to do. If I am critical in what I say of their screen personas, it is because I feel it was in a way harmful for two or three generations of Americans — indeed people all over the world — to be brought up believing fervently in these mythical characters. The men who played these characters could not support the contradictions this entailed and I seriously doubt if it was very different for the viewers who watched them and wanted to believe in them. My critique, if I have one, of the Western is not so much on aesthetic but on psychological grounds and, quixotic though it might seem, on *ethical* grounds.

According to Autry and Herskowitz in *Back in the Saddle*, Autry did not importune Nat Levine for a chance to appear in pictures; Autry did not even seek out Levine. Rather Levine, because he owed a laboratory bill to Herbert J. Yates and wanted financing from Yates for *In Old Santa Fe*, sought out Autry, who was recording for the American Record Company, in which Yates was a major stockholder. The coauthors further claim that Gene was dubious about a film career, actually for a time did not want one, and was hired for a flat $500 by Levine — without knowing that this was to be the sum until Autry left Chicago after their initial interview and showed up at Mascot — and a similar amount for *Mystery Mountain*, and that then, reluctantly, Autry agreed to star in *The Phantom Empire*, which they claim was a thirteen-chapter serial, rather than a twelve-chapter serial.

I doubt if even in 1934 Gene Autry would have gone anywhere for anybody without knowing beforehand how much he was to be paid. But that to one side, the narrative of events this chapter presents concerning Autry's first coming to work for Mascot has been checked and rechecked and confirmed by several individuals — Yakima Canutt, who was charged over a four-month period *prior* to *In Old Santa Fe* with training Autry in horsemanship, the late Joe Kane who first met Autry at that party Nat Levine arranged for Autry at his home and who was one of the original nay-sayers, Maurice Geraghty who worked on the screenplay for *The Phantom Empire* and had several sessions with Autry so he might better learn how to put him across on the screen, the late Smiley Burnette who was signed when Autry was and who was at the time under a personal contract to Autry whereby many of his songs eventually became the property of Autry's music publishing company, and Ken Maynard who was introduced to Autry by Nat Levine before they were to work together so as to get Maynard's approval. The narrative is borne out by the original contracts and agreements between Mascot and Autry. It is not the role of the historian to take sides; the preponderance of evidence, physical and verbal, is in support of Levine's version, not Autry's.

"We constantly strove to be pathfinders," Levine once remarked to me. "*The Phantom Empire* was one of the innumerable productions which proved it. Here was science fiction that would be readily acceptable today, and not considered old-fashioned." One cannot but agree with him, since *The Phantom Empire* was remade as part of the short-lived television series *Cliffhangers* (NBC, 1979). Had there been no *Phantom Empire*, there may well have been no *Flash Gordon* from Universal in 1936, budgeted at $360,000, or *Buck Rogers* from the same studio in 1939, and two more Flash Gordon serials. There for sure would have been no *Undersea Kingdom* from Republic in 1936 produced by Nat Levine and directed by Reeves Eason and Joe Kane, nor would science fiction have become so much a staple of serial production for the next fifteen years. Yet there is nothing more absurd than an empire 25,000 feet below the Earth's surface and a singing cowboy for whom the cliffhanger usually meant whether he would make it back to Radio Ranch in time for his daily two o'clock broadcast.

Part of the plot to *The Phantom Empire* we owe to James Church-ward, who wrote a series of books in the early thirties devoted to his scientific and mystical discovery of a strange civilization which vanished from the surface of the Earth more than 12,000 years before. The first book in the series was entitled *The Lost Continent of Mu* (I. Washburn, 1931). Churchward was anything but an empiricist and (as did Erich von Däniken with *Chariots of the Gods* [Putnam's, 1968] in our own time) he managed to make a tenable if farfetched hypothesis appear all the more sensational and incredible because of his own weird quirks and pet beliefs. The remains of the Muranian rock quarries might be what has been found on Easter Island and perhaps it is the statues of their gods which still survive. Churchward was convinced that Mu had been located in the Pacific Ocean, where today only the mountain tops remain as numerous islands. The unusual lump which in our age observers on the Moon have recorded in the Earth's contour in the area of Europe was anticipated by Churchward who hypothesized that some great suction process occurred within the Earth's interior, realigning the levels above the molten center. When this happened, according to Churchward, land jutted out in one place, a continent disappeared in another. Churchward, basing his record on ancient writings found in the Orient, called this continent Mu. Perhaps, he suggested, certain of the American Indian tribes are their descendants. The Mascot story department concocted another theory.

Wallace MacDonald, Gerald Geraghty, Maurice Geraghty (without credit), and Hy Freedman were employed on the screenplay. MacDonald, who had worked as an actor for many years, having starred in the chapter play *Breaking Through* (Vitagraph, 1921), and who had appeared with Ken Maynard at KBS as noted before, claimed at the time that the plot for *The Phantom Empire* came to him while he was in a dentist's chair, under the influence of nitrous oxide, or laughing gas. Maybe so. Here's his plot. When Mu sank beneath the Earth's surface, not all of its inhabitants were destroyed. Some survived and created a city within the interior. Basing his conception of this world on a combination of Jules Verne's *Journey to the Center of the Earth* (1864) and Edgar Rice Burroughs' novels of Tarzan's adventures inside the Earth's core, MacDonald conceived of a wholly advanced miraculous world, calling its citizens, aptly, Muranians. Even the credit crawl to each episode, with the theme from *Mystery Mountain* played beneath it, showed three different views of the scientific city of Murania. Undisturbed by the continual wars and conflicts of the surface people, the Muranians have lived for centuries in peace. They have developed a great many scientific wonders which, by surface standards, are nearly magical. Among their medical triumphs, they can resuscitate the dead. Almost all physical labor is performed by robots (which, I have been told, was wholly consistent with MacDonald's waggish sense of humor). The Muranians' work in the area of television permits them to record and perceive events at tremendous distances, while a series of special facial masks, covering the olfactory organs, permits them to breath the much drier air on the surface. Without these masks, they would be reduced to gasping inactivity. Surface men, conversely, do not seem inhibited by Muranian air, and do not apparently need any protection when they descend to the depths. Because of immense radium deposits, the Muranians have devised very powerful ray-projecting machines, one of which indeed brings about the ultimate destruction of their kingdom.

Mascot serials have always stressed fantasy elements, but none before had gone so far as *The Phantom Empire*. The Muranians have their own social order, although the viewer cannot help but think, as their society crumbles, that the dissent among certain elements, led by Wheeler Oakman as the Lord High Chancellor Argo, came only as a result of undue contact with the disorganized, perpetually warring world of the surface men. This is the one chapter play in which Mascot stepped beyond the confines of pure adventure and firmly into that realm which sober critics these days call "social relevance." There is both wistful sadness and aristocratic pride in the voice of Queen Tika, portrayed by Dorothy Christie, as she watches the behavior of the surface people, rushing about their business, obsessed with fighting and killing each other so that one man may gain control over another. The more the contact with the surface people, the stronger becomes these latent impulses among the Muranians, finally heralding the dissolution of their mighty, tranquil, enlightened civilization.

Gene Autry, the blandest of screen personalities, beginning here but throughout his career was incapable of showing emotion convincingly. For this reason, Levine felt he must be surrounded with a singing group, a stock company of competent performers, and between the two let them play on the feelings of the audience which Autry could never touch. In *The Phantom Empire* every sentence he uttered was spoken with painstaking care, his mind obviously on enunciation and diction, not meaning. But ultimately this did not matter. Without completely realizing it, the Mascot story department, Levine, and Autry himself had created the Autry fantasy. The Autry fantasy was totally divorced from reality. So, too, were Ken Maynard and Tom Mix, but the Autry fantasy, embodying as it did the notion of Gene Autry as a Western hero, differed from all the others associated with movie cowboys.

A fable may best illustrate what I mean. It is the fable of the little tailor. The little tailor was seated in his pantry one day, eating a jelly sandwich. Flies were attracted by the jelly and the tailor, in a fit of temper, swatted several of them. Proud of his accomplishment, he immediately sewed a championship belt for himself, imprinted with the words "Seven at One Blow." Unwittingly, people from all over the countryside attributed to the tailor the reputation of being a giant killer. They wanted to believe that such an inconsequential, diffident little man could be a giant killer. While walking in the forest one day, the tailor happened upon two particularly horrible and very powerful ogres. They had fallen into a deep sleep. The tailor, keeping his presence amongst them a secret, managed cunningly to invoke a fight between them, the upshot of which was that they killed each other in mortal combat and, standing on the sidelines, he emerged the victor, winning not only his own kingdom but the fair princess in the bargain.

Prior to Autry's arrival on the screen, Western heroes were customarily portrayed as being strong, capable, occasionally austere men, believable frontier types who might actually have undertaken many of the heroic exploits attributed to them by the scenarios. In Autry's case this was not so because, physically and dramatically, it could not be so. So he had to be surrounded by a different kind of aura, if no less magical. He lived, it had to seem, a charmed life whereby, battling against frequently staggering odds, he invariably triumphed.

Autry was born on September 29, 1907, at Tioga, Texas, to Delbert and Nora Autry. After attending high school in Tioga, he went to work for the railroad as a night telegrapher and was working at the depot in Chelsea, Oklahoma, one night — as he tells the story — when he met Will Rogers who heard him strumming his guitar and singing and suggested he go on the radio. The character actor, Guinn "Big Boy" Williams, who had been cast in *Mystery Squadron,* and who had been given his nickname "Big Boy" by Rogers in 1919, once observed to me that it was interesting that Autry never told this story about himself and Will Rogers until after Rogers was dead. It does not matter if the story is true or apocryphal; what matters is that it is wholly consistent with the Autry fantasy. In Autry's Westerns, this meant that he never initiated any of the action, but rather was drawn into it. In his autobiography, Autry did not think of being a professional singer until Will Rogers encouraged him to do it; nor did Autry want to be in films, not until Nat Levine repeatedly pleaded with him. Autry and Herskowitz articulated this far better than I could hope to in *Back in the Saddle.* "So many singers would go on, like Jolson, and not only sing *at* the audience and down their throats, they had to have a runway so they could get closer," they wrote. "They just overpowered you. I could never do that. I just laid back and let the audience come to me. It was like listening to the boy next door sing. I thought of myself as a showman, not a great entertainer. I never tried to be more or less than Gene Autry."

The reader may recall how the screenplay for *Harmony Lane* could have been compared to one long series of song cues. When, in his auto-biography, Autry came to tell of his songwriting activities and his hit songs, it reads the same way. When an amorous female fan wrote Autry a letter, she remarked "'I looked at the stars in the heavens.... I saw millions of them. But *you* are the only star in my blue heaven.' And that was where I got the idea, and the title, for one of my early hits: 'You're the Only Star in My Blue Heaven.' ... I recorded more than three hundred tunes, helped write a third of them, mostly with Fred Rose, had *nine* that sold a million or more, and can't read a note of music." One hastens to point out that the Autry fantasy was not an entirely isolated phenomenon in the thirties. One of the most popular, perhaps even *the* most popular film director of that period was Frank Capra, whose films projected similarly diffident and improbable leading men, even if it meant casting against type as in the case of Gary Cooper in *Mr. Deeds Goes to Town* (Columbia, 1936), or the roles enacted by a young James Stewart in *You Can't Take It with You* (Columbia, 1938) and *Mr. Smith Goes to Washington* (Columbia, 1939); indeed the conflicts in *You Can't Take It with You* are solved by a song.

It is to Nat Levine's credit that he gambled on Autry, that he both discovered Autry and risked starring him in a chapter play, that, rather than use the usual star build-up when so pressed for time, he had Autry use his own name to give him maximum exposure, even if it meant that the private Gene Autry and the public Gene Autry would become even more inextricably intertwined, but Levine was rather hesitant about Autry's value as a screen property and this led to an animosity between the two men. Because of Levine's opinion of Autry, the first Republic star biographies stressed elements more closely associated with the Tom Mix legend than with the Autry fantasy, that Autry had supposedly learned to ride before he could walk; that, like Ken Maynard, Autry had run away from home at fourteen to join a traveling show; that, also like Maynard, Autry had been a rodeo champion. When Tom Mix came to work on the Mascot lot, Autry fell in love with a light-tailed sorrel Mix used in hard riding sequences to double for Tony, Jr. He offered to buy the horse from Mix, and Tom sold him. The sorrel had been foaled the day Lindbergh had flown the Atlantic and was called Lindy. Autry changed his name to Champion. It was the first of three movie Champions that he would use. Autry also had his screen costumes, initially, designed by Trem Carr to closely resemble Ken Maynard's.

"I know that I owe about all I have to the devotion and support of the kids," Autry commented when his career on the screen reached its apex. "... To youngsters, Gene Autry is not simply a human being, but a kind of superman. They accept anything he does or says as the right thing. That's why Gene Autry has to be so careful about the way he handles himself."

Whereas William Boyd hated children, beginning with *The Phantom Empire* Autry liked to have them in his films, Frankie Darro and Betsy King Ross in *Empire* forming a sort of a vocal fan club, urging Gene on to daring feats in the serial, and Autry knew how to capitalize on it. Betsy King Ross, unfortunately, had grown several inches since she had appeared in *Fighting with Kit Carson*, to Levine's irk, and so she had to go through *Empire* with her shoulders hunched so as not to appear taller than Darro, when in fact she was.

While in the first few films Autry made for Republic following *Empire*, he would wind up with the girl, the Autry fantasy soon dispensed with this cliché. After all, if he was Gene Autry in every film, he could not possibly marry every girl he met. Romance, so long a vital ingredient of the Western, was thus done away with in the Autry vehicles and the heroine's role was confined to smiling when Gene sang, being upon occasion – when she was unduly spoiled – spanked by Autry, and often a victim to the villains' evil designs.

Levine made another, very substantial contribution to the Autry fantasy. I have commented on Levine's penchant for stooge comedy. When it came to Autry, given Levine's doubts about Gene's virility, a stooge was more vital than ever, if only to offset and exaggerate the Autry persona. Now a stooge and a sidekick are not the same thing. William S. Hart had used Lucien Littlefield as a sidekick in *Tumbleweeds* (United Artists, 1925), and, since that time, Western heroes would frequently have a saddle partner of somewhat less intelligence and capacity than they possessed. But for Autry, the sidekick had to be replaced by the stooge, a person without dignity. In *The Phantom Empire*, Smiley Burnette and William Moore provided the stooge comic relief, but their comedy was confined to slapstick antics and preposterous stupidity. In Autry's early years at Republic, Burnette moved right along with him as his stooge, and thus, in tandem, they made way for countless other "B" Westerns to imitate their example and nearly every cowboy star during the forties had at least one stooge, some of them two or more.

Autry's films enjoyed a large following almost at once, but principally in rural areas where Saturday night at the local movie theatre would see farmers and their families forsaking traditional barn dances to attend the latest Autry opus. Autry's Westerns for these rural sectors provided much of the atmosphere of the cowboy jamboree and attracted much the same kind of middle American audiences that Lawrence Welk would during many successful years on television. Beginning in 1938, when Nat Levine left Republic and Autry and Armand Schaefer, who was Autry's production manager all his years making films, had at last wrenched control over the formats of the films, the Radio Ranch idea from *The Phantom Empire* was expanded, whereby action became somewhat incidental to the singing and the music-making. Only in the late forties and early fifties was this trend diminished in favor of increased action.

What did remain unchanged from 1935, when Autry made his first feature Western, and 1953 when he made his last one, was the Autry fantasy. In *Red River Valley* (Republic, 1935), when a group of dam workers refuse to return to their jobs unless they are paid, Autry solves the problem in what became for him the characteristic Autry fashion: he leads them in the title song. When it is over, he comments: "Don't you feel better? There's nothing like a song." In *Mexicali Rose* (Republic, 1939), Noah Beery, Sr., playing a Mexican bandit, captures Autry and Burnette. Tied up at the campfire, Autry discovers that Beery has a secret passion. Not women, or liquor, or gambling; it's collecting Gene Autry records. When a member of the gang accidentally kicks over Beery's portable phonograph, on which he is playing Autry's rendition of the title song, smashing the record, before Beery can shoot the offender, Gene takes up the song. Beery, thus learning Autry's identity, asks him to sing another song, which Autry does. It brings tears to Beery's eyes and he resolves to reform and commits himself to helping Autry save an orphanage from the schemings of oil speculators.

The Autry fantasy said, in point of fact, that every human problem, every dislocation, every tragedy, could be dispelled, not with hard riding, not with straight shooting, but with the magic of a song. Maybe the people who attended Autry's films actually believed this, at least while they were in the theatres. Even later, in films like *The Cowboy and the Indians* (Columbia, 1949), when Autry was confronted with the sufferings and poverty of a tribe of Indians, triumphantly at the end of the film Autry rode into their village laden with gifts and singing "Here Comes Santa Claus."

In the sixth episode of *The Phantom Empire*, when Autry is in Murania, the notion is advanced that perhaps his lungs should be dissected to learn why he insists on singing all the time. Obviously, even with their advanced science, the Muranians were insufficiently perspicacious to grasp the significance of the Autry fantasy.

Yet Autry stopped singing eventually, not, as he would have it, entirely of his own volition. Johnny Bond—who played guitar for him on the opposite side of the microphone on radio—all the years, after the war, that Autry went out on the road, went with him, taking 8mm home movies. His earliest films are of Autry's appearances at Madison Square Garden in New York where Autry would play to audiences of 25,000 people twice a day. The last film is from 1960, after Autry had been off the radio since 1956— when the Wrigley people, who had sponsored him, had fired him and replaced him with his stooge of those years, played by Pat Buttram (in private life neither Smiley Burnette nor Pat Buttram were the roles they portrayed as part of the Autry fantasy)—after he had been off television since 1955, after he had been out of the theatres since 1953. In it, Autry, very heavy and somewhat inebriated, is playing to an audience of less than a hundred people. The Autry fantasy may not have changed, but perhaps the willingness of the American public to believe in it had.

The question arises, if Autry himself so believed in the Autry fantasy, how did he accumulate his millions? Do nice people like Gene Autry become millionaires and remain nice? This leaves out one factor, a factor which Nat Levine above all would recognize: luck. A group of oil speculators from Texas once approached Autry and offered him a percentage of the profits of their syndicate, should they discover oil, simply for the use of his name and what it symbolized. Nineteen of the twenty wells drilled came in gushers. Autry used his share to start his own syndicate, with nearly identical results. Yet Autry's role in business was usually a passive one, letting people come to him, investing when he thought it opportune, withdrawing when it seemed precarious. Autry in fact fared best where he remained personally uninvolved, almost indifferent, in much the same way that he sang nonchalantly through his films and recording sessions. The acquisition of wealth itself, however, preoccupied Autry throughout his career, even when he was a showman and entertainer. The one time where he permitted his passion to become a factor, in the building of a championship team out of the Los Angeles Angels, he had less than a marked success. On the occasions I have talked with Autry, I have come away with the distinct feeling that he had been sizing me up, testing me to see just how much of the Autry fantasy I was willing to believe and, to the extent he perceived I did not accept it, he became hostile and distant.

Autry should perhaps be given the final word. "I can't do much now about the rumors and exaggerations. I believe my success in business answers the worst of them. ... The best way to silence a detractor anytime is to prosper. That always confounds them. There is a satisfaction that comes from success in business that is less personal, but also less selfish, than success in show business or sports." If success in business is to be the criterion, then in Gene Autry's case belief in the Autry fantasy worked.

Levine budgeted *The Phantom Empire* at $70,000, most of which went into the special effects. It became the third top-grossing serial in Mascot history.

The late Stanley Edgar Hyman wrote in "A Critical Look at Psychology" in his book *The Promised End* (World, 1963) that Jung "has made an impressive range of occultisms part of his dogmatic system, of which the possibility of flying saucers is only the latest and funniest." There are a number of issues that might be taken with this statement, but I will forego all but one. Hyman could not have read Jung's book *Flying Saucers: A Modern Myth of Things Seen in the Skies*, now contained in Volume X of Jung's *Collected Works* (Princeton University Press, 1970), although the book originally appeared in 1958. If he had read it, he would have found in the preface that Jung wrote for the first English edition, Jung's query: "Why should it be more desirable for saucers to exist than not? The following pages are an attempt to answer this question."

"In [H.G.] Wells' time," Issac Asimov wrote in his introduction to a new edition of Wells' *The War of the Worlds* (Fawcett, 1968), "the nations of Europe controlled virtually all of Africa and large sections of Asia. They did not seriously consider that the 'natives' of these regions had much in the way of rights. They dominated the Africans and Asians as the Martians dominated Earthmen and felt justified in doing so, as, no doubt, the Martians did." If, as Jung surmised, we began in the fifties to look to the heavens and to project onto them all our desperate hopes for salvation, in the mid thirties contact between one culture and another, alien culture still meant one or another of them must be destroyed, just, as I've said, Western films nearly always insisted that when the superior white man's civilization confronted the Native American, one of them, the latter, had to vanish. Murania, in one sense, might be a metaphor for the unconscious, but a metaphor for salvation it could not be.

Eleven

Tom Mix Rides Again

The state's rights system of marketing which Mascot had used since its inception was an outgrowth in the twenties and thirties of the battles of pioneers like William Fox and Carl Laemmle with the Motion Picture Trust in the first decade of the twentieth century. While major producing companies, including in time those of Fox and Laemmle, set up their own exchange networks for the distribution of their product, many of the small, independent motion picture manufacturers could not afford it. For one thing, their annual production schedule was insufficient to occupy fully a series of exchanges in key cities, much less service ten or fifteen thousand low-grade theatres in which their pictures regularly played. In some cases, as with the Educational Film Corporation of America, several of these small producing companies banded together for purposes of financing and distribution, combining their joint product, and used the exchanges of one of the major producing companies for dissemination. Until the mid thirties, Educational used the Fox exchanges. Trem Carr of Monogram attempted a similar set-up independently in the early thirties.

While flat rentals without percentage terms were still common in the thirties, rental fees were higher than before and, faced with the Depression, thousands of theatres could not afford to play pictures distributed by the majors even if they had been inclined to do so. Some of the majors, like Paramount and Fox, owned sizable theatre chains in which their pictures customarily played, while Loew's, Inc., owned Metro-Goldwyn-Mayer; some of the majors, like Universal and the rapidly growing Columbia Pictures, owned no theatres. Satisfied with serving a different audience, the low priced theatres booked through the independent exchanges. Rentals were as low as $15-$25 for three days. The exchange, working with several producing firms, would purchase distribution rights to the films they distributed, in the mid thirties as before, for a period of from three to five years, and in that period would attempt to get as many play-offs as they could.

From the start, of course, Nat Levine had worked through these independent exchanges. They handled his serials and, eventually, his features. The serials were booked at $5 a chapter (or, if pressure was very great from Universal, somewhat less). During the years in which Universal principally competed with Mascot, Levine came to control a sizable portion of the chapter play market. In 1934-1935 a few independent companies still tried making an odd serial or two, also marketed via state's rights, with prices even lower than Mascot's — the thinking being that as Mascot improved its product and raised its franchise fee to the exchanges such inexpensive chapter plays would have a better chance. Sherman Krellberg's *The Lost City* (Krellberg, 1935) was one such serial. In general a wretched chapter play, worse than anything Mascot ever produced, Krellberg made enough money on it to purchase rights to re-release the first six Hopalong Cassidy pictures Harry Sherman produced originally for Paramount release.

It was natural enough that as Mascot's reputation solidified and their serials improved in terms of production values, Levine should try to raise his franchise fees to the exchanges. Yet, even so, no matter how he might increase production, he had no exclusive contract with any exchange because he still had inadequate product to dominate their sales volume or the market demand. He had to put up with the packaging of Mascot features and serials by the exchanges with product from other companies. In 1935 Mascot released eight features and four serials. It was scarcely enough to warrant any kind of distribution other than state's rights. Because of this persistent situation, Levine was inclined to lend Herbert J. Yates an ear with his talk about merging several independent producing companies and setting up a series of corporate exchanges to handle the united product. He would then be able to process all bookings directly, charge still higher rental rates, and participate more significantly, corporately and personally, in the popularity of the films he produced.

Once the thirties came to a close, state's rights distribution was nearly at an end. It is to Yates' credit that he foresaw this development. Independent producers increasingly would band together and form their own corporately controlled distribution outlets. Monogram Pictures, reorganized after Trem Carr sold out his interest in Republic, was but a notch above the lowliest of all such companies, Producers Releasing Corporation. Monogram, PRC, Astor Pictures (a successor to Grand National combining new product with the vintage product of Tiffany, WorldWide, KBS, Reliable, Supreme, Freuler, Diversion, Allied, Ambassador, and several other small firms), and their like, bought up or completely dominated most of the remaining independent exchanges in the forties. Producers actually got a better deal this way, with the releasing company packaging the product from all of these individual production firms, or just from their own firm, rather than the exchanges doing it themselves, and charging the theatres directly for play-offs.

It is anything but astonishing that Universal made a million dollars on *The Indians Are Coming* when one considers their exchange network, the cost of the film at $160,000, the hoopla, the free Indian headdresses given to the first 100 children in attendance, the novelty of sound, and the following Tim McCoy had from his M-G-M Westerns and Allene Ray had from her Pathé serials. *The Miracle Rider* (Mascot, 1935) was Levine's second serial for 1935 and with its negative cost of $80,000 — $40,000 of which went to Tom Mix at the rate of $10,000 a week for four weeks' work—it cost half of the Universal effort, yet Levine so excelled at marketing it that it equalled the gross receipts of *The Indians Are Coming* and on the state's rights market! The first chapter was released in five reels and, it was suggested, should be marketed as the bottom half of a double bill to attract wider audiences. Rental was $15 for the initial episode and $5 for each subsequent chapter. It was Mascot's first fifteen chapter serial and Levine used this fact to convince exchange men and exhibitors alike that his costs were commensurately greater. It cost the exhibitor $85 to play the entire serial and the chapter play was effectively booked into over 12,000 theatres, winning the day over Universal's summer entry, *The Roaring West* (Universal, 1935), with Buck Jones—on the whole an unspectacular and, for Jones, disappointing entry. *The Phantom Empire* had been very strong competition for *Rustlers of Red Dog* (Universal, 1935) with Johnny Mack Brown and further disposed the market to accept the latest Mascot production. But maybe most of all it was Tom Mix's return to the screen that made the difference. Adults who remembered him from two decades before turned out with legions of youngsters to see the film. *The Miracle Rider* was a testament to the enduring magic of Tom Mix's appeal, the massive following he still retained, engendered by reissues of his Universal Westerns, his continuing circus appearances, and the radio show using his name. He was as much a legend as Daniel Boone and Davy Crockett. In the prologue to the picture, these folk heroes were shown, each in his own era representing the distinct values of the great American frontier hero, until the present day when all such values were to be found embodied in Tom Mix. As Mascot publicity expressed it at the time, Tom Mix was the "Idol of Every School Boy in the World," which included a lot of old-timers.

Despite Paul E. Mix's *The Life and Legend of Tom Mix* (A.S. Barnes, 1972), Gene Autry and Mickey Herskowitz in *Back in the Saddle* paid lip service to the Tom Mix legend. In their words: "Tom was the genuine article, an adventurer, a soldier of fortune who saw action in the Spanish-American War, in the Philippines, in the Boxer Rebellion in China, and on both sides of the Boer War. He punched cows in Texas, Oklahoma, and Kansas, and once left Mexico a few hours ahead of a firing squad. Tom deserted from the Army in 1902—according to Ripley's Believe It or Not—and never completed his military service. But no charges were ever brought against him. He was even a lawman, once a Texas Ranger and briefly a deputy U.S. marshal. Could anyone have written a character more colorful than Mix? He was no longer young when I met him, but he drove cars that were custom built and he wore lavish Western outfits. He was especially proud of a horsehair belt, fastened with a diamond-studded buckle, engraved with the legend: 'Tom Mix, America's Champion Cowboy'."

The true facts of the matter are far less romantic. Mix was born Thomas Edwin Mix on January 6, 1880, in a little hollow in Pennsylvania between the Pennsylvania railroad line and Bennett's Branch of the Susquehanna River, known as Mix Run, of Ed and Elizabeth Mix. His older brother, Harry, was six years old, his sister, Emma, three. As a child of ten, Mix attended the Buffalo Bill Wild West Show at the Clearfield, Pennsylvania, fairgrounds and was struck by a burning desire to go West and become a lawman. As a child, Mix believed that whatever you may do, you must do it better than anyone else. He attended school at Dubois, Pennsylvania, where his family moved when he was four, and on April 26, 1898, the day after war had been declared on Spain, Tom enlisted in the Army, attached to Battery M, 4th Regiment, United States Artillery. He saw no action. While Mix was stationed in Virginia, he fell in love with Grace Allin and, during a furlough, the two were married on July 18, 1902.

Grace did not want a soldier for a husband. She put it to Tom succinctly, it was either her or the Army. In October, 1902 Mix ran off with Grace and by November was listed as a deserter. The military was quite casual in those days about desertion when a war was not in progress, much of the thinking still consistent with the Colonial notion of a volunteer army except in times of national emergency. Nothing was done to apprehend Mix and no charges were ever brought against him even when he became one of the most famous Americans of his generation, although, when he died, it took John Ford, who had once directed him, to intercede with the War Department to get special permission to have Mix's coffin draped with the American flag, a permission granted because of what Mix had come to represent about the United States.

Grace's father was not quite so lenient. He felt it outrageous for his daughter to be married to a deserter. Tom and Grace migrated to Guthrie, Oklahoma, where Grace taught school and Mix held classes in physical fitness. Grace finally deserted Mix, and her father was successful in getting the marriage annulled.

Mix took to odd jobs, including bartending at a saloon on Robinson Avenue in Oklahoma City. The saloon owner had a daughter, Kitty Jewel Perrine, with whom Mix promptly fell in love. Mix met Joe Miller while tending bar and asked him for a job with the 101 Ranch Wild West Show which quartered near Bliss, Oklahoma, and which was owned by the Miller brothers. Joe discussed the matter with his brothers, George and Zack, and Tom was offered $15 a week as a starting wage to go to work for them. Mix and Kitty were married at the Perrine Hotel on November 20, 1905. It was a foolish move. Mix felt compelled to conceal his marriage from the guests wintering at the Miller brothers' ranch—he was hired on as a greeter and was expected to charm and escort vacationing women from the East—and this did not set very well with Kitty. They were soon divorced.

Mix wanted to learn the cowboy arts—riding, roping, bulldogging, broncobusting, expert rifle and pistol shooting, knife throwing—but Zack Miller was not particularly impressed with his potential and Mix had to struggle doubly hard to convince Miller to give him a chance. In December, 1908, in Dewey, Oklahoma, Mix met and fell in love with Olive Stokes, a girl on vacation from a Montana ranch. Apparently Mix could not go to bed with a woman with whom he was not at least three-quarters in love, or without convincing himself that he was. For all that women would cost him – virtually all of the six million dollars he made during his career – what he wanted of them, it would appear, remained very simple. Other than occasional sexual companionship, Mix preferred being left to his own resources. He loved speed and danger and masculine conversation. He also had a tremendous penchant for fabricating tall tales about himself which delighted him the more when they were gullibly believed by his auditors. It was due to this that all of those fabulous exploits were ascribed to Mix later during his motion picture career, exploits which had no foundation whatsoever in reality.

On January 19, 1909, Tom and Olive were married and went to Miles City, Montana, for their honeymoon. When Mix returned, he thought he would try for a job with the Widerman Wild West Show on the basis of his three years' experience with the Miller brothers. Mix's specialty with this show was a rope act. When the show ended its season, back in Dewey, Oklahoma, on a lark, Mix borrowed a horse from the Miller brothers in order to enter a rodeo. He ended up breaking his leg in the competition and stabled the horse temporarily at the Mulhall ranch. The horse disappeared and the Miller brothers brought charges of theft against Mix. Mix offered Zack Miller a trade whereby he would appear with their show when it next played in Mexico City, which Miller accepted provisionally, but the entire matter would come up again when Miller was pressed for money and Mix had become a millionaire.

Sid Jordan, a friend of Mix's in Dewey, introduced Tom to his father, Sheriff John Jordan, and Mix told the sheriff that he needed steady employment now that he was married. Jordan assisted Mix in getting a job as night marshal in Dewey and it was while working in this capacity that Mix came to the attention of Francis Boggs, who was a film director with the Selig Polyscope Company that had come to Dewey to film a semidocumentary titled *Ranch Life in the Great Southwest* (Selig, 1910). Mix regaled Boggs, who was a ready believer, with stories about himself and his experiences. Boggs hired Mix as a stock handler on the picture and, when the unit was packing up to move to Flemington, Missouri, Boggs invited Tom and Olive to come along.

Mix had found a staunch ally in Boggs. Boggs thought it might be a good idea to get some of Mix's real-life, or supposedly real-life, adventures on film, even before *Ranch Life* was released. Mix starred in two short action films, *Briton and Boer* (Selig, 1909) and *Up San Juan Hill* (Selig, 1909), which had such a salutary effect on Colonel Selig, the head of the company, that Selig put Mix under contract. Mix appeared in all kinds of films, not just Westerns, and he was not always the star. In 1912, Mix left Selig briefly to try the rodeo circuit and also worked a short stint for Will A. Dickey's Circle D Wild West Show, but by 1913 he was back before the cameras. In the interim, Selig, in view of the continuing popularity of the Broncho Billy Anderson Western two-reelers from Essanay, had decided to concentrate on his own Western series, and he put Mix in charge of production, sometimes writing the stories himself, sometimes directing them, and, of course, starring in them.

When Mix began using Selig contract actress Victoria Forde regularly in his films as the girl, it should not come as too much of a surprise that he fell in love with her off screen as well as on. Divorcing Olive, once Mix and Vicky Forde were signed in 1917 by William Fox to star together, Mix declared his feelings and in 1918 they were married. Although Mix had had ambitions of settling down on the ranch he and Olive had acquired near Prescott, Arizona, and there to live with their small daughter, Ruth, it was not to be, and Mix settled instead in Hollywood permanently.

It may seem incredible today the way Tom Mix was worshipped in the twenties when a star at Fox. He asked for, and the studio was doubtless justified in paying him, $17,500 a week by 1922. He bought a $250,000 mansion with a neon sign on top which flashed his name at the heavens all night long; he filled a seven car garage with fancy imports; and he built permanent sets for his Westerns at Mixville, a tract of some sixty acres located in the Fox Hills. When Buck Jones joined Fox and began making Westerns, Mix, looking over his studio biography and noting that Jones had broken horses for the British during the Boer War and had served in the U.S. Army in the Philippines, quickly added these credits to his own screen biography.

Mix's first screen horse had been Old Blue. When Old Blue died in 1917, Tony succeeded him. When, in 1933, Mix decided to retire Tony because of age, Tony presumably related his protest to Jack Hill for an article in *Movie Classic* for the January, 1933, number. The article is interesting because it points up so graphically how much a world legend Tom Mix had become, and Tony with him. "If I were to circulate a petition for reinstatement," Tony the horse was quoted as saying, "there would be plenty of signers—people I've met, prominent ones, too. There would be ex-President Coolidge—I've been photographed with him; likewise President Hoover. I also knew Presidents Taft, Wilson, and Harding. Four times I visited the White House, once inside to meet Mrs. Harding. Forty-eight governors including Alfred E. Smith and Franklin D. Roosevelt, and mayors by the hundreds are my personal friends. Furthermore, royalty and foreign notables would come to my rescue. The Prince of Wales chatted with me in Tetterhalls, London. I met President von Hindenburg in Berlin, and the late President Gaston Doumergue in France. Sir Arthur Harris, Lord Mayor of London, looked me over and said I was a fine horse, and der Herr Sehr Hoch-geboren Heinrich von Kleinberg, Burgermeister of Berlin, had the same idea, only in German. On the same trip, I was presented to Prince Henry of Prussia; Queen Marie of Roumania; the Prince and Princess of Belgium; the Duke of Veraga, in Spain; Cardinal Merry del Val in Brussels and the Burgermeister of Amsterdam...." The list goes on and on.

It was William Fox's conviction in 1927 that the coming of sound spelled doom for the Western film. Earlier he had let Buck Jones go and now he did not renew Tom Mix's contract, despite the fact that Mix's

Westerns were still doing very well. Joseph P. Kennedy, with Film Booking Office, acted with alacrity, and Mix was signed to make a series of Westerns and to be paid $15,000 a week for doing so. Kennedy was in the midst of the merger plans mentioned previously and he wanted a series of pictures that would rack up impressive grosses; he felt Tom Mix's name alone sufficient to guarantee a substantial box office. The Westerns, unfortunately, were very cheaply made and they were of little credit to either Mix or Film Booking Office. *Photoplay*, whose reviews were reliable in those days, said of *The Drifter* (FBO, 1929) that it was Mix's "swan song, his last picture on his last contract. It won't emblazon the famous Mix initials in film history. Just another Western...."

Tom Mix announced his retirement from motion pictures. He began that year, 1929, to make personal appearances with the Sells-Floto Circus, owned by John Ringling. His name as a headliner brought in the crowds and by means of a percentage agreement Mix's earnings climbed as high as $20,000 a week. And Mix needed the money. The stock market crash had wiped out over a million dollars in paper assets. Mix felt constrained to sell property he had purchased in Arizona and was even tempted to dispose of his home. Zack Miller, opening the old lawsuit about the stolen horse, wanted money, and Mix finally agreed to pay off $20,000 in notes held against Miller, discounting them to about $2,000.

In 1930 matters went from bad to worse. Mix's jaw had been shattered as a result of an accident and he had false teeth which, he felt, impeded his ability to deliver dialogue. He was terrified at the prospect of sound films. He had no alternative but to work with the circus. What this meant in actuality was that for forty-odd weeks a year Mix was on the go, doing one and sometimes two performances a day. In October, 1929, at the time of the crash, Mix had been drinking heavily, fell from his horse during a performance in Dallas, and shattered his shoulder. It was wired together. Several weeks later the shoulder bothered him to the point where it had to be rewired. By November, 1930, he was hospitalized, complaining of back trouble. The wiring had to be removed because it was found to be causing arthritis of the back.

In addition to the physical discomfort, in March, 1930, Mix was forced to appear in tax court and was fined $175,000 in back taxes plus $1,000 each on three counts of accidental tax evasion. In June, 1930, Mix tried to prevent his daughter Ruth from marrying Douglas Gilmore at Yuma, Arizona. When he failed, he cut off her allowance of $225 a month which he had been paying her since his divorce from Olive. Ruth brought suit against him. The case was settled in Mix's favor on July 5, 1930 and, ironically, on July 9, 1930, Ruth's marriage ended in an annulment.

Vicky Forde Mix, who had not bargained on Tom's being on the road so much and who was terrified by his drinking and unhappiness – she told the divorce court that Tom would frequently twirl a .45 on his finger during their arguments – wanted out of their marriage and was awarded a handsome property settlement, including the Mix mansion. Tom was in despair. "When a man's been married half a dozen times," he remarked with some exaggeration, "any sentiment about anniversaries is as cold as the ashes of last year's campfire. Payin' all them alimonies sorta drowns out the romance." This did not stop him, however, from marrying a fifth time, to Mabel Ward, an aerial performer with the Sells-Floto Circus, in Mexico in February, 1932.

"You're asking me if I'll go back to the pictures again?" Mix said in an interview for *Shadowplay Magazine*. "I figger it this way. A fella can't live on buttons. And that's all we were gettin' paid at the studios a while back. So I figgered anyhow that if I left the studios, I had enough buttons on my breeches and enough silver on Tony to let me and Mrs. Mix eat for a while yet.... But I may go back. Anyway, it isn't for lack of offers." Presently it was revealed that Tom Mix would be returning to the screen as a Universal star.

Mix was fifty-two. Even if he got past his fear of sound recording equipment, kept dying his hair a shiny black, overcame his difficulty with his dentures, tried his best to make it as a dramatic actor, he had always taken pride in doing his own stunts and he did not feel the years he was carrying, and the amount of injuries which he had had and which now were plaguing him, were conducive to making action films. Yet an offer of $10,000 a week coupled with renewed exposure on the screen and the boost it would give his personal appearances was impossible to turn down.

His first film on the new contract was *Destry Rides Again* (Universal, 1932), based on a novel by Max Brand, many of whose stories he had brought to the screen when he had been a star at Fox. The films which followed were of unusually high quality and certainly superior to any other Western series produced in the decade. But it was arduous. While filming *Hidden Gold* (Universal, 1932), Tony took a spill and injured his hip, Mix breaking three ribs, complicated by internal injuries. As the gruelling schedule continued of a new picture every seven weeks, Mix began increasingly to feel that he was too old and tired to keep pace. Finally, after his ninth film, he went to Uncle Carl Laemmle and asked to be released from his contract.

"I've nearly died twice makin' these films," he told Laemmle. "The risks aren't worth it any more."

Mix signed for the 1933-1934 season with the Sam B. Dill Circus, which traveled some 14,000 miles in its motorized units. In 1935 Mix bought out Dill, renaming the enterprise the Tom Mix Circus. He paid $400,000 for it. Under his ownership, the show traveled 13,275 miles in 1935. Mix thought that perhaps another film series might help popularize the Circus. It was at this opportune juncture that Nat Levine happened upon the scene.

"I was mad at conditions I saw and read about each day," Mix commented in a press conference, explaining his decision to return to the screen. "Criminals on the loose. Boys and girls learning Communist propaganda in schools. Crime news filling the papers. So I figured I could help by returning to the screen in a picture which would set an example for kids to follow — one with good old-fashioned virtues and Western justice. When Mascot Pictures Corporation showed me the story *The Miracle Rider*, I knew I had the kind of rip-snortin', he-man chapter play which would thrill every kid in town."

The outline of the story which Mix read showed him to be the champion of the Indians against modern, organized gangsters and munitions manufacturers. Many have since claimed that Mix should not have made the serial; that it is tedious, slow, flimsily plotted; and that his dramatic portrayal does not show him at his best. All of this is true. But it was to be the Tom Mix picture most people, following his death, were to see. His Universal features were reissued by Realart in 1936, but after that they virtually disappeared and were never released to television except for an odd title here or there in one or another isolated market.

To keep on schedule, each scene was shot rapidly with no attention to Mix's performance, or anyone else's. Mix was doubled by Cliff Lyons in nearly all the exteriors. The doubling permitted two and sometimes three units to be shooting at once, whereas Mix confined his work week to five days with limited calls. The rest of the cast was not particularly notable. Joan Gale, who had had a minor role in *The Last of the Mohicans*, was cast as the romantic interest. Charles Middleton was the chief villain, but not a mystery man, heading up the standard heavies.

The Mascot publicity department mounted an impressive campaign, including a massive pressbook along with numerous press releases and news stories. This was coordinated with the M.M. Cole Company in Chicago issuing *Tom Mix's Song Book* with a song to which Tom wrote the lyrics, several that he had nothing whatsoever to do with, and a centerfold filled with production stills from *The Miracle Rider*. Armand Schaefer was assigned to direct Mix's scenes and Breezy Eason handled all the exteriors and much of the second unit work. In view of the concentration of talent which collaborated on the story—including Wellyn Totman who had worked on *Ladies Crave Excitement*, *Waterfront Lady*, and *Confidential*, Barney Sarecky who, in addition, supervised the serial, and Gerald and Maurice Geraghty—certainly it should have been better. Only the idea of calling the heavies by peculiarly memorable names was inspired, if that is the right word for it.

The prologue for the first episode—the chapter was titled "The Vanishing Indian"—opened in 1777 with the original thirteen colonies. Jay Wilsey, who had been Buffalo Bill, Jr., in a low-grade Western series in the silent era, although no real relation to William F. Cody, played Daniel Boone, to whom greedy white men remark: "The sooner we kill off the Indians, the better it will be for all of us." When Boone cannot prevent the pillaging of Indian lands, a massacre of the whites is the result, with the footage being lifted from the Huron attack on a wagon train leaving Fort William Henry in *The Last of the Mohicans*. In 1825 there are twenty states and two heavies knife an Indian chief which leads to an attack on a wagon train extrapolated from *Fighting with Kit Carson*. When there are thirty-four states in 1877, character actor Earl Dwire as Buffalo Bill tries to prevent a heavy from shooting a buffalo which leads to a pitched fight between the Cavalry and the Indians. In 1912, according to this mini-lesson in American history, the Indians have literally been driven back into a twenty-mile stretch of land ceded them as a reservation. Tom Mix's screen father is murdered trying to protect the Indians' rights. It is this wanton act which motivates Mix in 1930 to become a Texas Ranger and in this guise he becomes the lone paternalistic champion of the Indian cause, defeating Middleton and his gang in their efforts to steal a miracle explosive which they are secretly mining on the reservation. No triad hero here. As in the case of Ken Maynard, Tom Mix was his own show.

Now, however, since so many negative comments have been made about the scenario, I should also like to point out what unusual qualities it did possess. First, it did have Tom Mix, and, although he himself, off screen, may have become weary of playing Tom Mix, on screen he was still able to suggest at least in part the magic that had been for so long associated with his public persona. Second, unlike nearly all the previous Mascot chapter plays, *The Miracle Rider* did have a sensible development of plot along linear lines; indeed, this probably contributed to the sense of slowness, when compared to the hectic action of an illogical Mascot storyline. Third, and lastly, it perpetuated the Mascot attempt to combine the contemporary world, circa 1935, with the Old West, and in the radio-controlled firebird, an airplane, and in the miracle explosive, called X-94 in the script, it included science fiction ingredients as had *The Phantom Empire*.

"I was paid $25 a week," Maurice Geraghty recalled for me, "and worked six days a week, from 8:30 to 6:00, and I mean worked. It was a real sweatshop operation, but jobs were hard to come by at the time — the drag end of the Depression. Offices were located in a cement factory ... on the second floor above where they made cement, and studio space was rented when the pictures went into production [this was prior to Levine's leasing of the Sennett lot]. Across the street was a cemetery. You had a feeling that it wouldn't be long before you ended up there. ... I was appointed serial story supervisor, with Barney Sarecky as my boss-associate producer, for the Tom Mix serial.... We worked in conference, five or six writers. When an episode was blocked out satisfactorily, it was divided up among the writers to be put on paper in synopsis form. If you didn't know how to type, you learned fast, or got fired. Secretaries, who were also secretaries for the executives, were strictly for final script, typing stencils for mimeo. They did furnish paper and carbons, pencils and erasers, and rented typewriters, Underwoods, and they kept meticulous track of supplies so nobody could take anything home for private use. Synopses of each episode were sent into the executive offices for okay, also the screenplays, when written, but to my knowledge Nat Levine never got involved in the creative end of making the pictures, aside from determining what was to be made and who would be in it, also director, crew, etc. He was a promoter and money man, but you have to give him credit for picking the right things to make and the right men to create them for him."

Bob Kortman was again cast as an Indian, this time the treacherous halfbreed Longboat who betrays his tribe because he aspires to be a chief. Individual chapter titles used as a background a clip of Chief John Big Tree offering up a sacrifice, one of the few genuine Native Americans in the cast. The Indian village—the tribe was referred to as the Ravenhead Indians—was located on the Sennett studio back lot and was a Hollywood Poverty Row version of Navaho/Pueblo architecture.

Although presumably a Ravenhead maiden, Joan Gale was given the screen name of Ruth. This may, in its way, have symbolized Tom Mix's rapproachment with his daughter, Ruth Mix. In 1936 Mix traveled 12,236 miles with his Tom Mix Circus, making 217 stands, and 10,521 miles in 1937 making 195 stands. Ruth Mix joined him and stayed on tour with him, in part to watch over him since his fifth marriage had not been altogether successful. *The Miracle Rider* had been filmed in four weeks in spring, 1935. On October 4, 1935, Mix broke his leg when his horse fell during a performance at Alva, Oklahoma. He was injured again when the tent was flattened during a storm on May 20, 1936. His fortunes were sinking rapidly. His troupe had to be reduced from over a hundred performers to fewer than fifty, the band members were cut to eleven. Mix increasingly turned to drink, disillusioned, bitter, occasionally not answering his calls. He would become so depressed and violent that many were afraid of him. Sometimes, in the middle of the night, he would get into his high-powered sports car and drive for hours at great speeds to rid himself of his despair. Once he got into a fistfight with a spectator outside his circus tent and was taken to court for aggravated assault. In 1938, a very, very bad year for all circuses, the Tom Mix Circus closed for good.

On April 11, 1938, the Ralston Purina Company renewed their license to use the Tom Mix name on the *The Tom Mix Ralston Straightshooters* radio show, but with the additional provision that they be permitted to have Tom Mix's image endorse their products. A similar practice was being pursued by *The Lone Ranger* radio show, which was sponsored by Silvercup Bread, and a child could get his Lone Ranger badge only if he was able to persuade three neighbors to buy the sponsor's bread on their next trip to the food store. A good deed, therefore, had become by this time being a good American consumer and consuming precisely those products which good American heroes told you to consume, and to enlist others in conforming to the American way by also consuming those products.

Mix had an even more violent falling out with Ruth than he had had over her abortive marriage. In May, 1938, with a huge white stallion he called Tony II, Mix embarked on a second European tour. When he arrived in England, he was relieved of eight pistols and five rifles, the press commenting that Tom Mix represented "the largest armed force that has tried to land on British soil since the last attempt by the Stuarts, almost 200 years ago." Tom and Tony II were a big hit at the Birmingham Hippodrome in September, 1938. Having regained his firearms, Mix amazed the British public with his marksmanship. He could shoot a .45 slug at a butcher knife and put out burning candles situated on both sides with only one shot.

When he returned to the States, Mix moved his livestock to a small ranch about twenty miles from Hollywood, became better friends with his daughter Thomasina, from his marriage to Vicky, and the trip had brought him closer to Mabel. He went on personal appearance tours in the Southwestern states. He had just finished one such appearance in Tucson, Arizona, and was on his way to Phoenix on October 12, 1940, while his custom-built Cord roadster sped along the lonely highway. He was wearing fancy boots, a diamond-studded belt buckle — the one he had shown off to Gene Autry, and a white ten-gallon Stetson. In his pockets he had stuffed $6,000 in cash and $1,500 in traveler's checks. "I ride into a place owning my own horse, saddle, and bridle," he had once summed up the Tom Mix screen persona. "It isn't my quarrel, but I get into trouble doing the right thing for somebody else. When it's all ironed out, I never get any money reward."

Tom came upon a highway detour. He swerved his car, but he was going too fast. The Cord went down a dry wash and up the other side, where it overturned, pinning him beneath. He may have known no pain. A metal suitcase, on the back ledge of the car, broke his neck upon impact. When his crushed body was finally freed, Tom Mix was dead. His white suit was nearly unwrinkled.

He left behind an estate of $115,000, divided between Mabel and Thomasina. The Arizona Highway Commission erected a memorial to him, a riderless horse on the spot where he met his death. "In memory of Tom Mix," the inscription read, "whose spirit left his body on this spot and whose characterizations and portrayals in life served to better fix memories of the old west in the minds of living men." Gene Autry regarded the occasion as an opportunity to give a special show at Madison Square Garden, paying tribute to Mix as one of the leading promoters of cowboy sports. A different time had found a different hero.

Twelve
The End of the Trail

Mascot produced and released only two more chapter plays following *The Miracle Rider.* The first of these was *The Adventures of Rex and Rinty,* the first episode of which was released on August 31, 1935. It was essentially a race horse drama uniting Rex once again with Rin Tin Tin, Jr. Kane Richmond, later to be a familiar figure in chapter plays, was cast as Frank Bradley, a popular polo player. Mischa Auer appeared as Tanaga, a high priest of a kingdom called Sujan where the natives worship a God-Horse, the latter portrayed of course by Rex. When chief heavy Harry Woods and his gang kidnap Rex in order to race him, it is Richmond, accompanied by Rex's new pal, "the dog with human intelligence" according to the chapter résumé, Rinty, who returns Rex to Sujan. Woods continues pursuit of the horse, attempting to turn the natives against worshipping him. Norma Taylor was cast as the girl and her role consisted of little save being photographed charmingly in tight riding pants. Smiley Burnette joined the cast for comic support, a variation of his "stooge" portrayal, but there was as little humor in his antics as there was, in retrospect, in the mockery the script made of the rights of the Sujanese to have unconventional religious beliefs.

Ford Beebe and Reeves Eason directed *The Adventures of Rex and Rinty* and, interestingly, Joseph H. Lewis, who would eventually become a film director with a cult following particularly in Europe, was credited with being supervising editor, as he had been on *The Miracle Rider,* replacing Wyndham Gittens. Gittens, on a freelance basis, supplied the script for *Ghost Patrol* (Puritan, 1936), a Western with Tim McCoy which employed a science fiction plotline, a gismo invented supposedly by Lloyd Ingraham which, when focused on an airplane in the sky, causes the engine to malfunction, forcing the plane to land. Beyond this, Gittens had been hired away from Mascot to work in the Universal serials story department where he collaborated on the story for *Ace Drummond* (Universal, 1936) and, with Ford Beebe, codirected *Tim Tyler's Luck* (Universal, 1937). Barney Sarecky, who supervised production on both *The Adventures of Rex and Rinty* and the final entry, *The Fighting Marines* (Mascot, 1935), would soon follow Gittens to Universal. Joseph H. Lewis would also join Universal briefly, following the Mascot merger, being assigned the direction of some of that studio's Bob Baker singing Westerns.

Jack Marta, who would have a long career as a contract cinematographer with Republic Pictures, joined William Nobles to film *The Fighting Marines.* Joseph Kane, nearly all of whose years would be spent working for Republic, joined Reeves Eason as the codirector. *The Fighting Marines* was released through the Republic exchanges, beginning with the first chapter on November 23, 1935, to the final episode on February 8, 1936. The subtitle for the serial read "U.S. Marines Follow the Trail of Adventure" and, in more than one sense, the chapter play could conceivably be regarded as a U.S. Marines recruiting film.

The story line had it that the Marines in trying to establish a landing field on Halfway Island were being sabotaged in their efforts by a mysterious criminal known as The Tiger Shark. Grant Withers, who had played second lead to Buck Jones in *The Red Rider* (Universal, 1934) and who would presently star in both *Jungle Jim* (Universal, 1937) and *Radio Patrol* (Universal, 1937) as a result of his work in *The Fighting Marines,* was cast as Corporal Lawrence while Adrian Morris, brother to actor Chester Morris and usually a heavy, was cast as Sergeant McGowan. Ann Rutherford, in an early role, was given the feminine lead and George Lewis, who had appeared in *The Wolf Dog,* was also in the cast. Jason Robards, Sr., cast as a diffident servant, is revealed in the final chapter to be The Tiger Shark.

Although he did not receive screen credit, the remarkable special effects connected with the model work for the radio gravity gun, used by The Tiger Shark and his minions, was the work of Howard Lydecker, Jr., who would soon become head of the special effects department at Republic Pictures. Unfortunately, despite the amount of writing talent assigned to the chapter play — including Wallace MacDonald, Maurice Geraghty, and Barney Sarecky — the plot was exceedingly thin, as if everyone working on the chapter play realized that it was being made only to fulfill existing contracts with exhibitors.

The Tiger Shark's motivation was to safeguard his secret hideout on Halfway Island. This of itself was not a common ingredient at Mascot. Most often it was the prospect of protecting or gaining possession of hidden wealth. Not that this ingredient could not be found in other pictures produced during the Depression, but at Mascot it was very nearly an obsession. In *The Lightning Warrior,* the Wolf Man wanted a rich gold deposit running underground throughout the district; in *Burn 'em Up Barnes* there were rich oil deposits on Lola Lane's property. The Voice had hoped to steal the oil fields in which Harry Carey was drilling. The Rattler wanted to keep his discovery of gold from the railroad. In *The Phantom Empire* a group of crooked scientists wished to avail themselves of the rich lode of radium ore beneath Radio Ranch and in *The Miracle Rider* Charles Middleton was secretly mining an extremely precious explosive.

Sometimes the wealth sought by the heavies was of a different kind, if no less real. In *Fighting with Kit Carson* it was a bullion shipment as it was also in *The Last of the Mohicans.* El Diablo held out the prospect of unbounded riches at the race track in *The Devil Horse* as did Rex in *The Adventures of Rex and Rinty*.

Greed is an easily comprehended motive because it is so widespread. But at Mascot, motive went beyond greed. A world view was projected in which possession of a fortune constantly in jeopardy was worth the risk of one's life at least eleven times, occasionally more often. After all, what did all these risks matter, if on the last throw, at the last moment, sustaining wealth was assured? It was aptly characteristic of the gambler's psychology.

At Universal, world dominion was the predominant theme of that studio's serials. Not so at Mascot where this element could only be found rarely, in *The Whispering Shadow*, in *The Three Musketeers* (confined to France's North African colonies), and, above all, in *The Miracle Rider* where the outside world was pictured as being poised for war, which indeed it was, and where the immense destructive capability of X-94 would make Charles Middleton, in the words of the screenplay, "the most powerful man in the world."

The value of human relationships began to matter in the Mascot chapter plays significantly in *The Last of the Mohicans* and even more so in *The Devil Horse*. In this fantasy world, the good at heart, those with strong loyalties, became rich in a nonmaterial sense. Frankie Darro and Harry Carey, having lost their families, still had each other at the end of *The Devil Horse*; Hawk-eye and Uncas were thrown together, in defiance of James Fenimore Cooper's original plot, at the conclusion of *The Last of the Mohicans*.

Nat Levine was a man of quick emotion, at times a difficult and obstinate executive, a cost-watcher, an egotist, but at the same time capable of sudden generosity. He was quite probably unaware of the spirit of the Mascot stock company as it grew up around him, filled with imaginative, hard-working, dedicated employees. Wyndham Gittens, Colbert Clark, Barney Sarecky, Reeves Eason (between terminations), Terry Kellum, Armand Schaefer, Yakima Canutt, Ernest Miller, William Nobles, Maurice and Gerald Geraghty — they loved the pictures they were making as much as any unit attached to a major studio, in some ways more. I am reminded that Louis B. Mayer used to say that his business was the only one he knew of where all the corporate assets went home at night through the studio gates. Nat Levine did not think like that. Unlike Mayer, whom he personally admired, he was not paternalistic. He did not make beautiful pictures with expensive budgets, pictures that often only glittered; he made inexpensive, delightful, exciting, entertaining pictures, and he was good at it. His people were not cowed the way even the biggest names in movies were at Metro-Goldwyn-Mayer. They were passionately creative. Levine gave them freedom and never demanded they exchange immediacy for slickness. They had a kinship at heart with the young; it never devolved into mere manufactured optimism. Only one thing did they have in common with all of the Hollywood studios: they lied about the character and quality of life on this planet as glibly, enthusiastically, and hopefully as any.

No Mascot film ever won an award. They were all formulary pictures, but innovative ones, made neither for prestige nor to please a sophisticated public, but to make money at the box office. They were made for fun. In 1935 Louis B. Mayer appraised Levine's stature. He was encouraged by what he thought Levine might be able to do given substantial budgets. As the merger to form Republic loomed on the horizon, Mayer offered Levine $3,500 a week to come to Culver City as an associate producer. Mayer wanted him to specialize in juvenile pictures. Levine considered Mayer's proposal.

"I leased it with an option to buy," Levine commented with regard to the old Sennett studio, "but never exercised the option, principally because I always needed all our additional funds to expand film production." Herbert J. Yates' proposal to Levine came to this: Mascot should merge with Monogram Pictures and Consolidated Film Industries to form Republic Productions while this new corporate entity would simultaneously buy out Liberty Pictures, Majestic Pictures, and Chesterfield Pictures, including all contracts and any corporately-owned distribution outlets. It sounded good. Levine would be in charge of production. Trem Carr would work in production supervision. It is doubtful if either Trem Carr or Nat Levine guessed Yates' ultimate design at this time. They were too wound up with their own production and distribution problems and sales figures to engage in advanced corporate scheming.

To make adequate use of his studio, Levine had had to increase production; in order to better control his distribution, Levine had to have more product. Mascot's annual production, for a long time, had been insufficient to amass much capital. Accounting was done on an accrual basis and monthly returns were used to meet monthly operational costs. Levine did not have the money to buy the Sennett studio in 1933 and by 1935, when he did have the money, he was taken up with Yates' grand concept of a combined facility.

There is perhaps no greater villain in business life and practice than the intimidating spectre of the future. A business attains a state where its direction becomes so obvious to its executives that they become impatient to reach further than their existing resources permit at the moment and so feel constrained to invite outside financial assistance. The wise businessman, confronted by this spectre, sells out because he knows that whatever it was inside of him that produced his success is now at an end because of his impatience, that his discipline is about to give way to self-indulgence. The foolish businessman merges and usually ends up with others exploiting his success for their own profit. Levine had become convinced that the way production costs were mounting, the days of independent producing companies without massive financing were numbered. It was evident to him that small producing companies could not match the distribution networks and the quality product of the bigger studios. This was Yates' central argument. By merging resources, production could be increased both in quantity and quality. Republic would have its own exchange network and the state's rights marketing system could be scrapped.

The Miracle Rider had earned a million dollars. M-G-M would never have made this picture, or any of the others Levine had produced. A cobbler should stick to his last, the old saying went. At Republic, Levine would still be in a position of authority over production and he would be a stockholder. He decided in favor of the merger.

Many years hence, Levine would comment to me that this was his major mistake. "For it was taking me," he went on, "from an operation that I owned with complete control to an operation of being subject to partners and ones who knew little about production. When I joined Republic, my serials were the most successful on the market, Autry and the musical Westerns were completely my own venture, and the studio in North Hollywood was mine. All of this went into Republic and it was established at the time that without my contribution they would have gone into bankruptcy." He added, a trifle wistfully, "my thoughts were to remain with Republic for five years and establish it as an important entity, then to sell out and become an independent producer." Yates could not have afforded a direct buy-out instead of a merger. It is doubtful, too, if Levine would have agreed to sell out completely in 1935. He wanted to press his luck as far as it would go. The only way for Yates to get Mascot was to merge and eventually discard Levine once he had the money to buy him out, and that is precisely what Yates did.

No sooner had the merger become a fact than Yates closeted himself with Levine and suggested they buy out the Trem Carr/Monogram interests, ostensibly on the grounds that the productions which Carr supervised, chiefly the John Wayne series Westerns, were of inferior quality. Contract players like Wayne, however, would stay on at Republic. Trem Carr together with W. Ray Johnston, who had founded Monogram and been titular head of the company since 1931, presently organized the new Monogram Pictures. They were given $1,000,000 for their shares in Republic. While they left behind the twenty franchise holders and nineteen company-owned exchanges they had brought to the merger to provide the distribution system for Republic, they held a new stock issue in 1937, generated at a million shares, and opened branch offices in New York, Philadelphia, and Washington, D.C. Trem Carr also freelanced to raise money. When the new management at Universal began to make the competing Bob Baker series of musical Westerns, some of which were directed by Joseph H. Lewis, Carr took over as production supervisor on the pictures. Monogram, in the meantime, began independent production of low budget feature films, mostly Westerns.

"Prior to becoming Herb Yates' partner," Levine told me, "I was considered the leading independent producer and my ambitions were to become the leading *major* producer, divorcing myself from distribution and become affiliated with M-G-M or Paramount. I felt my affiliation with Republic would expedite my career." In 1937, when Levine was thirty-seven years old, only two years after their partnership had begun, with Levine producing four Republic serials a year, the Gene Autry singing Westerns, the Three Mesquiteer trio Westerns, Yates was ready to move against him, buying him out for $2,000,000. Mascot Pictures, at the time of the original merger, had probably been worth in excess of that figure, but Levine had subsequently merged everything that mattered, his staff — what remained of it — and success formulae, his production unit and his lot, his contracts and his players. Now these were half Yates' property. Once Yates gained complete control, he held onto Republic until the mid fifties when, a very old man, he determined to liquidate all of his assets and retire from film production.

When Levine left Republic, he was not certain of what course to follow. He soon learned that he could not start over. Too much of the market for the kinds of pictures he had been making was dominated by Republic and he would have a difficult time competing against his own ideas. The new Monogram, he knew, would never be successful the way Republic already was.

"Under what was described as the 'friendliest of conditions'," the *Film Daily Yearbook* for 1937 put it, "Nat Levine resigned his post as president of Republic Productions, last February, 1937, due, it was said, to differences which arose concerning future policies. He also sold his half interest in the enterprise, but did not formally leave until April, employing the two intervening months to finishing work on product. Then he headed for New York, saying that he was 'on a vacation,' and to prove it boarded the *Rex* for Europe and spent some eight or ten weeks there." On July 8, 1937, having returned to the States, Levine signed a long-term contract with M-G-M as an associate producer.

Evidently Levine did not take readily to the peculiar regimen at M-G-M. In March, 1938, he resigned. He was then approached by E.W. Hammons to participate in the proposed merger of the facilities of Grand National with Hammons' Educational Film Corporation. Grand National had been started initially by Edward Alperson, a former sales manager from Warner Bros., and Spyros Skouras, head of the Fox West Coast theatres and also long associated with Warner Bros. They negotiated $2,000,000 in financing for the new company. James Cagney, on suspension from Warner Bros. at the time, contracted to make a picture a year in exchange for 2,500 shares of stock. George Hirliman was added along with independent producer-director Al Herman, who had originally discovered Mickey Rooney for Larry Darmour. The firm put $900,000 into *Something to Sing About* (Grand National, 1937) which, consequently, was way over budget and did not gross. Cagney patched up his quarrel with Jack L. Warner and went back to work on the Burbank lot with a reduced annual film quota and a chance at roles other than playing gangsters. Edward Finney, who had been producing the Tex Ritter singing Westerns for Grand National release, brought suit against the company. Ritter was under contract to Finney and Finney wanted to switch to the newly organized Monogram for financing and release, which eventually he did. After a series of conferences with Alperson, Hammons, and Hirliman, Levine withdrew from the project, proclaiming it unfeasible. He returned to M-G-M, this time as an independent producer, commencing in August, 1938. He produced a low budget film, *Four Girls in White* (M-G-M, 1939), and took credit at least for conceiving the idea behind *Lord Jeff* (M-G-M, 1940) which starred Freddie Bartholomew and Mickey Rooney. But this new association did not work out either.

Levine took to spending all his time at the race track gambling. Fyodor Dostoyevsky had an intimate knowledge of the gambler's psychology as a result of his own obsession with the gaming tables and in his short novel, *The Gambler* (1866), he provided a revealing portrait of a man suffering from such an obsession. "I have only for once to show will power and in one hour I can transform my destiny," he had his gambler declare. "The great thing is will power. Only remember what happened to me seven months ago at Roulettenburg just before my final failure. Oh! it was a remarkable instance of determination: I had lost everything then, everything.... I was going out of the Casino, I looked, there was still one gulden in my waistcoat pocket: 'Then I shall have something for dinner,' I thought. But after I had gone a hundred paces I changed my mind and went back. I staked that gulden, ... and there really is something peculiar in the feeling when, alone in a strange land, far from home and from friends, not knowing whether you will have anything to eat that day – you stake your last gulden, your very last. I won, and twenty minutes later I went out of the Casino, having a hundred and seventy gulden in my pocket. That's a fact. That's what the last gulden can sometimes do. And what if I had lost heart then? What if I had not dared to risk it?"

Levine was correct about the Grand National merger. The newly merged corporation went into receivership in 1940, selling out most of its negatives to Astor Pictures which then reissued the films. Levine became more and more convinced that he could and would have success at the race track. All the money he had accumulated, all he owned was consumed by his passion for gambling. When, in the mid forties, he negotiated the sale of all the Mascot negatives he still owned to Irvin Shapiro, Levine's wife divorced him, feeling his situation was hopeless.

Shapiro was a speculator. He leased the Mascot sound serials and features to Unity Television Service. Unity rented them to television stations, making as much as $3,000 for a single booking of *The Miracle Rider*. Unity's head booker was Sid Weiner. When Unity was purchased by Screen Gems, the television arm of Columbia Pictures, Weiner went along. He became Director of Administration for Columbia Pictures Television and was in that position when Columbia surrendered all of the original negatives of the Mascot productions to the Library of Congress so that they might be transferred to acetate and thus preserved for future generations.

Nat Levine, who had brought so many people into the motion picture business, some mentioned herein, others not, like Sol C. Siegel who came from the real estate industry and later succeeded Levine as head of production at Republic — or even Nathanael West who worked briefly in the Mascot writing department — joined ZIV-TV for a time as a studio manger before he became a theatre manager for the California Sterling Theatres. In 1979, Levine confessed to me that it was all gone, even his copies of scripts, and that he was trying to make ends meet on Social Security. He had developed, he claimed, a distaste for gambling.

"I ran into old man Yates when I was in Italy," Yakima Canutt recalled once in his trophy room in his North Hollywood home. "He had sold Republic. Now he was living comfortably with Vera Ralston, whom he'd married. He threw his arms around me and treated me like a long lost friend. He told me that when I got back to California, I should come and visit him. When I did get back, I said, 'What the hell! I might as well go and see him.' And I did. I went out to his house and told the servant whom I was and that I had come to visit Mr. Yates."

Yak paused and a smile played around the corners of his mouth. "The servant came back. I was told: 'Mr. Yates can't be disturbed.' It was probably Vera's doing. During his last years, she wouldn't permit anyone from the old days to see him."

Yak reclined in his chair. "I never did see him again."

All of which leaves us ultimately with the Mascot films themselves and the images that gave them life. "In the saga," Mircea Eliade wrote in *Myth and Reality* (Harper & Row, 1968), "the hero is placed in a world governed by the gods and fate." This is certainly the atmosphere into which one is plunged almost at once when watching a Mascot chapter play.

In his essay "Psychologie und Dichtung" [Psychology and Poetry] contained in Volume XV of his *Gesammelte Werke*, titled *Über das Phänomen des Geistes in Kunst und Wissenschaft [On the Phenomenon of the Spirit in Art and Science]* (Walter-Verlag, 1971), C.G. Jung made a valuable distinction between the psychological mode and the visionary mode. The psychological mode in art is that which pertains strictly to the conscious life of the individual and the conflicts with which it deals are realistic conflicts from a person's conscious life. The visionary mode, in comparison, is not derived from conscious or personal experience; often its imagery is reminiscent of the fantasies of the insane insofar as it follows no logical course of development. Yet it is the visionary mode through which art transcends personal meaning and becomes general in significance, even though that significance cannot readily or logically be explained. "The repeated submersion into that primal condition of 'participation mystique' is the secret of artistic creation and works of art," Jung wrote in this essay, "for from this stuff of experience is seen not the experience of the individual but rather that of the people, and it consists no longer of the weal and woe of the individual but rather of the life of the people. For this reason the great work of art is objective and impersonal and yet moves us deeply as individuals. For this reason what is personal to the poet is advantageous or disadvantageous for his art, but not essential. His personal biography can be that of a Philistine, a brave man, a neurotic, a fool, or a criminal: interesting and unavoidable, but with regard to the poet inessential."

I am not making the claim for the Mascot serials that they were great works of art, only that viewed in terms of their imagistic and fantastic content they are allied more with the visionary mode than with the more mundane psychological mode. In another essay in the same book, "Über der Beziehungen der analytischen Psychologie zum dichterischen Kunstwerk" [On the Relationship of Analytical Psychology to Works of Poetry], Jung wrote of the social significance of the visionary mode. "The relative nonconformity of the artist is his truest advantage," he remarked; "it makes it possible for him to remain aloof from the great thoroughfares and to pursue his own yearning and to find what others are lacking without knowing it. So, just as the single individual corrects the one-sidedness of his conscious attitude through unconscious reactions on the path to psychic self-regulation, so art represents a process of spiritual self-regulation in the life of nations and of the times."

The Mascot chapter plays in their emphasis on hectic activity compensated for the spiritual lethargy of the times in which they were made. In their use of heroes willing to risk their lives in the pursuit of fabulous wealth, they offered an alternative to the vision of bleak poverty which held the United States tightly in its clasp. In their penchant for master villains they compensated for the suspicion that evil might be ambiguous rather than specific and identifiable; and by masking these master villains and making them mystery figures they managed to make the hostility one might feel toward a master villain cautious rather than committed. In their triad heroes, they argued against the isolation of the hero which had been true of chapter plays previously; Gene Autry and his music-making gave the people something to sing about when there seemed nothing worth singing about; while Ken Maynard and Tom Mix sought to restore via their screen personas the belief that the individual could still triumph over adversity.

In a spoof on the Mascot serials, James A. Stringham claimed in an article in the *Film Fan Monthly* (April, 1968) that he had just come upon the pressbook of a "lost" Mascot chapter play based on William Shakespeare's stage drama of the same title, *Hamlet*. The cast, according to Stringham, was as follows: Hamlet (Frankie Darro), Claudius, King of Denmark (Robert Frazer), Gertrude, Queen of Denmark (Eileen Sedgwick), Ophelia (Betsy King Ross), Horatio (Jack Mulhall), Polonius (Henry B. Walthall), Laertes (Lane Chandler), Rosencrantz (Walter Miller), Guildenstern (William Desmond), Hamlet, Sr. [Ghost] (Noah Beery, Sr.), Fortinbras (Joe Bonomo), and as pirates Yakima Canutt, Robert Kortman, and Glenn Strange. Richard Thorpe was credited with the direction. In a prefatory statement, Nat Levine himself is supposedly quoted, making the assertion that "in transforming Shakespeare's *Hamlet* into a twelve-chapter serial I am again demonstrating my faith that the popular type serial has the greatest box-office value of any running exploitation device. Now, in addition, I have been able to include an element of culture which had been the only thing lacking in my previous efforts."

In the publicity section of the pressbook, there was a notation that "during research for their serial production of *Hamlet,* Mascot's writers discovered that a character, appropriately called 'Prologue,' spoke the introduction to many of his [Shakespeare's] plays. Since they were concerned with the introduction to each episode of the all-talking chapter play..., they immediately realized that the answer had been handed them across the centuries. Each chapter of the adventures of Frankie Darro and the all-star cast will begin with a plot résumé spoken by ... well, call him Prologue."

How did Mascot's *Hamlet* end? On this subject, the pressbook had only this to say: "Threatened by a bared blade, a poisoned point, and a fatal drink, his death seems certain. Yet, he triumphs in a climax unequalled for action and suspense."

However ludicrous this all may appear, it does embody the unique quality which was the hallmark of the Mascot serials and which distinguished them from chapter plays made by any other company. And there is one thing more. The imagination of disaster and narrow escape, which informed every episode of a Mascot serial, was itself a pattern of narration that could, and often did, draw on any source for its imagery, if not Shakespeare, then nevertheless the primordial dreams and fantasies, not of the individual, but, as Jung put it, of *das Volk,* of the people.

Appendix I

The Mascot Serials

The Silent Flyer (Universal, 1926), directed by William Craft. *Cast*: Silver Streak (dog), Malcolm MacGregor, Louise Lorraine, Thur Fairfax, Hughie Mack, Anders Rudolph, Edith Yorke. *Chapter titles*:

1. The Jaws of Death
2. Dynamited
3. Waters of Death
4. The Treacherous Trail
5. Plunge of Peril
6. Fight of Honor
7. Under Arrest
8. Flames of Terror
9. Hurled Through Space
10. Love and Glory

The Golden Stallion (Mascot, 1927), directed by Harry Webb. *Original story*: Karl Kusada and William Lester. *Cast*: Maurice "Lefty" Flynn, Joe Bonomo, White Fury (horse), Molly Malone, Joseph Swickard, Burr McIntosh, Billy Franey, Tom London. *Chapter titles*:

1. The Golden Stallion
2. The Flaming Forest
3.
4. The Stallion's Fury
5.
6.
7.
8.
9.
10. The Lost Treasure

Isle of Sunken Gold (Mascot, 1927), directed by Harry Webb. *Cast*: Anita Stewart, Bruce Gordon, Evangeline Russell, Curtis "Snowball" McHenry, Duke Kahanamoku, Alfred Sabata, Ammett Wagner, Jay J. Bryan, K. Nambu. *Chapter titles*:

1. The Isle of Sunken Gold
2. Trapped in Mid-Air
3. Engulfed by the Sea
4. The Volcano's Pit
5. The Hulk of Death
6. The Prey of Sharks
7. Fire of Revenge
8. The Battle of Canoes
9. Trapped by the Ape
10. The Devil Ape's Secret

Heroes of the Wild (Mascot, 1927), directed by Harry Webb. *Cast*: Jack Hoxie, Josephine Hill, Joe Bonomo, Tornado (dog), White Fury (horse). *Chapter titles*:

1. Heroes of the Wild
2. Sword to Sword
3. The Plunge of Peril
4. The Slide of Life
5. The Trap of Death
6. The Flaming Fiend

| 7. The Clutching Hand | 9. The Fatal Arrow |
| 8. The Broken Cable | 10. The Crown of the Incas |

Vultures of the Sea (Mascot, 1928), directed by Richard Thorpe. *Original story*: Wyndham Gittens and William Burt. *Cast*: Johnnie Walker, Shirley Mason, Tom Santschi, Boris Karloff, Frank Hagney, John Carpenter, George Magrill, Joe Bennett, Arthur Dewey, Joseph Mack, J.P. Lockney, Lafe McKee. *Chapter titles*:

1. The Hell Ship	6. The Stolen Ship
2. Cast Adrift	7. At the Mercy of the Flames
3. Driven to Port	8. The Fight for Possession
4. Scum of the Seas	9. The Traitor
5. The Harbor of Danger	10. The End of the Quest

The Vanishing West (Mascot, 1928), directed by Richard Thorpe. *Cast*: Leo Maloney, Jack Daugherty, Jack Perrin, Yakima Canutt, William Fairbanks, Eileen Sedgwick, Fred Church, Little Mickey Bennett, Helen Gibson, Bobby Burns, Harry Lorraine, Aaron Edwards, Tom Bay. *Chapter titles*:

1. The Trail to Yesterday	6. Roaring Wheels
2. The Flaming Trap	7. The Phantom Roper
3. Thundering Hoofs	8. The Tunnel of Terror
4. The Balance of Fate	9. The Fatal Second
5. The Chasm of Danger	10. The End of the Trail

The Fatal Warning (Mascot, 1929), directed by Richard Thorpe. *Original story*: Wyndham Gittens. *Production supervisor*: Ben Schwab. *Cast*: Helen Costello, Ralph Graves, George Periolat, Phillip Smalley, Lloyd Whitlock, Boris Karloff, Sid Crossley, Thomas Lingham, Symona Boniface, Martha Mattox. *Chapter titles*:

1. The Fatal Warning	6. Into Thin Air
2. The Phantom Flyer	7. The House of Horror
3. The Crash of Doom	8. Fatal Fumes
4. The Pit of Death	9. By Whose Hand
5. Menacing Fingers	10. Unmasked

King of the Kongo (Mascot, 1929), directed by Richard Thorpe. *Original story*: Wyndham Gittens. *Cast*: Jacqueline Logan, Walter Miller, Richard Tucker, Boris Karloff, Larry Steers, Harry Todd, Richard Neill, Lafe McKee, J.P. Leckray, William Burt, Gordon Russell, Robert Frazer, Ruth Davis. *Chapter titles*:

1. Into the Unknown	6. The Fight at the Lion's Pit
2. Terrors of the Jungle	7. The Fatal Moment
3. The Temple of Beasts	8. Sentenced to Death
4. Gorilla Warfare	9. Desperate Chances
5. Danger in the Dark	10. Jungle Justice

The Lone Defender (Mascot, 1930), directed by Richard Thorpe.

Cast: Rin-Tin-Tin (dog), Walter Miller, June Marlowe, Buzz Barton, Joseph Swickard, Lee Shumway, Frank Lanning, Robert Kortman, Arthur Morrison, Lafe McKee, Bob Irvin, Julian Barlano, Victor Metzetti, Bill McGowan, Arthur Metzeth. *Chapter titles*:

1. The Mystery of the Desert
2. The Fugitive
3. Jaws of Peril
4. Trapped
5. The Circle of Death
6. Surrounded by the Law
7. The Ghost Speaks
8. The Brink of Destruction
9. The Avalanche
10. Fury of the Desert
11. Cornered
12. Vindicated

Phantom of the West (Mascot, 1930), directed by D. Ross Lederman. *Cast*: Tom Tyler, William Desmond, Tom Santschi, Dorothy Gulliver, Joe Bonomo, Tom Dugan, Philo McCullough, Kermit Maynard, Frank Lanning, Frank Hagney, Dick Dickinson, Halee Sullivan, Al Taylor, Ernie Adams. *Chapter titles*:

1. The Ghost Riders
2. The Stairway of Doom
3. The Horror in the Dark
4. The Battle of the Strong
5. The League of the Lawless
6. The Canyon of Calamity
7. The Price of Silence
8. The House of Hate
9. The Fatal Secret
10. Rogues' Roundup

King of the Wild (Mascot, 1930), directed by Richard Thorpe. *Cast*: Walter Miller, Nora Lane, Dorothy Christy, Tom Santschi, Boris Karloff, Arthur McLaglen, Carroll Nye, Victor Potel, Martha Lalande. *Chapter titles*:

1. The Tiger of Destiny
2. Man Eaters
3. The Avenging Horde
4. The Secret of the Volcano
5. The Pit of Peril
6. The Creeping Doom
7. Sealed Lips
8. The Jaws of the Jungle
9. The Door of Dread
10. The Leopard's Lair
11. The Fire of the Gods
12. Jungle Justice

The Vanishing Legion (Mascot, 1931), directed by Reeves Eason. *Original story*: Wyndham Gittens, Ford Beebe, and Helmer Bergman. *Supervising editor*: Wyndham Gittens. *Photography*: Benjamin Kline, Ernest Miller, and Jo J. Novak. *Editor*: Ray Snyder. *Sound engineer*: George Lowerre. *Cast*: Harry Carey, Edwina Booth, Rex (horse), Frankie Darro, Philo McCullough, William Desmond, Lafe McKee, Bob Kortman, Edward Hearn, Paul Weigal, Olive Fuller Golden, Dick Hatton, Frank Brownlee, Tom Dugan, Al Taylor, Pete Morrison, Joe Bonomo, Dick Dickinson, Bob Walker, Charles "Rube" Schaeffer, Yakima Canutt.

1. The Voice from the Void
2. The Queen of the Night Riders
3. The Invisible Enemy
4. The Fatal Message
5. The Trackless Trail
6. The Radio Riddle
7. The Crimson Clue
8. The Doorway of Disaster
9. When Time Stood Still
10. Riding the Whirlwind
11. The Capsule of Oblivion
12. The Hoofs of Horror

The Galloping Ghost (Mascot, 1931), directed by Reeves Eason. *Associate director*: Armand Schaefer. *Supervising editor*: Wyndham Gittens. *Original story*: Helmer Bergman, Ford Beebe, and Wyndham Gittens. *Photography*: Benjamin Kline, Ernest Miller, and Tom Galligan. *Editor*: Ray Snyder and Gilmore Walker. *Sound engineer*: George Lowerre. *Musical director*: Lee Zahler. *Cast*: Harold Grange, Dorothy Gulliver, Tom Dugan, Gwen Lee, Francis X. Bushman, Jr., Theodore Lorch, Walter Miller, Edward Hearn, Ernie Adams, Tom London, Frank Brownlee, Edward Peil, Joe Mack, Stepin Fetchit, Dick Dickinson, Wilfred Lucas, Snowflake. *Chapter titles*:

1. The Idol of Clay
2. The Port of Peril
3. The Master Mind
4. The House of Secrets
5. The Man Without a Face
6. The Torn $500 Bill
7. When the Lights Went Out
8. The Third Degree
9. The Sign in the Sky
10. The Vulture's Lair
11. The Radio Patrol
12. The Ghost Comes Back

The Lightning Warrior (Mascot, 1931), directed by Armand Schaefer and Benjamin Kline. *Supervising editor*: Wyndham Gittens. *Original story*: Wyndham Gittens, Ford Beebe, and Colbert Clark. *Photography*: Ernest Miller, William Nobles, and Tom Galligan. *Editor*: Ray Snyder. *Sound engineer*: George Lowerre. *Cast*: Frankie Darro, Hayden Stevenson, George Brent, Pat O'Malley, Georgia Hale, Theodore Lorch, Lafe McKee, Frank Brownlee, Bob Kortman, Dick Dickinson, Yakima Canutt, Frank Lanning, Bertee Beaumont, Helen Gibson, Kermit Maynard, Rin-Tin-Tin (dog). *Chapter titles*:

1. The Drums of Doom
2. The Wolf Man
3. Empty Saddles
4. Flaming Arrows
5. The Invisible Enemy
6. The Fatal Name
7. The Ordeal of Fire
8. The Man Who Knew
9. Traitor's Hour
10. The Secret of the Cave
11. Red Shadows
12. Painted Faces

Shadow of the Eagle (Mascot, 1932), directed by Ford Beebe. *Supervising editor*: Wyndham Gittens. *Original story*: Ford Beebe, Colbert Clark, and Wyndham Gittens. *Photography*: Benjamin Kline and Victor Scheurich. *Editor*: Ray Snyder. *Sound engineer*: George Lowerre. *Cast*: John Wayne, Dorothy Gulliver, Edward Hearn, Richard Tucker, Lloyd Whitlock, Walter Miller, Edmund Burns, Pat O'Malley, Kenneth Harlan, Little Billy, Ivan Linow, James Bradbury, Jr., Ernie Adams, Roy D'Arcy, Bud Osborne, Yakima Canutt, Billy West, Monty Montague. *Chapter titles*:

1. The Carnival Mystery
2. Pinholes
3. The Eagle Strikes
4. The Man of a Million Voices
5. The Telephone Cipher
6. The Code of the Carnival
7. Eagle or Vulture?
8. On the Spot
9. When Thieves Fall Out
10. The Man Who Knew
11. The Eagle's Wing
12. The Shadow Unmasked

The Last of the Mohicans (Mascot, 1932), directed by Reeves Eason and Ford Beebe. *Supervising editor*: Wyndham Gittens. *Original story*: James Fenimore Cooper. *Screenplay*: Colbert Clark, John Francis Natteford, Ford Beebe, and Wyndham Gittens. *Photography*: Ernest Miller and Jack Young. *Editor*: Ray Snyder. *Sound engineer*: George Lowerre. *Cast*: Harry Carey, Hobart Bosworth, Junior Coughlan, Edwina Booth, Lucile Browne, Walter Miller, Bob Kortman, Walter McGrail, Nelson McDowell, Edward Hearn, Mischa Auer, Yakima Canutt, Chief Big Tree, Joan Gale, Tully Marshall. *Chapter titles*:

1. The Last of the Mohicans
2. Flaming Arrows
3. Rifles or Tomahawks
4. Riding with Death
5. Red Shadows
6. The Lure of Gold
7. The Crimson Trail
8. The Tide of Battle
9. A Redskin's Honor
10. The Enemy's Stronghold
11. Paleface Magic
12. The End of the Trail

The Hurricane Express (Mascot, 1932), directed by Armand Schaefer and J.P. McGowan. *Supervising editor*: Wyndham Gittens. *Original story*: Colbert Clark, Barney Sarecky, and Wyndham Gittens. *Screenplay*: George Morgan and J.P. McGowan. *Photography*: Ernest Miller and Carl Webster. *Editor*: Ray Snyder. *Sound engineer*: George Lowerre. *Cast*: Tully Marshall, Conway Tearle, J. Farrell MacDonald, John Wayne, Shirley Grey, Edmund Breese, Lloyd Whitlock, Al Bridge, Mathew Betz, Joseph Girard, James Burtis, Ernie Adams, Charles King, Al Ferguson, Glenn Strange. *Chapter titles*:

1. The Wrecker
2. Flying Pirates
3. The Masked Killer
4. Buried Alive
5. Danger Lights
6. The Airport Mystery
7. Sealed Lips
8. Outside the Law
9. The Invisible Enemy
10. The Wrecker's Secret
11. Wings of Death
12. Unmasked

The Devil Horse (Mascot, 1932), directed by Otto Brower. *Second unit*: Yakima Canutt and Richard Talmadge. *Supervising editor*: Wyndham Gittens. *Screenplay*: George Morgan, Barney Sarecky, George Plympton, and Wyndham Gittens. *Photography*: Ernest Miller and Carl Webster. *Editor*: Victor Scheurich and Ray Snyder. *Sound engineer*: George Lowerre. *Cast*: Harry Carey, Noah Beery, Sr., Frankie Darro, Greta Granstedt, Barrie O'Daniels, Edward Peil, Jack Mower, Al Bridge, Jack Byron, J. Paul Jones, Carli Russell, Lou Kelley, Dick Dickinson, Lane Chandler, Fred Burns, Apache, the Devil Horse. *Chapter titles*:

1. Untamed
2. The Chasm of Death
3. The Doom Riders
4. Vigilante Law
5. The Silent Call
6. The Heart of the Mystery
7. The Battle of the Strong
8. The Missing Witness
9. The Showdown
10. The Death Trap
11. Wild Loyalty
12. The Double Decoy

The Whispering Shadow (Mascot, 1933), directed by Albert Herman and Colbert Clark. *Supervising editor*: Wyndham Gittens. *Original Story*: Barney Sarecky, George Morgan, Norman Hall, Colbert Clark, and Wyndham Gittens. *Photography*: Ernest Miller and Edgar Lyons. *Editor*: Ray Snyder and Gilmore Walker. *Sound engineer*: Homer Ackerman. *Cast*: Bela Lugosi, Viva Tattersall, Malcolm MacGregor, Henry B. Walthall, Robert Warwick, Roy D'Arcy, Karl Dane, Lloyd Whitlock, Bob Kortman, Lafe McKee, Jack Perrin. *Chapter titles*:

1. The Master Magician	7. The Double Doom
2. The Collapsing Room	8. The Red Circle
3. The All-Seeing Eye	9. The Fatal Secret
4. The Shadow Strikes	10. The Death Warrant
5. Wanted for Murder	11. The Trap
6. The Man Who Was Czar	12. King of the World

The Three Musketeers (Mascot, 1933), directed by Armand Schaefer and Colbert Clark. *Supervising Editor*: Wyndham Gittens. *Original story*: Norman Hall, Colbert Clark, Ben Cohn and Wyndham Gittens. *Photography*: Ernest Miller and Tom Galligan. *Editor*: Ray Snyder. *Sound engineer*: Homer Ackerman. *Music*: Lee Zahler. *Cast*: Jack Mulhall, Raymond Hatton, Francis X. Bushman, Jr., John Wayne, Ruth Hall, Creighton Chaney, Hooper Atchley, Gordon DeMain, Robert Frazer, Noah Beery, Jr., Al Ferguson, Edward Peil, Sr., William Desmond, George Magrill, Robert Warwick, Wilfred Lucas, Yakima Canutt. *Chapter titles*:

1. The Fiery Circle	7. Naked Steel
2. One for All and All for One	8. The Master Strikes
3. The Master Spy	9. The Fatal Circle
4. Pirates of the Desert	10. Trapped
5. Rebel Rifles	11. The Measure of a Man
6. Death's Marathon	12. The Glory of Comrades

Fighting with Kit Carson (Mascot, 1933), directed by Armand Schaefer and Colbert Clark. *Supervising editor*: Wyndham Gittens. *Original story*: Barney Sarecky, Colbert Clark, Jack Natteford, and Wyndham Gittens. *Photography*: Alvin Wyckoff, Ernest Miller, and William Nobles. *Editor*: Earl Turner. *Sound engineer*: Terry Kellum. *Music*: Lee Zahler. *Cast*: Johnny Mack Brown, Betsy King Ross, Noah Beery, Sr., Noah Beery, Jr., Tully Marshall, Edmund Breese, Al Bridge, Edward Hearn, Lafe McKee, Jack Mower, Maston Williams, Lane Chandler. *Chapter titles*:

1. The Mystery Riders	7. Law of the Lawless
2. The White Chief	8. Red Phantoms
3. Hidden Gold	9. The Invisible Enemy
4. The Silent Doom	10. Midnight Magic
5. Murder Will Out	11. Unmasked
6. Secret of Iron Mountain	12. The Trail to Glory

The Wolf Dog (Mascot, 1933), directed by Colbert Clark and Harry Frazer. *Supervising editor*: Wyndham Gittens. *Original story*: Barney Sarecky and Sherman Lowe. *Screenplay*: Al Martin, Colbert Clark, and

Wyndham Gittens. *Photography*: Harry Neumann, Tom Galligan, and William Nobles. *Editor*: Earl Turner. *Sound engineer*: Cliff Ruberg. *Cast*: Rin-Tin-Tin, Jr. (dog), George Lewis, "Boots" Mallory, Frankie Darro, Hale Hamilton, Henry B. Walthall, Donald Reed, Gordon DeMain, Stanley Blystone, Tom London, Lane Chandler, Lafe McKee. *Chapter titles*:

1. The Call of the Wilderness
2. The Shadow of a Crime
3. The Fugitive
4. A Dead Man's Hand
5. Wolf Pack Law
6. The Gates of Mercy
7. The Empty Room
8. Avenging Fangs
9. The Wizard of the Wireless
10. Accused!
11. The Broken Record
12. Danger Lights

The Mystery Squadron (Mascot, 1933), directed by Colbert Clark and David Howard. *Supervising editor*: Wyndham Gittens. *Original story*: Sherman Lowe and Al Martin. *Screenplay*: Barney Sarecky, Colbert Clark, David Howard, and Wyndham Gittens. *Photography*: Alvin Wyckoff, Ernest Miller, and William Nobles. *Editor*: Earl Turner. *Sound engineer*: Terry Kellum. *Cast*: Bob Steele, Guinn "Big Boy" Williams, Lucile Browne, Jack Mulhall, Purnell Pratt, Robert Frazer, J. Carrol Naish, Bob Kortman, Lafe McKee, Edward Hearn, Kernan Cripps, Edward Peil, Jack Mower, Jack Perrin. *Chapter titles*:

1. The Black Ace
2. The Fatal Warning
3. The Black Ace Strikes
4. Men of Steel
5. The Death Swoop
6. Doomed
7. Enemy Signals
8. The Canyon of Calamity
9. The Secret of the Mine
10. Clipped Wings
11. The Beast at Bay
12. The Ace of Aces

The Lost Jungle (Mascot, 1934), directed by Armand Schaefer and David Howard. *Supervising editor*: Wyndham Gittens. *Original story*: Sherman Lowe and Al Martin. *Screenplay*: Barney Sarecky, David Howard, Armand Schaefer, and Wyndham Gittens. *Photography*: Alvin Wyckoff and William Nobles. *Editor*: Earl Turner. *Sound engineer*: Terry Kellum. *Cast*: Clyde Beatty, Syd Saylor, Cecilia Parker, Edward LeSaint, Warner Richmond, Wheeler Oakman, Lou Meehan, Max Wagner, Wally Wales, Ernie Adams, Jack Carlyle, Maston Williams, Wes Warner, Charles Whitaker, Jim Corey, Mickey Rooney. *Chapter titles*:

1. Noah's Ark Island
2. Nature in the Raw
3. The Hypnotic Eye
4. The Pit of Crocodiles
5. Gorilla Warfare
6. The Battle of Beasts
7. The Tiger's Prey
8. The Lion's Brood
9. Eyes of the Jungle
10. Human Hyenas
11. The Gorilla
12. Take Them Back Alive

Burn 'em Up Barnes (Mascot, 1934), directed by Colbert Clark and Armand Schaefer. *Supervising editor*: Wyndham Gittens. *Original story*: John Rathmell and Colbert Clark. *Screenplay*: Al Martin, Armand Schaefer, Barney Sarecky, and Sherman Lowe. *Photography*: Ernest Miller and William Nobles. *Editor*: Earl Turner. *Sound engineer*: Terry Kellum. *Cast*:

Jack Mulhall, Frankie Darro, Lola Lane, Julian Rivero, Edwin Maxwell, Jason Robards, Sr., Francis McDonald, Lloyd Whitlock, Bob Kortman, Tom London, Stanley Blystone, Al Bridge. *Chapter titles*:

1. King of the Dirt Track
2. The News Reel Murder
3. The Phantom Witness
4. The Celluloid Clue
5. The Decoy Driver
6. The Crimson Alibi
7. Roaring Rails
8. The Death Crash
9. The Man Higher Up
10. The Missing Link
11. Surrounded
12. The Fatal Whisper

The Law of the Wild (Mascot, 1934), directed by Armand Schaefer and Reeves Eason. *Supervising editor*: Wyndham Gittens. *Original story*: Ford Beebe, John Rathmell, and Al Martin. *Screenplay*: Sherman Lowe and Reeves Eason. *Photography*: Ernest Miller and William Nobles. *Editor*: Earl Turner. *Sound Engineer*: Terry Kellum. *Cast*: Rex, King of the Wild Horses, Rin-Tin-Tin, Jr. (dog), Ben Turpin, Bob Custer, Lucile Browne, Richard Cramer, Ernie Adams, Edmund Cobb, Charles Whitaker, Dick Alexander, Jack Rockwell, Lafe McKee, George Chesebro. *Chapter titles*:

1. The Man Killer
2. The Battle of the Strong
3. The Cross-eyed Goony
4. Avenging Fangs
5. A Dead Man's Hand
6. Horse Thief Justice
7. The Death Stampede
8. The Canyon of Calamity
9. Robber's Roost
10. King of the Range
11. Winner Takes All
12. The Grand Sweepstakes

Mystery Mountain (Mascot, 1934), directed by Otto Brower and Reeves Eason. *Supervising editor*: Wyndham Gittens. *Original story*: Sherman Lowe, Ben Cohn, Barney Sarecky, and Reeves Eason. *Photography*: Ernest Miller and William Nobles. *Editor*: Earl Turner. *Sound engineer*: Terry Kellum. *Music*: Lee Zahler (uncredited). *Cast*: Ken Maynard, Verna Hillie, Carmincita Johnson, Syd Saylor, Edward Earle, Hooper Atchley, Edward Hearn, Al Bridge, Bob Kortman, Lou Meehan, George Chesebro, Tom London, Lynton Brent, Lafe McKee, Jack Rockwell, Wally Wales, William Gould, Edmund Cobb, Steve Clark, Gene Autry, Smiley Burnette, Frank Ellis, Philo McCullough, Jim Mason, Tarzan (horse). *Chapter titles*:

1. The Rattler
2. The Man Nobody Knows
3. The Eye that Never Sleeps
4. The Human Target
5. Phantom Outlaws
6. The Perfect Crime
7. Tarzan the Cunning
8. The Enemy's Stronghold
9. The Fatal Warning
10. The Secret of the Mountain
11. Behind the Mask
12. The Judgment of Tarzan

The Phantom Empire (Mascot, 1935), directed by Otto Brower and Reeves Eason. *Production supervisor*: Armand Schaefer. *Original story*: Wallace MacDonald, Gerald Geraghty, and Hy Freedman. *Continuity*: John Rathmell and Armand Schaefer. *Photography*: Ernest Miller and William Nobles. *Editor*: Earl Turner. *Sound engineer*: Terry Kellum. *Music*: Lee Zahler. *Cast*: Gene Autry, Frankie Darro, Betsy King Ross, Dorothy

Christie, Wheeler Oakman, Charles K. French, Warner Richmond, Frank Glendon, Smiley Burnette, William Moore, Edward Piel, Jack Carlyle, Wally Wales, Jay Wilsey, Fred Burns, Stanley Blystone, Richard Talmadge, Frank Ellis. *Chapter titles*:

1. The Singing Cowboy
2. The Thunder Riders
3. The Lightning Chamber
4. Phantom Broadcast
5. Beneath the Earth
6. Disaster from the Skies
7. From Death to Life
8. Jaws of Jeopardy
9. Prisoners of the Ray
10. The Rebellion
11. A Queen in Chains
12. The End of Murania

The Miracle Rider (Mascot, 1935), directed by Armand Schaefer and Reeves Eason. *Production supervisor*: Victor Zobel. *Original story*: Barney Sarecky, Wellyn Totman, Gerald Geraghty, and Maurice Geraghty. *Screenplay*: John Rathmell. *Supervising editor*: Joseph H. Lewis. *Photography*: Ernest Miller and William Nobles. *Editor*: Dick Fantl. *Sound engineer*: Terry Kellum. *Cast*: Tom Mix, Joan Gale, Charles Middleton, Jason Robards, Sr., Bob Kortman, Edward Earle, Edward Hearn, Tom London, Niles Welch, Edmund Cobb, Ernie Adams, Max Wagner, Charles King, George Chesebro, Jack Rockwell, Stanley Price, George Barton, Wally Wales, Jay Wilsey, Dick Curtis, Frank Ellis, Dick Alexander, Earl Dwire, Lafe McKee, Hank Bell, Pat O'Malley, Slim Whitaker, Robert Frazer, Art Ardigan, Chief Big Tree, Forrest Taylor, Fred Burns, Black Hawk, Chief Standing Bear, Tony, Jr. (horse). *Chapter titles*:

1. The Vanishing Indian
2. The Firebird Strikes
3. The Flying Knife
4. A Race with Death
5. Double-Barreled Doom
6. Thundering Hoofs
7. The Dragnet
8. Guerilla Warfare
9. The Silver Band
10. Signal Fires
11. A Traitor Dies
12. Danger Rides with Death
13. The Secret of X-94
14. Between Two Fires
15. Justice Rides the Plains

The Adventures of Rex and Rinty (Mascot, 1935), directed by Ford Beebe and Reeves Eason. *Supervisor*: Barney Sarecky. *Original story*: Reeves Eason, Maurice Geraghty, and Ray Trampe. *Screenplay*: John Rathmell and Barney Sarecky. *Supervising editor*: Joseph H. Lewis. *Photography*: William Nobles. *Editor*: Dick Fantl. *Cast*: Rex, King of the Wild Horses, Rin-Tin-Tin, Jr. (dog), Kane Richmond, Norma Taylor, Mischa Auer, Smiley Burnette, Harry Woods, Pedro Regas, Hooper Atchley, Wheeler Oakman, Victor Potel, Allan Cavan, Al Bridge, Edmund Cobb, Charles King, George Chesebro, Jack Rockwell. *Chapter titles*:

1. The God Horse of Sujan
2. Sport of Kings
3. Fangs of Flame
4. Homeward Bound
5. Babes in the Woods
6. Dead Man's Tale
7. End of the Road
8. A Dog's Devotion
9. The Stranger's Recall
10. The Siren of Death
11. New Gods for Old
12. Primitive Justice

The Fighting Marines (Mascot, 1935), directed by Reeves Eason and Joseph Kane. *Supervisor*: Barney Sarecky. *Original Story*: Wallace Mac-Donald, Maurice Geraghty, and Ray Trampe. *Screenplay*: Barney Sarecky and Sherman Lowe. *Supervising editor*: Joseph H. Lewis. *Photography*: William Nobles. *Editor*: Dick Fantl. *Sound engineer*: Cliff Ruberg. *Sound effects*: Roy Granville. *Cast*: Grant Withers, Adrian Morris, Ann Rutherford, Robert Warwick, George Lewis, Pat O'Malley, Victor Potel, Jason Robards, Sr., Warner Richmond, Robert Frazer, Frank Glendon, Donald Reed, Max Wagner, Richard Alexander, Tom London, Jim Corey. *Chapter titles*:

1. Human Targets
2. Isle of Missing Men
3. The Savage Horde
4. The Mark of the Tiger Shark
5. The Gauntlet of Grief
6. Robbers' Roost
7. Jungle Terrors
8. Siege of Halfway Island
9. Death from the Sky
10. Wheels of Destruction
11. Behind the Mask
12. Two Against the Horde

Appendix II

The Mascot Features

Pride of the Legion (Mascot, 1933, 70 min.) [alternate title: **The Big Payoff**], directed by Ford Beebe. *Adaptation*: Ford Beebe. *Original story*: Peter B. Kyne. *Photography*: Ernie Miller, Carl Webster, and S.W. Brown. *Editor*: Ray Snyder. *Cast*: Barbara Kent, J. Farrell MacDonald, Lucien Littlefield, Sally Blane, Glenn Tryon, Matt Moore, Ralph Ince, Victor Jory, Jason Robards, Sr., Rin-Tin-Tin, Jr. (dog).

Laughing at Life (Mascot, 1933, 71 min.), directed by Ford Beebe. *Original story*: Ford Beebe. *Adaptation*: Prescott Chaplin and Thomas Dugan. *Photography*: Ernie Miller and Tom Galligan. *Musical director*: Lee Zahler. *Sound engineer*: Earl Crane. *Cast*: Victor McLaglen, Conchita Montenegro, William "Stage" Boyd, Regis Toomey, Ruth Hall, Noah Beery, Sr., Tully Marshall, J. Farrell MacDonald, Lois Wilson, Guinn "Big Boy" Williams, Henry B. Walthall, Dewey Robinson, Ivan Lebedeff, Mathilde Comont, Henry Armetta, Edmund Breese, Frankie Darro, Buster Phelps, Pat O'Malley, William Desmond, Lloyd Whitlock, Philo McCullough, George Humbert.

The Lost Jungle (Mascot, 1934, 68 min.). See serial version.

Young and Beautiful (Mascot, 1934, 63 min.), directed by Joseph Santley. *Story and adaptation*: Joseph Santley and Milton Krims. *Screenplay*: Dore Schary. *Additional dialogue and construction*: Al Martin and Colbert Clark. *Photography*: John Stumar. *Editor*: Thomas Scott. *Sound engineer*: Karl Zint. *Cast*: William Haines, Judith Allen, Joseph Cawthorn, John Miljan, Shaw and Lee, James Bush, Vince Barnett, Warren Hymer, Franklin Panghorn, James Burtis, Syd Saylor, Greta Meyer, Fred Kelsey, Andre Beranger, Ray Mayer, Lester's Hollywood Singers, Edward Hearn.

Crimson Romance (Mascot, 1934, 71 min.), directed by David Howard. *Original story*: Al Martin and Sherman Lowe. *Screenplay*: Milton Krims. *Additional Dialogue*: Doris Schroeder. *Photography*: Ernest Miller. *Editor*: Doris Draught. *Sound engineer*: Terry Kellum. *Cast*: Ben Lyon, Sari Maritza, Erich von Stroheim, Hardie Albright, James Bush, William Bakewell, Herman Bing, Bodil Rosing, Vincent Barnett, Arthur Clayton, Oscar

Apfel, Purnell Pratt, Jason Robards, Sr., William von Brincken, Eric Arnold, Fred Vogeding, Harry Schultz.

In Old Santa Fe (Mascot, 1934, 67 min.), directed by David Howard. *Original story*: Wallace MacDonald and John Rathmell. *Screenplay*: Colbert Clark and James Gruen. *Photography*: Ernest Miller and William Nobles. *Editor*: Thomas Scott. *Sound engineer*: Terry Kellum. *Cast*: Ken Maynard, Evalyn Knapp, H.B. Warner, Kenneth Thomson, George Hayes, Wheeler Oakman, George Burton, George Chesebro, Gene Autry, Smiley Burnette, Cliff Lyons, Edward Hearn, Stanley Blystone, Jack Rockwell, Frank Ellis.

The Marines Are Coming (Mascot, 1934, 70 min.), directed by David Howard. *Original story*: John Rathmell and Colbert Clark. *Screenplay*: James Gruen. *Photography*: Ernie Miller and William Nobles. *Editor*: Thomas Scott. *Sound engineer*: Terry Kellum. *Cast*: William Haines, Esther Ralston, Conrad Nagel, Armida, Edgar Kennedy, Hale Hamilton, George Regas, Broderick O'Farrell, Michael Visaroff, Dell Henderson.

Little Men (Mascot, 1934, 72 min.), directed by Phil Rosen. *Production supervisor*: Ken Goldsmith. *Original story*: Louisa May Alcott. *Screenplay*: Gertrude Orr. *Photography*: Ernest Miller and William Nobles. *Editor*: Joseph Kane. *Sound engineer*: Lambert Day. *Musical setting*: Dr. Hugo Riesenfeld. *Cast*: Junior Durkin, Frankie Darro, David Durand, Dickie Moore, Tad Alexander, Richard Quine, Tom Bupp, Ronnie Cosbey, Bobby Cox, George Ernest, Buster Phelps, Dickie Jones, Donald Buck, Eddie Dale Heiden, Erin O'Brien-Moore, Ralph Morgan, Cora Sue Collins, Jacqueline Taylor, Hattie McDaniels.

Burn 'em Up Barnes (Mascot, 1934, 68 min.). See serial version.

Behind the Green Lights (Mascot, 1935, 68 min.), directed by Christy Cabanne. *Original story*: Capt. Cornelius W. Willemse. *Screenplay*: James Gruen. *Photography*: Ernest Miller. *Editor*: Joseph Lewis. *Sound engineer*: Terry Kellum. *Cast*: Norman Foster, Judith Allen, Sidney Blackmer, Purnell Pratt, Theodore von Eltz, Ford Sterling, Kenneth Thomson, Lloyd Whitlock, Edward Hearn, Jane Meredith, Edward Gargan, J. Carrol Naish, John Davidson, Hooper Atchley, Marc Loebell, Fern Emmett, John Ince, Ralph Lewis.

One Frightened Night (Mascot, 1935, 66 min.), directed by Christy Cabanne. *Original story*: Stuart Palmer. *Screenplay*: Wellyn Totman. *Photography*: Ernest Miller and William Nobles. *Editor*: Joseph Lewis. *Sound engineer*: Terry Kellum. *Cast*: Charles Grapewin, Mary Carlisle, Arthur Hohl, Evalyn Knapp, Wallace Ford, Hedda Hopper, Lucien Littlefield, Regis Toomey, Fred Kelsey, Clarence Wilson, Adrian Morris, Rafaela Ottiano.

The Headline Woman (Mascot, 1935, 71 min.), directed by William Nigh. *Original story and screenplay*: Jack Natteford and Claire Church.

Photography: Ernest Miller. *Editor*: Joseph Lewis. *Sound engineer*: Terry Kellum. *Cast*: Heather Angel, Roger Pryor, Jack LaRue, Ford Sterling, Conway Tearle, Franklin Pangborn, Jack Mulhall, Russell Hopton, Syd Saylor, Theodore von Eltz, George Lewis, Ward Bond, Harry Bowen, Wade Boteler, Wheeler Oakman, Warner Richmond, Lynton Brent, George Hayes, Edward Hearn, Jack Raymond, Lillian Miles, Robert Gleckler, Allen Bridge, Joan Standing, Lloyd Ingram, Tony Martelli, Charles Regan, Guy Kingsford.

Ladies Crave Excitement (Mascot, 1935, 73 min.), directed by Nick Grindé. *Production supervisor*: Armand Schaefer. *Original story*: John Rathmell. *Screenplay*: Wellyn Totman and Scott Darling. *Supervising editor*: Joseph H. Lewis. *Photography*: Ernest Miller and William Nobles. *Editor*: Ray Curtiss. *Sound engineer*: Terry Kellum. *Sound effects*: Roy Granville. *Cast*: Norman Foster, Evalyn Knapp, Eric Linden, Esther Ralston, Purnell Pratt, Irene Franklin, Emma Dunn, Gilbert Emery, Russell Hicks, Christian Rub, Francis McDonald, Matt McHugh, Jason Robards, Sr., Syd Saylor, George Hayes, Stanley Blystone.

Harmony Lane (Mascot, 1935, 89 min.), directed by Joseph Santley. *Production supervisor*: Colbert Clark. *Original story*: Milton Krims. *Screenplay*: Joseph Santley and Elizabeth Meehan. *Photography*: Ernest Miller and Jack Marta. *Editor*: Joseph Lewis and Ray Curtis. *Sound engineer*: Terry Kellum. *Cast*: Douglass Montgomery, Evelyn Venable, Adrienne Ames, Joseph Cawthorn, William Frawley, Clarence Muse, Gilbert Emery, Florence Roberts, James Bush, David Torrence, Victor DeCamp, Edith Craig, Cora Sue Collins, Lloyd Hughes, Ferdinand Munier, Mildred Gover, James B. Carson, Rodney Hildebrand, Mary McLaren, Al Herman, Earl Hodgins.

Streamline Express (Mascot, 1935, 71 min.), directed by Leonard Fields. *Production supervisor*: George Yahalem. *Original story*: Wellyn Totman. *Screenplay*: Leonard Fields, Dave Silverstein, and Olive Cooper. *Supervising editor*: Joseph H. Lewis. *Photography*: Ernest Miller and Jack Marta. *Sound engineer*: Terry Kellum. *Sound effects*: Roy Granville. *Cast*: Victory Jory, Evelyn Venable, Esther Ralston, Erin O'Brien-Moore, Ralph Forbes, Sydney Blackmer, Vince Barnett, Clay Clement, Bobby Watson, Lee Moran, Syd Saylor, Libby Taylor, Edward Hearn, Allan Cavan, Joseph Girard, Tommy Bupp, Harry Harvey.

Waterfront Lady (Mascot, 1935, 70 min.), directed by Joseph Santley. *Production supervisor*: Colbert Clark. *Original story and screenplay*: Wellyn Totman. *Additional dialogue*: Joseph Fields. *Supervising editor*: Joseph H. Lewis. *Photography*: Ernest Miller. *Editor*: Ray Curtiss. *Sound engineer*: Terry Kellum. *Sound effects*: Roy Granville. *Songs*: Smiley Burnette. *Cast*: Ann Rutherford, Frank Albertson, J. Farrell MacDonald, Barbara Pepper, Charles C. Wilson, Grant Withers, Purnell Pratt, Jack La Rue, Ward Bond, Paul Porcasi, Mary Gordon, Mathilda Comont, Robert Emmett O'Connor, Clarence Wilson, Victor Potel, Wally Albright, Smiley Burnette.

Confidential (Mascot, 1935, 65 min.), directed by Edward L. Cahn. *Original story*: John Rathmell and Scott Darling. *Screenplay*: Wellyn Totman. *Additional dialogue*: Olive Cooper. *Photography*: Ernest Miller and Jack Marta. *Editor*: Ray Curtiss. *Cast*: Donald Cook, Evalyn Knapp, Warren Hymer, J. Carrol Naish, Herbert Rawlinson, Theodore von Eltz, Morgan Wallace, Kane Richmond, Clay Clement, Reed Howes, James Bur-Edward Hearn, Allan Bridge, Earl Eby, Lynton Brent, Monte Carter, George Chesebro, Mary Gwynne, Frank Marlowe, Lillian Castle, Donald Kerr, Edwin Argus, Jack Gustin, David Worth, Allen Connor, Tom Brower.

Doughnuts and Society (Mascot, 1936, 63 min.), directed by Lewis D. Collins. *Production supervisor*: William Berke. *Original story and screenplay*: Karen DeWolf, Robert St. Clair, and Wallace MacDonald. *Additional dialogue*: Gertrude Orr and Matt Brooks. *Photography*: William Nobles. *Editor*: Arthur Brooks. *Cast*: Louise Fazenda, Maude Eburne, Ann Rutherford, Eddie Nugent, Hedda Hopper, Franklin Pangborn, Rafael Corio, Smiley Burnette, Harold Minjir, Olaf Hytten, Robert Light, Claudell Kaye.

Radio Ranch (Mascot, 1940, 71 min.). See serial version of **The Phantom Empire.**

Index